FISHING ALASKA
ON DOLLAR$
A DAY

A Comprehensive Guide
to Fishing, Hunting
& Outdoor Recreation
*in Alaska's
National Forests*

By Christopher and Adela Batin

Published by Alaska Angler® Publications
Fairbanks, Alaska

Published by Alaska Angler® Publications, P. O. Box 83550, Fairbanks, Alaska 99708, (907) 455-8000.

First Edition, March 1990
Revised Edition, January 1992

Book and cover design: Adela Ward Batin
Cover illustration: Jeff Schuler
Typography and production: Award Design, Fairbanks, Alaska
Photo of authors, page 339: Jim Bailey

Library of Congress Cataloging in Publication Data
Batin, Christopher—
    Fishing Alaska on Dollars a day: a comprehensive guide to fishing, hunting & outdoor recreation in Alaska's national forests

    Includes index.
    1. Fishing—Alaska. 2. Forest reserves—Alaska—Recreational use. 3. United States. Forest Service. Alaska Region. I. Batin, Adela. II. Title

SH467.B38 1991

Library of Congress Catalog Card Number: 91-076370
ISBN 0-916771-26-1 (Trade Edition)

Produced in the State of Alaska
Printed in the United States of America

FISHING ALASKA
ON DOLLAR$
A DAY

To Ernest
Good fishing

Chris Batin

This book is dedicated

To the men and women who help maintain Alaska's National Forests, our gratitude;

To the fish and game resources of the Tongass and Chugach, our respect;

To our parents, who shared with us their love and sense of adventure,
and encouraged us to explore this Great Land of Alaska;

And our most humble thanks and praise to the Almighty,
for allowing us to witness the special beauty of His handiwork,
and to proclaim the immense joy of His creation.

Rise to the FUTURE

Fish Your National Forests

Trophy pink salmon, like this one held by Adela Batin, are found in coastal southeastern Alaska waters, on Kodiak Island and several southcentral watersheds.

Table of Contents

Table of Contents

When fishing for rockfish, veteran anglers prefer Flowering Floreo jigs, Gibbs Depth Charge jigs in chrome and white, and white, six-inch Mr. Twister baits on a two-ounce leadhead. Chris Batin admires an average-size black rockfish.

Acknowledgements

This book is the collective effort of many people. A special thanks goes to Sharon Durgan Wilson for her invaluable assistance in planning and production, and the long hours spent in editing and typesetting this book.

Ample credit belongs to the U.S. Forest Service. Thanks to Jim Kaplan, who first introduced us to the remarkable beauty of the Tongass. Another round of applause goes to Wanita Williamson for her patience in answering numerous questions and for being there when we became lost in a mound of paperwork.

The Alaska Department of Fish and Game deserves a round of applause for the ample sportfishing and hunting information they provided.

Special thanks to Ned Pleus for showing us parts of the Tongass we never would have seen otherwise, and to Stan Stephens for showing us the wonders of Prince William Sound.

And last but not least, thanks to the (d-2) U.S. Forest Service Alaska Planning Team: Sigurd Olson, Hatch Graham, Barney Coster, John Galea, Ray Steiger, Pam Wilson and Gerry Coutant for their past efforts in promoting new national forests in Alaska.

If we've forgotten anyone in this listing, our apologies and heartfelt thanks and appreciation for your help.

Christopher and Adela Batin
Fairbanks, Alaska

Alaska's National Forests

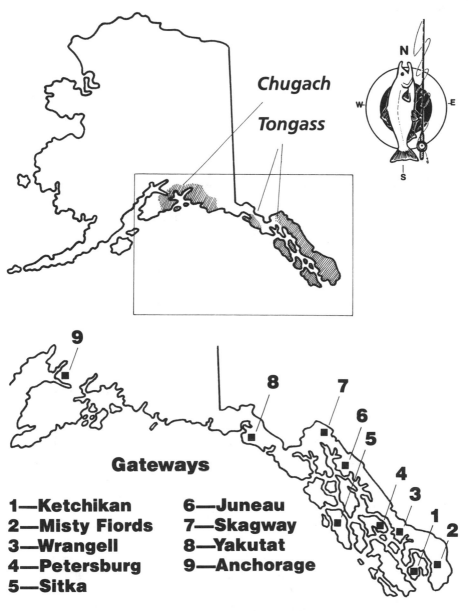

Chugach

Tongass

Gateways

1—Ketchikan
2—Misty Fiords
3—Wrangell
4—Petersburg
5—Sitka
6—Juneau
7—Skagway
8—Yakutat
9—Anchorage

Alaska has two national forests: The 17-million acre **Tongass National Forest** covers more than 90 percent of southeast Alaska. It contains about 120,000 acres of fish-bearing lakes and 23,000 miles of streams. Over one-third—5.5 million acres— is wilderness. Located in southcentral Alaska, the 5.99-million acre **Chugach National Forest** contains about 70,000 acres of lakes and 8,000 miles of streams. Together, they offer sportsmen some of the richest fisheries in the state.

WANTED

Anglers to enjoy world-class salmon and trout fishing on remote Alaska rivers, streams and lakes. Plenty of fun and relaxation. Fishing experience helpful but not necessary. Boat and accommodations included. Cost: Just dollars a day. Read this book for more information.

Are you a candidate for fishing Alaska on dollars a day?

Before you fling yourself to the head of the line, let me set the scene so you'll know what to expect. In the distance, a bluish crown of glacial ice hangs heavy on a mountain's craggy brow. To the left, and down a short ways, mountain goats begin to feed in a lush-green alpine meadow. Above them the sky is the deep, transparent blue of a sapphire held up to the light. To the south, cumulus clouds merge and separate into a kaleidoscopic display of images that only a dreamer fully appreciates. Closer to earth, the surroundings are equally impressive. The stream at your feet gurgles with purity. No trash, not even footprints, are seen. A mink swims through the shallows on the other side, causing salmon fry to leap in unison for safer cover. Nearby, bushes heavy with blueberries, huckleberries and salmonberries entice you to sample their all-you-can-eat bounty. But there's a stronger call appealing to your senses. In the river, hundreds of silvery salmon fin slowly against the current.

After a series of casts, a salmon on the outside edge of the school charges across the river and inhales your fly and charges back to its hole. Set the hook! The fish retaliates with a series of head-over-tail aerial leaps. It rockets upstream, bounces off a gravel bar, and sizzles through another series of acrobatics that has you well into your backing. An eagle glides quietly overhead, checking out the activity. With trembling hand, you salute it, and it flies on. By now the fish has beached itself in the shallows; a wild and crazy, chrome-bright, fresh-from-the-sea coho salmon, its thrashing tail covered with sea lice. While reviving the fish, you notice three cutthroat trout in a nearby backeddy. You chuckle and shake your head. Their husky girth is from dining on helping after helping of salmon egg omelette.

There's more. Near a log jam, pink and sockeye salmon are holding near their redds. What an environment for fish, and fishermen! With a massive tail splash, the coho swims off. The excitement, the energy of the moment, swells up inside of you. With trembling fingers you examine the fly. It's still good. Yet, no sense in overdoing it. Take a break. You'll be here for the next five days. At Alaska's best lodges, the going rate for this type of fishing costs anywhere from $2,000 to $4,000 a week.

Now here's my offer. If you don't mind doing your own cooking, operating a boat and motor, and releasing your own fish, you can have the same quality fishing for $20 a day. Impossible you say? Not in Alaska's National Forests.

Don't stereotype Alaska's National Forests with those found in the Lower 48.

There, campgrounds are often packed with visitors, and hikers dot the mountainsides. When fishing is available, it is often intense. Traffic can be horrendous during peak tourist season.

But Alaska's National Forests are different. They invigorate the soul with their pristine beauty. They are an elixir for those who crave adventure. And the fishing is spectacular! If your fishing arm isn't twitching and your heart racing at the thought of wetting a line in waters that seldom get fished, it's obvious that you haven't been properly introduced.

Allow me the honor: Alaska has two national forests: The 17-million acre Tongass National Forest covers more than 90 percent of southeast Alaska. It contains about 120,000 acres of fish-bearing lakes and 23,000 miles of streams. Over one-third—5.5 million acres—is wilderness.

The 5.99-million acre Chugach National Forest, located in southcentral Alaska, contains about 70,000 acres of lakes and 8,000 miles of streams. Together, they offer sportsmen some of the richest fisheries in the state that include all five species of salmon (king, coho, sockeye, chum and pink) arctic grayling, Dolly Varden, rainbow and cutthroat trout, steelhead, eastern brook trout, kokanee, lake trout, northern pike, halibut, rockfish, lingcod, and eulachon.

To fully appreciate the quality and quantity of the fishery resource in Alaska's National Forests, it's necessary to examine the state's entire commercial, sport and subsistence fisheries. Take salmon for instance. Over the five-year period from 1981-86, about 80 percent of the total United States commercial salmon harvest was landed in Alaska. That's impressive. In 1985 alone, total commercial salmon landings in Alaska exceeded 673 million pounds and accounted for almost 85 percent of the Nation's salmon harvest. Now here's the clincher. In recent years, salmon production from Alaska's National Forests has accounted for nearly 40 percent of the state's total salmon catch. That's a boatload of salmon going to market, and even more available to sportfishermen.

But fish abundance is only one of the many points to consider when planning a fishing trip in Alaska's National Forests. Equally as important is remoteness. During peak seasons, many of of these streams, rivers and lakes receive heavy fishing pressure. However, most do not. There is a good chance you won't see another angler during your stay, especially in the fly-in, wilderness regions. Some fisheries are so remote they receive only a handful of visitors each year.

The best way to sample these fisheries, and the surrounding plethora of outdoor activity, is through the public recreation cabin system managed by the USDA Forest Service. Currently, there are almost 200 of these cabins dispersed throughout the Tongass and Chugach forests, offering environments ranging from tidewater to remote alpine.

From these cabins, you have unlimited access to not only the nearby fisheries, but also to wild berries, clams, mussels, seafood, hiking, wildlife photography and a host of other resources and activities.

At most cabins, the price includes a boat for your own personal use. And at day's end, forget about climbing into a tent. Relax in a comfortable A-frame or Pan-abode cabin furnished with a wood or oil stove, bunks, outhouse, tables, benches and other amenities. Dinner attire is informal, but meals are usually exquisite. For instance, smell the rich aroma of that sockeye salmon you caught as it sizzles on an alder fire. No where else will you find, for the price, accommodations like this in the Alaska wilds. And if you're a hunter, many of the cabins are located in some of the finest waterfowl, upland game and big game hunting country you'll find in the state. And again, once you are there, it will only cost $20 a day for the accommodations.

Need more convincing?

A study entitled *Forest Service Cabin Use—A Survey of Eight Cabins in the Ketchikan Area,* by Gary Sanders reveals much about why people select a particular cabin; what activities they participate in at the cabin site; expenditures associated with cabin use, including transportation to the site; average trip length and party size; how closely trip experiences match expectations, and other information. Here is a synopsis of the study:

• Fishing was the primary consideration in selecting a USFS cabin for 88 percent of the non-residents and 59 percent of Alaska residents. Two other characteristics listed as important in choosing a USFS cabin were "getting away (solitude)" and "aesthetic setting (scenery)."

• The majority of the respondents (77 percent) rated the daily bag and possession limits "just right," on salmon, trout and steelhead.

• The vast majority of respondents did not encounter any outfitted/guided parties. However, the majority voiced strong opinions about the perceived effect that such an encounter would have on their recreational experience; 76 percent indicated that encountering a commercially outfitted/guided party would decrease the quality of their experience.

- Approximately 67 percent of the reservations for cabins surveyed were made by Alaska residents and 33 percent were made by non-residents.
- The average length of a trip to a USFS cabin was 2.5 days for Alaska residents and 5.6 days for non-residents.
- When an Alaska resident made the USFS cabin reservation, the average party included 2.7 Alaska residents, and when a nonresident reserved the cabin, the average party included 3.5 nonresidents.
- The non-residents surveyed spent 666 recreational days at the USFS cabins while Alaska residents only accounted for 466 recreational days.
- Visiting the National Forest and fishing were the main reasons indicated by non-residents respondents for visiting southeast Alaska.
- Alaska residents using the USFS cabins tended to be younger than the non-residents—69 percent of the Alaska residents were 35 years old or younger versus 42 percent for non-residents.
- The mean gross annual income bracket for Alaska residents was $30,000 to $39,000 versus $40,000 to $49,000 for non-residents.
- The average Alaska resident respondent's party spent $248 per trip for transportation to and from their permanent residence(s) and the USFS cabin, plus an additional $350 associated with activities while at the cabin site, for a total expenditure of $598. Thus, the average Alaska resident spent approximately $221.50 for his share of the cost of visiting one of the surveyed cabins.
- The average non-resident respondent's party spent approximately $1,809 as its total expenditure, which includes overall travel costs. However, on the average, only 75.2 percent of the party's time was spent at a USFS cabin. Therefore, that portion of overall travel cost attributed to visiting the USFS cabin is $1,360 ($1,809 x 75.2 percent). An additional $500 was spent on costs associated with using the cabin, for a total expenditure of approximately $1,860. The average non-resident spent approximately $531 for his share of the cost to visit one of the surveyed cabins.
- The average cost per recreational day was approximately $89 for Alaska residents and $95 for non-residents. (Editor's Note: By taking food from home and using your own fishing tackle, sleeping bags and camping equipment, the only cost to you, after reaching the cabin, is the daily rental fee of $20).
- Eighty-seven percent of all respondents expressed medium to high satisfaction with the USFS cabin reservation system.

Keep in mind that some cabins near popular fishing and hunting areas are often booked six months in advance. Use of cabins in the Sitka, Wrangell and Petersburg areas is increasing. Prince of Wales Island is receiving more and more anglers who have discovered the excellent sportfishing on this island.

The good news is: there are plenty of cabins and opportunities for remote fishing away from the crowds. For instance, cabin use in the Sitka area is decreasing, due to an increase in local airfares, while cabin use in the Chugach is increasing.

To make the most of your trip takes planning, which is the purpose of this book.

There's no question about it: I'm in love with Alaska's National Forests. As editor of The Alaska Angler® , The Alaska Hunter and author of several books on Alaska sportfishing and hunting, I've traveled and fished the state's best fisheries, sampled her best lodges, and have experienced wilderness where I was probably the first person ever to wet a line in her waters.

Many of my most memorable experiences have not been the expensive, $3,000-a-week excursions, but rather, the remote fishing opportunities in the Misty Fjords, or fishing for small-stream steelhead on Prince of Wales Island. It was that weekend vacation to Alexander Lake, or that wilderness fly-in to scenic Goat Lake with pilot Ned Pleus. No pressure, no competition, only scenic beauty and chunky fish.

Indeed, the sportfish of Alaska's National Forests are special. I talk to them during the releasing process, something I couldn't do at a crowded lodge without being labeled strange. I am sure that in many cases I was the first person to catch a particular fish, and probably the last person to ever see it. It's a sad, yet wonderfully satisfying experience. These fish are waiting to be enjoyed in a truly grand environment. They are the essence of what an Alaska fishing adventure is all about.

In this book we provide much of the information you need to make informed decisions about where to stay and what to fish for. It makes no sense to book a five-day trip to the Situk River cabin in April when you want solitude and a chance to fish a small mountain stream at your own pace.

Here's a bit of advice: Plan on doing more than just fishing. Alaska's National Forests offer recreational opportunities that have yet to be tapped to their fullest potential. Experience wildlife photographic opportunities that rival world-famous Denali National Park. Hunt for birds, hares and big game such as moose, goat, wolf, deer and bear. Kayak the Inside Passage, raft a glacial river, or delight in birding and plant collecting. Sleep next to a glacier, and listen to the booming of the ice. Or stand atop a wilderness peak, put your face into the wind, and feel the power of Nature in all her raw, unharnessed fury.

Add these experiences to the fabulous fishing, and you'll understand why the state's best-kept secret is Alaska's National Forests.

Christopher Batin
Fairbanks, Alaska

This book separates the Tongass and Chugach National Forests into nine gateways. Within those gateways, detailed descriptions of fishing areas and their accompanying cabins are listed.

Many **prime fishing waters** within the forests do not have cabins. We've listed several of the most popular waters in the fishing facts section at the beginning of each **gateway**, mainly as alternate locations for anglers who want to explore other fisheries. The **fishing tips** listed for a particular water often work well in other watersheds. Before your trip, read the fishing notes for each region and learn about the various types of lures, techniques, and equipment needed for optimum fishing success and enjoyment. This information is culled from experts and our own extensive field research. For the most comprehensive work on the best techniques to use throughout this region, obtain a copy of *"How to catch Alaska's Trophy Sportfish"* by Christopher Batin, Alaska Angler Publications, P.O. Box 83550, Fairbanks, Alaska 99708.

Because fishing and hunting areas can be opened and closed at random, it's wise to check with the Alaska Department of Fish and Game prior to planning a hunting or fishing trip into any of these areas.

Flight times are generally one-way, unless otherwise noted. Multiply this figure times four to get the total flight time an air taxi service will charge you. Some services offer package fly-out deals that may be cheaper than their per-hour charge. Be sure to inquire about this before your trip.

Study the **cabins and facilities** sections under each geographic location. Cabins are listed by name and Forest Service number; their physical location and structure are described, and amenities are listed. Some are located on salt water, and no boat is available. To enhance your trip, we recommend that you bring your own boat. Some cabins have oil stoves instead of wood-burning stoves, while still others may not have an adequate water supply, requiring you to bring your own.

The listing of **precautions** offers advice regarding strict access times, dangers and possible inconveniences you are likely to encounter at some cabins. A listing of **user comments** provides input from people who have stayed at the featured cabin, and who have taken time to fill out the U.S. Forest Service comment card.

In the **planning** section of this book, read about the flora and fauna you are likely to see, precautions to take, insect pests, shellfish poisoning and other items of concern.

Pack light, have fun, and respect the resources. Allow the beauty of Alaska's National Forests to enrich your soul, and leave the forests as you found them for future generations to likewise enjoy. See you in the field!

The Sportfish of Alaska's National Forests

While staying at one of the U.S. Forest Service cabins, it is likely that you will catch, and hopefully release, plenty of fish. Keep in mind, however, that most waters won't have "fish a cast" angling. In Alaska waters, many species are seasonal in availability. But don't be disappointed. Consult each cabin listing or the "fishing facts" section of the gateway (ranger district) you'll be visiting for specific information on timing of anadromous runs, and availability of freshwater species.

The following is an introduction to the major sportfish species found throughout the Tongass and Chugach forests. My philosophy is, "The more you know about a sportfish species, the better your chance of success."

Cutthroat Trout

Throughout southeast Alaska, cutthroat trout are found in hundreds of lakes and streams in both resident and anadromous forms. The appellation "cutthroat" is derived from the reddish-orange slash along the inner edge of the fish's lower jaw. A cutt exhibits a greenish-blue dorsal area, with silvery sides and angular or round black spots often organized into irregular patterns on the back and sides. It has a large mouth, with the maxillary extending beyond the back of the eye. A cutthroat will have teeth on its vomer (tongue). An anadromous cutthroat is a bluish silver with light markings and is often difficult to distinguish from a steelhead trout.

When a forage food base of kokanee is found in a watershed, or if cutthroats have access to the sea, they can reach trophy size. Lengths of 20 inches or more and weights of up to four pounds are possible. Conversely, when crustacean and non-salmonid food items are predominant, cutthroats rarely exceed 10 inches in length.

Cutthroat trout are available in over 200 lakes and streams throughout the Tongass National Forest.

Angling for trophy cutthroats is one of the highlights of a do-it-yourself southeast Alaska fishing adventure. Both anadromous and resident types can be found in the same watershed. The cutthroat in southeast Alaska's forests have an interesting life history. On the average, it takes three years for an anadromous cutthroat to reach smolt size, and six years for it to reach 10 to 12 inches. A lake-resident fish takes six to eight years to reach the same length.

Cutthroat populations are not overly abundant. Populations rarely exceed 2,000 fish in a single watershed. Some of the largest systems host populations of less than 500 fish. About half of all cutthroats entering fresh water are spawners, with actual spawning taking place from early May to early June.

Catching cutthroat is not difficult. When fishing muskeg streams or ponds, use egg patterns, chironomid patterns, stickleback, sculpin, leech and damsel fly nymph patterns. Black spinners, salmon eggs, and tiny spoons in the one-sixteenth-ounce category also work well. Use a 3- to 5-weight fly rod, or ultralight spinning tackle for best results.

In lakes with a forage food base of kokanee, a smolt, herring or fry pattern will invariably take the larger fish. Try silver/orange and blue/silver spoons, willow-leaf spinners or metal jigs for trophy cutts.

In streams, maggot patterns, drift lures in bright, fluorescent colors, smolt/fry patterns, and standard hardware are most effective in catching sea-run cutts. Cutthroats are especially fond of peach-colored egg patterns fished behind schools of holding or migrating pink and chum salmon. Fish the pattern with a small shot of lead and a 30-inch leader tapered to 5X.

Dolly Varden

Almost all freshwater systems in southeast Alaska support Dolly Varden. They are commonly taken from salt water throughout the year, but are also taken from the most unlikely places, such as tiny creeks and lakes of all sizes, including those without access to salt water.

In intertidal and saltwater areas, few lures can beat a Fjord spoon for catching Dolly Varden. Resembling needlefish, a favorite food of the Dolly, the spoon has an enticing wobble that signals an easy meal to the fish. Impart a twitching action while slowly retrieving the spoon along bottom, and you'll catch Dollies when other lures fail. Also try various sizes of Rooster Tails in yellow, green and chrome. In the spring, freshwater Dollies feed ravenously on out-migrating smolt and fry. In July through September, they gorge on salmon eggs. Any lures or flies imitating these food items will produce fish. My favorites include Aqua-cones, Glo-bugs in red and peach, Jansen minnows, Coronations, blue smolt and tinsel flies.

In lakes, Dollies can be caught on small Acme spoons, fluorescent red flatfish, flutter spoons, Storm Wee Warts and various aquatic nymph patterns.

The colors of Dolly Varden are extremely variable, ranging from silvery blue to olive green, brown, black or tan on the dorsal surfaces. Occasionally the sides of a Dolly turn a bright red/orange. They are almost always covered with pink, red or orange spots smaller than the pupil of the fish's eye. Weights range from two to ten pounds.

Eastern Brook Trout

Brook trout are identified by their dark, olive-green dorsal surface and upper sides. These spots are large, round and often encircled with a bluish halo. Irregular vermiculations are found on the dorsal fin and back, and the ventral fins usually have distinct white borders on the leading edge. Fish average one to eight pounds.

Eastern Brook trout are present in at least 17 lakes throughout southeast Alaska, and are the result of extensive stockings conducted by federal fisheries biologists in the early 1900s. About a thousand fish are harvested annually.

Very little biological data exist for this species in Alaska. On the average, it takes an Alaskan brookie four to five years to reach 10 inches. Because brook trout in Alaska are only found in a lake environment, heavy tackle is out. Ultralight tackle, using two-to four-pound line and small jigs, plugs, spin-bubble/fly combos, tiny Fjord spoons, and scud, mosquito emerger, leech and stickleback patterns take the most fish.

Rainbow Trout

Rainbow trout are present in all steelhead rivers listed throughout the Tongass Forest, but are numerous only in watersheds that have lakes at their headwaters and large runs of steelhead. Many rainbow populations in remote lakes are the result of stockings by the federal government that took place in the early 1900s. Today, over 60 lakes contain reproducing populations of wild rainbows, compared to 36 lakes that contain naturally occurring stocks of rainbow. These figures do not take into account lakes with small numbers of rainbow trout, or waters with greatly restricted access. Spawning takes place from late May to mid-June, although fish in high alpine lakes will spawn a short time after ice-out, usually in early July.

Use the same patterns for rainbows as those listed for cutthroat. Pack various nymphs and dries for catching rainbows in and around lily pads.

Rainbows lack the vomer teeth inherent to cutthroats, and sport a silvery, metallic blue/green dorsal area covered with black spots. A faint to dark pink to red stripe can be present.

Steelhead

The steelhead is the most preferred freshwater species among anglers surveyed by ADF&G.

There are over 330 streams in southeast Alaska with steelhead runs that take place in spring, summer and fall. Overall, spring fish are the most common, with summer-run fish being very rare. All southeast Alaska steelhead spawn in the spring, from May through June. Entry into these systems may be as early as February and March. Flyfishing for steelhead in the streams and rivers of southeast Alaska can be frustrating. Prince of Wales Island offers slick, neck-breaking wading. Expect impenetrable brush along the streambanks. Numerous obstacles such as logjams, boulders, and a rough bottom often prevent working a hole from various angles. A floating line with weighted fly is often the ticket here; however, take a sink-tip and braided loop lead-head system for the deeper holes and runs. Your choice of fly varies with the type of water fished and time of year. Crystal Bullet, Animated Alevin, Skykomish, Flashabou, Orange Roe and similar attractor patterns work well in both stained and clear water. The darker patterns, such as large black nymphs, purple Glo-Bugs, and matukas work well on steelies when water levels are low or if there is direct sun overhead. Steelhead are identifiable by their lack of teeth on the vomer, and metallic silver color. Males have a red stripe or band along their sides, especially after spending time in fresh water.

Alaska's National Forests have over 500 streams and lakes that contain rainbow trout and/or steelhead. Many are located in wilderness areas that seldom get fished.

Grayling

Grayling are not native to southeast Alaska. The transplants—restricted to lakes throughout the region—started in the 1950s and ended in 1976. The source was Tolsona Lake near Glennallen, Alaska, although reports indicate the earliest introductions were of Canadian origin.

As long as light tackle is used, grayling are not fussy about feeding. They are opportunistic feeders, and will take a variety of patterns from dry flies (Adams, humpy, caddis, bivisible, gray Wulff) to nymphs (hare's ear, muskrat, stonefly). They'll also take a variety of smolt and invertebrate patterns such as scuds, leech and beetle. The grayling's most identifying feature is its sailfish-like dorsal fin.

Chinook Salmon (King Salmon)

Nearly half of the chinook salmon catch in southeast Alaska is taken south of Frederick Sound, and approximately half of this harvest occurs near Ketchikan.

Of the area's major salmon rivers, 12 support chinook populations numbering less than 500 fish; six host populations of 500 to 5,000 chinooks. The Stikine is the largest producer, providing over 10,000 chinooks per year. Southeast Alaska chinooks are spring spawners. They begin entering intertidal areas in late April, and tail out by early July. Most have reached their spawning locations by July 30. Fish return at three to seven years of age. Saltwater bait and lures include herring, squid, hootchies and J-plugs. Where freshwater fishing is permitted, drift lures, plugs, Okies, Spin-N-Glos, and large fluorescent spoons regularly take king salmon. Use at least a 10-weight flyrod for kings or a stiff-spined, medium-heavy casting or spinning rod with stiff spine. Best flies include King Killer, Alaskabou, Baker Buster, Sockeye Pink, Flash Fly and Polar Shrimp. (See the king salmon chapter in *How to catch Alaska's Trophy Sportfish* for detailed information on how to fish these lures and flies.) Chinooks are identified by a black gumline and irregular black spots on the upper back. They can reach weights up to 90 pounds, with 20 to 30 pounds most common.

Grayling, the "sailfish of the North" are restricted to a handful of lakes and feeder streams located throughout the Chugach and Tongass National Forests.

Chum Salmon (Dog or Calico Salmon)

Southeast Alaska hosts both summer and fall runs of chum salmon, with the former being predominant. Chums are usually caught by anglers fishing for pink salmon. Many anglers do not consider the chum salmon a sportfish, probably due to its reluctance to strike lures. However, when congregated in intertidal areas, chums will strike flies, small spinners and spoons. Chum salmon can be caught consistently when you find them in or near the current at the mouth of a stream or river. Use blue or purple bucktails in clear water, and chartreuse or fluorescent purples, greens or reds in turbid water. Chum salmon lack the large black spots common to pinks and kings, although all fins except the dorsal are black tipped and sometimes speckled. Spawning fish show reddish, vertical markings of purple and green.

Coho Salmon (Silver Salmon)

There are approximately two thousand systems throughout southeast Alaska that support coho salmon populations. The coho is the region's second most preferred and caught salmon. Unlike other stocks, southern southeast coho have a four-year life cycle. However, fish can return anywhere from two to six years of age.

Most coho enter streams in September, and taper off in October. There are a few watersheds that receive runs of coho in July, and mid- to late August. These are generally systems with waterfalls or rapids that provide formidable obstacles to upstream migration during the October high-water period.

Stock a variety of lures for coho fishing. Use fluorescent spinners in slow-moving intertidal water and pools, and spoons in fast, deep pools, channels or in salt water. Herring, squid or hootchies are popular with marine trollers, as are various plugs in chrome and pearl. Fly fishers after coho use patterns that exhibit contrast, along with a healthy dose of flash from tinsel or mylar. I've found that weighted flies have a slight advantage over unweighted flies: they sink quickly and stay down, important prerequisites for catching coho on a regular basis. Coho have black spots along the dorsal area and top lobe of the tail, and a light-gray gumline. Fish range from two to 20 pounds.

Pink Salmon (Humpies)

According to an ADF&G survey, the pink salmon ranks eighth in angler preference. However, throughout all of southeast Alaska, pinks are the most frequently harvested salmon. Anglers catch over 40 thousand fish annually. Over 2,500 streams and intertidal areas throughout southeast Alaska contain fishable populations of pink salmon. Pinks are two-year fish, and average three to five pounds on returning to freshwater. Most spawn in intertidal areas (the best fishing) or no more than a few miles from salt water. Pink salmon are fun to catch on a 6-weight or lighter fly rod. Unusual as it may sound, chartreuse outfishes every other color in my inventory. Sockeye John, Sherry's Deliverer and The Chartreuse Yarn Fly are also effective patterns.

Top choices for lures include any small 0 to 3 Aglia-type spinner, half-ounce Pixee spoon with a chartreuse insert, or green Dardevle with red dots.

A pink has dark, oval spots covering its back and entire tail. Males develop a grotesque hump at maturity. Coloring ranges from olive green to silvery white.

Sockeye Salmon (Red Salmon)

Few spin fishermen pursue sockeyes because of the difficulty of catching this species in salt and fresh water. Each year, however, fly anglers take 20 to 50 percent of the 4,000-plus sockeye caught from the Tongass Forest's clearwater streams or rivers.

Sockeyes offer good sport on flies. Fish for them with either a fly rod and sink-tip or shooting head line, or spinning tackle and snag-proof, three-way or rubbercore sinker. Color is not as important as understanding the stream equation when angling for sockeyes. According to my sockeye equation, which appears in its entirety in *How to catch Alaska's Trophy Sportfish,* to catch sockeyes on a regular basis, you must have good visibility, structure to compress fish, and current.

Kokanee, a landlocked form of the sockeye salmon, are found in many lakes throughout southeast Alaska. They are a fighting fish that can reach lengths of 10 inches and are real tasty. Tiny Mirro-lures, flame Rooster Tails in sizes 2 and 3, and one-inch flutter spoons in silver and orange catch kokanee on a regular basis.

Sockeyes are silvery blue right out of saltwater. After spending time in freshwater, they turn green and crimson red. Weights range from two to 12 pounds.

Halibut

A survey of southeast Alaska anglers showed that halibut are tied with coho salmon for second place, surpassed only by chinook salmon as the most popular. Most of the halibut sport catch consists of small, immature fish ranging from five to 20 pounds. In recent years, anglers have been catching larger halibut, probably due to an increase in angling pressure, better angling techniques and increase in population numbers. In southeast Alaska, halibut are most abundant in mid- to late summer, when fish are moving through the region to feed on the abundance of marine life in bays and passages. However, early spring months offer excellent fishing in many areas.

Sockeye salmon are often referred to as "non-biters"; however, they can be caught consistently if anglers use the proper lures and techniques.

Halibut can be taken with either metal or leadhead jigs (from eight to 16 ounces) or bait herring, squid, octopus or salmon heads fished on a 10/0 hook and three to 20 ounces of weight. Jigging off the bottom before and after a slack tide is best, however, halibut can be caught throughout the entire range of tidal fluctuations.

There's no mistaking a halibut. Look for smooth, grayish skin and ''barn doors'' up to 400 pounds, although most fish will range from 10 to 30 pounds. Halibut have widely forked tails, while turbot and sole (other members of the flatfish family) exhibit more rounded tails.

Rockfish

The most common varieties of rockfish caught by anglers are the black, yellowtail, quillback, dusky and yelloweye (red snapper). Southeast Alaska rockfish are slow-growing, and can be found in the same locations year after year. Stock deterioration has already occurred in many of the more popular hotspots throughout southeast Alaska. However, remote areas still provide excellent fishing for trophy rockfish.

Successful anglers use a 1- to 6-ounce leadhead jig with a white, 6-inch Mr. Twister body. The Depth Charge by Gibbs Tackle is another effective rockfish producer. Deepwater yelloweye rockfish are commonly taken on 8-ounce silver Vi-ke jigs. A sharp, jigging action, allowing the lure to flutter to bottom, takes the majority of the fish.

Adela Batin with a large, yelloweye rockfish caught near Ketchikan.

Favorite Fishing Waters of the Tongass National Forest

Many of the sport fisheries in the Tongass National Forest (northern and southern southeast Alaska) are located in remote wilderness areas. A map is crucial in helping you locate these waters. Many streams that contain steelhead, for instance, have no names. Thus, the nearest reference point is given.

Because the Tongass National Forest covers over 90 percent of southeast Alaska, I've taken the liberty of including a few waters located immediately outside the forest boundaries, such as those found on city, national park or Native lands.

The United States Geological Survey office offers quad maps that will assist you in specifically locating these waters throughout the Tongass National Forest. Simply request the maps listed under the geographical identifier (Sitka, Ketchikan, etc.) The Yakutat (Russel Fiord Wilderness) or the Chugach National Forest watersheds are not included in this listing. Sportfish information on these waters can be found under their specific listings. To order USGS quad maps, see page 49.

Southeast Alaska has numerous watersheds that produce 20-pound silver or coho salmon. Brightly colored flies, fluorescent orange spoons and white-bladed spinners often take the largest fish.

USGS Quad Map— Skagway

Mosquito
Chilkat
Rustabach

Juneau

Shelter Island Windfall
Mendenhall
Auke Young

Taku River

Twin Glacier
Turner

Sitka

Florence
Thayer
Hasselborg
Davidson
McKinney
Distin
Freshwater
Guerin
Beaver
Alexander
Kanalku
Jims
Goulding #1
Goulding #2
Otter Lake (Goulding #3)
Goulding #4
Ford Arm
Pavlof
Kook
Sitkoh
Eva
Little Eva
Paddy
Baranof
Sadie
Buck #1
Buck #2
Buck #3
Leo
Anita
Klag Bay
Sea Level
Didrickson

Prince Rupert

Very Inlet
Hidden
Shrew
Nakat Mountain

Mount Fairweather

Hoktaheen
Surge

Port Alexander

Salmon
Big Bay #1
Big Bay #2
Banks
Ledge
Cool
Kutlaku
Alecks

Petersburg

Towers Arm
Bohemian
Kalinia
Irish
Kushneaheen
Kah Sheets
Petersburg
Colp
Harvey
Crane
Brown Cove
North Arm
Twin (Figure Eight)
Trout (Pat)
Thom's
Kunk
Burnett
Virginia

Bradfield Canal

Marten
Lower Harding
Anan
Boulder
Gene's
Eagle
Reflection

Craig

Hofstad
Scout
Three Islands
Bear
Upper Gold Standard
Lower Gold Standard

Ketchikan

Woodpecker
MacDonald
Helen
Wastra
Helm
Saks
Robinson
Wilson
Lower Checats
Winstanley Lakes
Bakewell
Porky
Badger
Nakat
Sykes
Kah Shakes
High Smith
Cobb
Humpback
Reef Point
Long Snipe Island
Orchard
Neets
Margarita Bay
Emma
Chamberlain
Patching
Heckman
Jordan
Salt Chuck
Shelter Cove #1
Shelter Cove #2
Leask Cove #1
Ingram
Connell
Ward
Mahoney
Upper Ketchikan
Lower Ketchikan
Swan
Manzanita
Mirror
Ella
Third
Big
Gokachin
Mesa
Basin
Low
Johnson
Otter

Cutthroat Trout Streams

USGS Quad Maps—
Skagway
Chilkat River

Juneau
Berner's River
Cowee Creek
Herbert River
Windfall Creek
Peterson Creek
Mendenhall River
Montana Creek
Bear Creek

Taku River
Taku River
Moose Creek
Yehring Creek

Sitka
Hasselborg River
Kanalku Creek
Pavlof River
Kadashan River
Sitkoh Creek
Goulding River
Ford Arm Creek
Eva Creek

Port Alexander
Salmon Creek
Kutlaku Creek
Alecks Creek

Bradfield Canal
Marten Creek
Tom Creek
Anan Creek
Eagle River
Hulakon River
Unuk River

Craig
Black Bear Creek

Petersburg
Kadake Creek
Hamilton River
Duncan Salt Chuck
Portage Creek
Big Creek
Blind Slough
Castle River
Tunehean Creek
Kah Sheets Creek
Totem Bay Creeks
Crystal Creek
Stikine River
Crittenden Creek
Thoms Creek
Kunk Creek
Streets Creek
Hatchery Creek
Red Bay Creek
Salmon Bay Creek
Exchange Creek
108 Creek
Sutter Creek
Shipley Creek
Trout Creek

Prince Rupert
Fillmore Creek
Sarkar Watershed
Log Jam Creek
Hatchery Creek
Eagle Creek
Staney Creek
Thorne River
Bear Creek
Karta River
Harris River
Klawak River
Hydaburg River
Miller Creek
Klakas Creek
Kegan Creek

USGS Quad Maps—
Skagway
Lower Dewey

Taku River
Dorothy

Port Alexander
Green
Long
Salmon

Sitka
Heart
Thimbleberry

Juneau
Annex

Craig
Bugge

Petersburg
Crystal

Bradfield Canal
Nellie

Ketchikan
Claude
Grace
Ketchikan
Perseverance
Whitman

Grayling Lakes

USGS Quad Maps—
Skagway
Herman

Juneau
Antler

Sitka
Beaver

Bradfield Canal
Halfmoon
Tyee
Minnie

Petersburg
Kane Peak Lake

Craig
Marge
Mellen
Summit

Ketchikan
Chamberlain
Goat
Little Goat
Manzoni
Orton
Patching
Snow

Rainbow Trout Lakes

USGS Quad Maps— Skagway
Lost
Lower Dewey

Sumdum
Lower Sweetheart
Deboer
Swan

Sitka
Swan
Blue
Sukoi
Sitkoh
Klag Bay

Mount Fairweather
Surge

Port Alexander
Salmon
Dianna
Biorka
Politofsky
Avoss
Grebe
Pass
Davidof
Plotnikof
Rezanof
Khvostof
Lower Khvostof
Lonieof
Deer
Fawn
Upper Rostislaf
Lower Rostislaf
Round
Sashin
Jetty
Betty
Alecks

Petersburg
Petersburg
Trout
Red
Salmon Bay
Shipley
Sutter

Bradfield Canal
Goat
Anan
Reflection
Gene's
Herman
Grant

Dixon Entrance
Johnson Cove

Craig
Sweetwater
Luck
Angel
Salmon
Karta
Wolf
Black Bear
Klawak
Eek
Hetta
Clover
Monie
Lower Clover
Paul
Moira
Kegan
Klakas
Crater
Rainbow
Kugel
Galea (Honker)
Rock

Ketchikan
Maude
Leduc
Walker
January
Punchbowl
Upper Checats
Lower Checats
High Smith
Notch Mountain
Goose
Donkey
Chopper
Ward
Connell
Lower Second Waterfall
Upper Second Waterfall
Lower Lunch Creek
Upper Lunch Creek
Harriet Hunt
Heckman
Jordan
Low
Rowena
Buckhorn
Venison
Upper Silvis
Lower Silvis
Steep
Cliff
Marten Arm
Downdraft

USGS Quad Maps— Port Alexander

Big Bay stream-Baranof
Redoubt Outlet
Salmon River
Kadake Creek
Kadake Creek tributaries
Kell Bay, Kuiu Island
Table Bay, Kuiu Island
SW Kuiu Island
Bear Harbor
Port Malmesbury
Petrof Bay
Gedney Harbor streams
Sashin Creek
Tumakof Creek
Alecks Creek
Piledriver Cove
Kwatahein Creek
Kutlaku Creek
Rowan Bay streams
Port Banks/Plotnikof
Gut Bay
Politofski River
Straight Creek
Head of Saginaw Bay stream
Saginaw Creek
Saginaw Creek tributary
Security Bay
Benzeman Lake tributary
Falls Lake Creek

Mount Fairweather

Surge Lake System
Topsy Creek
Steelhead Creek

Taku River

Taku River

Sitka

Sawmill Creek
Indian River
Fred's Creek
Gambier Bay tributaries
North Arm Hood Bay
    streams

Eva Creek
Suloia Creek
Gambier Bay streams
Mole River
Hasselborg River
Sitkoh Creek
Kook Creek
Kadashan River
Waterfall Cove
Ford Arm Creek
Ford Arm Creek
    tributary
Lake Anna tributary
Klag Bay
Chichagof Creek
Black Bay
Windfall Harbor
S. Fork Freshwater
    Creek
Stranger River

Juneau

Taku Harbor Creek
Admiralty Creek
Hilda Creek
Bear Creek
Peterson Creek
Salmon River (Gustavus)
Bartlett River
Cowee Creek
Mendenhall River
Montana Creek

Petersburg

Taylor Creek
Towers Arm
Hamilton River
Hamilton River
    tributaries
Kadake Creek
    and tributaries
Calder Bay
S.E. Kuiu Island stream
Eastern Passage
    stream
Crittenden Creek
Kunk Creek

Zarembo Island
    streams
Red Lake Creek
Red Lake Creek
    tributary
Totem Bay stream
Kushneahin Creek
Port Beauchler
    streams
Stikine River
Government Creek
North Arm Creek
Andrew Creek
Andrew Creek,
    South Fork
Shakes Slough
East Mitkof Island
    stream
Ohmer Creek
Falls Creek
Kah Sheets Creek
Kah Sheets Bay
    tributary
Middle Creek
Castle River
Castle River
    tributary
Duncan Canal
    watershed
Totem Bay
    watershed
Stream near
    Tunehean
Muddy River
Crystal Creek
Coho Creek
Petersburg Creek
Petersburg Creek
    tributaries
Twelve Mile Creek
Portage Creek
Duncan Creek
Duncan Salt Chuck
Head of Towers Arm
Indian Creek (mouth of
    Sweetwater

USGS Quad Maps— Craig

Kugel Creek
Miller Creek
Paul Creek
Klakas Inlet stream
Klakas Creek
Nutwa streams
Hetta Creek
W. Arm Cholm. Snd.
Hetta Inlet
Kasook watershed
Kasook Creek
Hydaburg River
Devil Lake Creek
Clover Bay
Clover Creek
Sunny Cove
Sunny Creek
Sunny tributary
Old Tom Creek
Cabin Creek
Dog Salmon Creek
Rock Creek
Twelve Mile Creek
Indian Creek
Survey Creek
Manhatten Creek
Harris River
Maybeso Creek (near Hollis)
Hydaburg
Trocadero streams
Point St. Nichols
Klawar River
Near Tlevak streams
Crab Creek
Head of Helm Bay
Black Bear Creek
Karta River
Paul Young Creek
Karta Bay streams
McGilvery Creek
Thorne River tributaries
Big Salt Lake Creek
Klawak River and Inlet
Shinaku Creek

#74 tributary
Shaheen Creek
Vixen Inlet
McHenry Anchorage
Little Ratz Creek
Ratz Creek
Luck Lake Outlet—
   Eagle Creek
Luck Lake Outlet—
   Luck Creek
Hatchery Creek
Lester Creek
Staney Creek
Sarkar Creek
Chuck Creek
   (Heceta Island)

Ketchikan

Carroll Creek
Choca Creek
King Creek
Leduc River
South Fork Chickamin
Barrier Creek
North Fork-Chickamin
Robinson Creek
Sake Creek
Bell Island Creek
Claude Lake Creek
Wasta Creek
Spacious Bay
Wolverine Creek
Santa Anna Inlet
Humpback Creek
Hugh Smith Creek
Cobb Creek
Buschmann Creek
Marten River
Marten River tributary
Vixen Bay stream
Badger Creek
Kah Shakes
Sykes Creek
Lucky Cove
Alava Bay
Bakewell Creek

Bakewell Arm
Keta River
Wilson River
Blossom River
Smeaton-Carp Creek
Bartholomew Creek
Smeaton Bay stream
Skull Creek

Outfitting Your USFS Boat

To best fish the lakes found throughout Alaska's National Forests, you'll need a boat. Bushwhacking is out, not only because of the likelihood of unexpectedly confronting a brown bear, but also because of the muskeg, swamp and downfall that hinders quick travel between fishing destinations.

Although many U.S. Forest Service cabins offer skiffs or boats, you'll need to bring your own if one's not available. You'll also need to bring an outboard motor.

I recommend a 4-hp engine for the smaller lakes and nothing larger than a 9.9 for the larger lakes and rivers. Oars come with each boat, but take a spare set. Pack an extra set of oarlocks, also.

Depending on the size of the lake, a five-gallon tank of gasoline for the outboard will generally last several days, unless you expect to do lots of trolling. Carry an extra gallon of gas in an approved container at all times. Also include a small tool kit, extra spark plug and shear pins.

Some anglers, especially fly fishers, are finding belly boats the key to successfully fishing these wilderness lakes. Fitted with neoprene waders and a pair of flippers, the angler boats over to the fishing spot, anchors the boat and fishes the area from his float tube. During the summer, this is the most effective means of fishing in and around lily and weedbeds, where rainbows and cutthroats often hide to escape the sun. The fish are often spooky, and nearly impossible to approach in a conventional boat. But the float tuber can ease into the weeds without alarming the fish. However, when the fish are holding deep, the troller has the advantage. A portable downrigger and sonar unit will contribute greatly to your success.

Wet weather prevails throughout southeast Alaska. Wise anglers take neoprene chest waders for lake and long-term river and stream fishing, and hip-boots for long hikes to and from fishing locations. The neoprenes make sense, even when fishing from a boat. They add an extra measure of warmth and keep you afloat should you fall overboard.

As for tackle, pack an ultralight rod and reel filled with 4- to 6-pound clear monofilament. Also take a medium-action level-wind or spinning outfit to handle the deep-water trolling and salmon fishing. Fly rodders should pack a lightweight 4- to 6-weight rod for trout, a sturdier 8-weight for salmon and steelhead, and a 10-weight for kings and Situk or Karta steelies, or for fishing in intertidal areas with lots of wind, such as those found near Yakutat and on Prince of Wales Island. Carry a full assortment of lines, all fitted with a braided loop leader system. I carry floating and short, sink-tip lines for the lighter rods, and stick to the heavy, shooting heads for the heavy tackle.

And last, but certainly not least, take along a catch and release philosophy. Keep a couple of fish for the pan, and release the rest, safely.

It's important to choose the right boat and outboard for the area you'll be fishing or hunting. Judging by what's left of this prop, this boater would have been better off using a jet unit. This is especially true when traveling glacial rivers.

Planning Your Trip

Cabin Types and Facilities

The two most common types of cabins in Alaska's National Forests are A-frames and Pan Abodes. Each can sleep at least four to six people. A-frame cabins have an additional second floor sleeping loft. Cabins generally come furnished with tables, benches, plywood bunks (without mattresses), wood or oil heating/cooking stoves, ax/maul, broom and outhouses. The cabins do not have electricity, bedding or cooking utensils. Be sure to take an air or foam mattress, propane cookstove, and personal flotation devices if you plan to be on the water.

Typical A-Frame

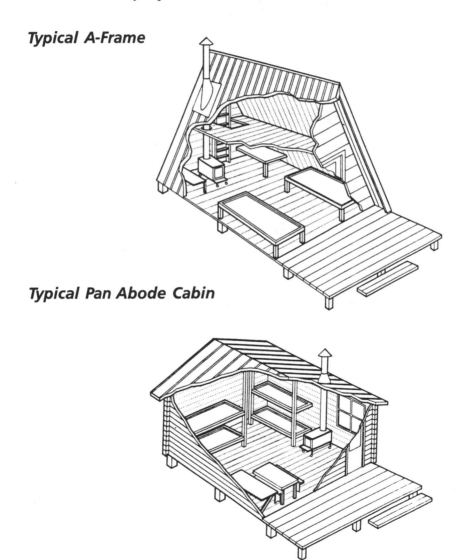

Typical Pan Abode Cabin

Cabin Reservations

Permits for public recreation cabins in the Chugach and Tongass National Forests are issued for non-commercial purposes to anyone 18 years of age or older on a first-come, first-served basis. Applications can be obtained by mail or by visiting any Forest Service office in the Alaska Region. Pay in cash or make checks or postal money orders payable to USDA Forest Service. For all mail applications or for applications in advance of the tenth day, send only check or money order.

In the Tongass National Forest, applications for permits may be postmarked or delivered in person no earlier than 190 days before the first day of planned use. Checks or money orders will be returned if the application was postmarked before the 190th day preceding the first day of planned use. If more than one application is received from 180 through 190 days in advance of intended use for a cabin for overlapping dates, a drawing will be held on the 179th day preceding the time of use to determine the successful permittee. Scheduled drawings are also held for some popular cabins during peak use periods. Drawing times and rules are available from the office administering the cabins. Payments will be returned to unsuccessful applicants, or if the requested cabin is unavailable.

In the Chugach cabin reservation system, reservations are assigned no sooner than 8 a.m. on the 179th day before the first day of intended use on a first-come, first-served basis. Applications must include payment of cabin use fees for the entire stay.

Permits are issued under provisions of the Granger-Thye Act, which requires the permittee to assist in cabin maintenance. Your signature on the maintenance agreement says you agree to these terms.

Any number of persons can occupy a cabin under a single permit. Use under most permits is limited to seven nights between April 1 and October 31, and 10 nights between November 1 and March 31. In the Chugach, from May 15 through August 31, permits for hike-in cabins on the Resurrection Pass, Russian Lakes, Crescent Lake and Crow Pass trails are valid for a maximum of three consecutive nights. Cabins are reserved from noon to noon.

Keep in mind that unauthorized use of these cabins is a violation of both state and federal laws and regulations. Violators are subject to a fine of $500, up to six months imprisonment, or both. Violations should be reported immediately to a Forest Service officer. Be certain to have your permit with you while using the cabin.

Burn combustible waste and pack out all other garbage, including unused food and fuel and pack out empty fuel cans. Leave a supply of firewood, using dead or downed trees. Do not cut live trees.

Refunds

To be eligible for a refund or transfer, a written request for the refund or change must be postmarked or delivered in person to the Forest Service office issuing the permit at least 10 days before the first day of scheduled use. The original permit must accompany the request. One change in a reservation (choice of cabin or reservation dates) may be granted if the request is made before the 10-day grace period. Refunds are not made if inclement weather conditions, frozen lakes, snow-covered trails and other acts of nature beyond Forest Service control prevent you from reaching the cabin, or if cabin-related equipment is not available.

Where to Obtain Permits

For information about reserving public recreation cabins in Alaska, contact the forest supervisor that manages the cabin(s) you are interested in:

Forest Supervisor—
Ketchikan Area
Tongass National Forest
Federal Building
Ketchikan, Alaska 99901
(907)225-3101

Craig Ranger District
Tongass National Forest
P.O. Box 500
Craig, Alaska 99921
(907) 826-3271

Thorne Bay Ranger District
Tongass National Forest
P.O. Box 1
Ketchikan, Alaska 99919
(907) 828-3304

Misty Fiords National Monument
P.O. Box 6137
3031 Tongass Avenue
Ketchikan, Alaska 99901
(907) 225-2148

Forest Supervisor—
Chatham Area
Tongass National Forest
204 Siginaka Way
Sitka, Alaska 99835
(907) 747-6671

Sitka Ranger District
Tongass National Forest
P.O. Box 504
Sitka, Alaska 99835
(907) 747-6671

Juneau Ranger District
Tongass National Forest
8465 Old Dairy Road
Juneau, Alaska 99803
(907) 586-8800

Admiralty Island National Monument
P.O. Box 2097
Juneau, Alaska 99803
(907) 586-8790

Hoonah Ranger District
Tongass National Forest
P.O. Box 135
Hoonah, Alaska 99829
(907) 945-3631

Forest Supervisor—
Stikine Area
Tongass National Forest
P.O. Box 309
Petersburg, Alaska 99833
(907) 772-3871

Petersburg Ranger District
Tongass National Forest
P.O. Box 1328
Petersburg, Alaska 99833
(907) 772-3871

Wrangell Ranger District
Tongass National Forest
P.O. Box 51
Wrangell, Alaska 99929
(907) 874-2323

Forest Supervisor—
Chugach National Forest
201 E. 9th Ave., Suite 206
Anchorage, Alaska 99501-3698
(907) 271-2500

Seward Ranger District
Chugach National Forest
P.O. Box 390
Seward, Alaska 99664
(907) 224-3374

Glacier Ranger District
Chugach National Forest
P.O. Box 129
Girdwood, Alaska 99587-0129
(907) 783-3242

Cordova Ranger District
Chugach National Forest
P.O. Box 280
Cordova, Alaska 99574
(907) 424-7661

Equipment

While offering full protection from the elements, recreation cabins do not have many items important for the comfort of your stay. Electricity is one such item. You'll need to bring your own **lantern, fuel** and **flashlights**. In extreme cases, some people pack in a **portable generator set**.

You'll need to bring a **sleeping bag**. A three-pound bag for summer and five-pound bag, with liner, for fall and winter will handle most of Alaska's varied weather.

Rain gear, ankle-fit hip boots and **warm clothing** are essential. Many recreationists take a small **daypack** to carry gear to and from the field. **Insect repellent** is a must during the summer months. To keep bites to a minimum, I use Ben's 100 for exposed skin and hands, and a spray such as Off! for hair and clothing. Some cabins near lakes or salt water do not have boats. If you intend to fish, hunt or explore these areas, a small **Porta-Bote** or **inflatable** with a **2-to 10-hp outboard** and a minimum of **five gallons of gas** will add to your enjoyment.

When reserving your cabin, be sure to check the specific stove information. The Forest Service does not provide stove oil for cabin users. Oil can be purchased from vendors in the various coastal communities. It must be **No. 1 diesel oil** for the stoves to operate properly. Oil use varies from five to 10 gallons per week, depending on the time of year and the weather.

At cabins furnished with wood stoves, wood may be provided but must be split. Check with the Forest Service office administering the cabin for information on wood availability. An ax or maul is provided at each cabin with a wood stove, but you should bring a **small ax** or **hatchet** just in case the tools at the cabin are not there. For all cabins, I recommend you take a **cooking stove** such as the Coleman Peak 1.

Checklist

- ☐ Ankle-fit hip boots
- ☐ Camp/hiking boots
- ☐ Casual shoes
- ☐ Raingear, either Goretex or PVC-type with pants
- ☐ Thinsulite vest or sweater
- ☐ Jacket
- ☐ Wool or cotton shirts
- ☐ Polar Fleece or wool-blend pants
- ☐ Hat and gloves
- ☐ Polypropylene longjohns
- ☐ Polypropylene/wool socks
- ☐ Extra shoelaces
- ☐ Extra eyeglasses
- ☐ Collapsible water jug
- ☐ Metal mess kit
- ☐ Food
- ☐ Synthetic fill sleeping bag
- ☐ Air mattress or pad
- ☐ First-Aid kit
- ☐ Camera, film/batteries
- ☐ Lighter and matches
- ☐ Candle
- ☐ Plastic trash bags
- ☐ Backpack
- ☐ Insect repellent
- ☐ Toilet articles
- ☐ Fishing equipment

Tips on Operating U.S.F.S. Oil Stoves

In areas without a supply of firewood, cabins are furnished with oil stoves for heating only. Here are several guidelines and tips to follow regarding oil stove use and operation:

- Fuel is not provided with cabin rental. You must bring your own supply of No. 1 stove oil (diesel fuel). No. 2 furnace oil will foul the stove burner.

- Never use gasoline, kerosene or Blazo in any combination for fuel.

- Carry fuel in a sealed, unbreakable container, especially if you are flying to the cabin. Air charter services will not haul any hazardous chemicals unless properly stored. It is best to buy and transport fuel in sealed, metal containers.

- Keep the fuel clean. Do not dump the bottom dregs or water into the oil tank. Water or dirt will foul the system.

- Do not leave fuel containers at the cabin. Fly them out with you when you leave.

Principles of Burning

In an oil stove, the oil must vaporize in the pot to properly burn. To vaporize fuel, the pot must be hot. The stove must burn at low fuel flow (number 1 on the fuel selector control) for at least 30 minutes before being turned higher.

Too much oil, too soon, cools and floods the pot. This prevents it from vaporizing the oil and soots the stove and pipe. An oil stove generally takes a couple of hours to heat a cabin to comfortable room temperature. Please be patient.

How to Light

Fill the tank, which is usually located outside the cabin. Leave the cap loose so air can enter the tank and the oil does not have to work against a vacuum. Open valve at tank (if equipped with one). Ensure the tank is above the stove's carburetor. Click the oil flow lever down (on carburetors equipped with one). Turn the fuel regulating knob to No. 1, and wait for the fuel to seep into the bottom of the pot.

Light a one-inch square of tissue or newspaper and drop it into the edge of the oil seep in the pot. Wooden matches and large wads of paper will foul ignition and burning canister.

Watch the pot carefully now to ensure that too much oil does not flow into the pot. If it does, turn off the fuel, and let the pot burn the excess oil. Turn on the oil just before the fire dies because oil going into a white-hot pot will atomize and cause an explosion. Now, allow the stove to burn for 30 to 40 minutes on the lowest setting to heat the pot enough to properly vaporize the oil.

When the pot warms to the burning temperature, gradually increase the fuel flow. The average setting is No. 3.

Filling the Tank

Fill the tank away from the cabin so spilled oil will not create a fire hazard. (NOTE: At some cabins, such as Karta and Staney Creek, tanks can't be moved).

Draining the Filter

If water appears in filter sediment bowl, put a can under the filter and loosen the bottom. Drain down to clean oil. Discard waste water away from the cabin.

Fuel Won't Flow?

It is imperative that the following steps be checked and followed, otherwise fuel won't flow:

- Oil regulator knob open, fuel flow lever clicked down (on those equipped with it)
- Ensure tank is above carburetor.
- Loosen cap on oil tank.
- Remove any water from sediment bowl filter.
- Remove the clean-out plug on the pipe that goes into the pot. It should be open. If not, run a wire through the pipe to open it.
- Clean the filter on the bottom of the carburetor. Unscrew the large nut or screws over an open oil can. If there is water or dirt in the carburetor, it will drain into the can.

Stove Runs Fine For Several Hours and Stops?

The oil tank cap is probably on too tight. Loosen and allow air into the tank.

Dirty Oil Pot?

With a spoon or hard piece of wood, scrape the inside of the pot, removing the scales and unclogging the airholes. Remove any material in the pot.

How Long Will the Fuel Last?

Lowest Setting: Ten hours per gallon of oil.
Average Setting (No. 3): Five hours per gallon of oil.
Highest Setting: Two hours per gallon of oil.

Damper Regulation

Oven damper: Turn the metal rod so it is pointing up to circulate more heat to the oven. Turn it down to start and for less heat to the oven. To efficiently heat the cabin, leave the oven door open and the damper handle up. Do not turn the adjusting, air control knob.

If the stove needs maintenance, advise the U.S. Forest Service. Remember, it's better to have a stove that works, even if not perfectly, than one that doesn't work after you've tried to fix the carburetor.

Outdoor Safety

I recommend extra food, as your stay may be prolonged by bad weather or poor visibility. In remote locations, take topographic maps, compass, knife, waterproof matches, knife with five-inch blade, first-aid kit, space blanket, small tent or emergency shelter, extra food, candles and flares. For those experienced with firearms, a rifle, .338 or larger, should be taken into areas with large concentrations of bears. You should also educate yourself on how to reduce your chances of a bear encounter. Contact the Forest Service for a copy of its informative pamphlet, "Bears and You."

Water

Many rivers and streams in the Tongass and Chugach forests are crystal clear and give the impression that the water is pure. However, clarity is not an indication of the absence of bacteria or *giardia*.

Giardiasis is a major problem. After ingestion by humans, *giardia* attach themselves to the small intestine. Disease symptoms usually include diarrhea, increased gas, loss of appetite, abdominal cramps and bloating. These discomforts may first appear a few days to a few weeks after ingestion of the *giardia* organisms and may last up to six weeks. If not treated, the symptoms may disappear on their own, only to reoccur intermittently over a period of many months. With proper diagnosis, the disease is curable with medication prescribed by a physician.

There are several ways for you to treat raw water to make it safe to drink. The safest way to destroy *giardia* is to boil water for at least one minute, preferably five. Boiling also destroys other disease-carrying organisms. At high altitudes, you should always boil water from three to five minutes for added safety.

Chemical disinfectants such as iodine or chlorine tablets or drops are not yet considered as reliable as heat in killing *giardia*, although these products do work well against most waterborne bacteria and viruses that cause disease. In an emergency where chemical disinfection is necessary, use an iodine-based product, since iodine is more effective than chlorine. If possible, filter or strain the water first, add iodine and wait for least 30 minutes before you drink the water. If the water is cold or cloudy, allow the iodine to work for at least an hour, or use more iodine.

Even though the lake or stream may look perfectly safe, make it a point to thoroughly boil all water before drinking.

Hypothermia

Hypothermia, the subnormal temperature of the body, is the number one killer of outdoor recreationists. Caused by exposure to cold, it is aggravated by wetness, wind and exhaustion.

The first step toward hypothermia is exposure and exhaustion. The moment you begin to lose heat faster than your body produces it, you are undergoing exposure. Two things happen. You voluntarily exercise to stay warm, and your body makes involuntary adjustments to preserve normal temperature in the vital organs. Both responses drain your energy reserves. The only way to stop the drain is to reduce the degree of exposure.

The second step is hypothermia. If exposure continues until your energy reserves are exhausted, cold reaches the brain, depriving you of judgement and reasoning power. You won't be aware that this is happening. You will lose control of your hands, and perhaps stumble. This is hypothermia. Your internal temperature is dropping. Without treatment, this drop leads to stupor, collapse and death.

How do you defend against hypothermia? Choose clothing that retains its insulating value when wet. Polar fleece is an excellent choice, as is Qualofil. Choose raingear that covers the head, neck, body and legs and provides good protection against wind-driven rain. Polyurethane-coated nylon is best. Avoid worn-out raingear, and some types of "breathable raingear." They don't hold up in Alaska's inclement weather.

And last, understand how cold affects the body. Most hypothermia cases develop in air temperatures between 30 and 50 degrees Fahrenheit.

Insect Pests

Alaska is home to various species of mosquitoes, and depending on the time of year, you may or may not encounter them. Mosquito bites usually leave welts that itch for several days. Scratching may result in secondary infections. Occasionally the bites cause an allergic reaction or low fever.

Alaska has some species of mosquitoes that winter as adults. Called "brown bombers," they emerge from hibernation before the snow has entirely disappeared. "Brown bombers," and the Aedes species, most disliked by sportsmen, peak in June and decline steadily thereafter. Mosquitoes are most active at twilight and early morning. A 5-mph wind grounds most mosquitoes, reducing the pest problem.

White-sox, also called black flies, simulids and buffalo gnats, start become active in May, and generally plague sportsmen until freeze-up. The reaction to bites is usually pronounced and the swelling and itching may last a week or more. Unlike mosquitoes, black flies crawl under loose clothing and into the hair and ears to bite.

No-see-ums, also called punkies, pester anglers from June through August. Along some coastal areas, they are the major biting fly pest, picking out exposed parts of the body. The bite is a most annoying, prolonged prick, after which the surrounding skin becomes inflamed, producing an itchy, small red spot. Clothing that covers as much of the body as possible offers the most protection. Products such as After-Bite offer some degree of relief.

Pack a small bottle of repellent with you at all times. Those repellents containing diethyl meta-toluamide (DEET) are most effective, especially when used in roughly 50 percent concentrations of the active ingredient. The best, of course, are the 95 percent active ingredients. A single application offers from two to 10 hours of protection.

Paralytic Shellfish Poisoning

Alaska has a significant problem with poisonous shellfish. This poison is commonly referred to as Paralytic Shellfish Poisoning (PSP). Alaska clams may be poisonous unless they have been harvested from an approved beach. Clams from approved beaches should still be eviscerated (gut removed) before eating them. The latest information on approved beaches is available from:

Alaska Division of Agriculture
Department of Natural Resources
P.O. Box 1088
Palmer, Alaska 99645
Tel: (907) 745-3236

Southeast Regional Laboratory
Alaska Department of Health and Social
Services
P.O. Box J
Juneau, Alaska 99811
Tel: (907) 586-3586

When PSP toxin is present, symptoms may appear soon after the clams are eaten; perhaps in less than an hour. The initial symptoms include a tingling numbness of the lips and tongue followed by tingling and numbness in the fingertips and toes. This may progress to loss of muscular coordination. Other possible symptoms are dizziness, weakness, drowsiness and incoherence.

Death from respiratory muscle paralysis may occur within three to 12 hours after the clams are eaten. Anyone who has eaten clams and has begun to experience symptoms like these should get prompt medical care. The current treatment is to administer an emetic to empty the stomach and a rapid-acting laxative. Emetics are available at most drug stores, and do not require a prescription. When breathing becomes difficult or ceases, artificial respiration may prove effective. Leftover clams should be saved for laboratory tests.

Razor clam digging is popular along the approved marine beaches of Alaska's National Forests. Photo by Sharon Durgan Wilson.

Wildlife

Alaska's National Forests offers a full complement of wildlife for everyone from the casual user to the professional wildlife photographer. The smaller residents include **mice, voles, squirrels, martens, hoary marmots, beavers** and **muskrats.** Larger animals include **moose, Sitka black-tailed deer, mountain goats, wolves,** and **black or brown bear.** In the Chugach and Yakutat area, expect to find **Dall sheep, caribou** and **Alaska-Yukon moose.**

The forest system offers ample hunting opportunities. During the 1988-89 hunting season, about 9,000 people hunted deer in southeast Alaska and harvested over 16,500 animals. Admiralty, Baranof and Chicagof Islands contributed over 60 percent of the take. On Admiralty Island, biologists estimate there is one brown bear for every square mile of habitat, one of the highest concentrations in North America. And the Cordova area of the Chugach National Forest is home to some of the largest moose in Alaska.

You don't need to be a hunter to enjoy Alaska's wildlife. In several areas, there are viewing platforms where you can photograph bears fishing for salmon, or watch goats graze in high alpine meadows. Either way, interacting with wildlife in such a grand setting is sure to be a highlight of your trip.

The marshlands and lakes are popular nesting and rearing areas for birds and waterfowl. The **bald eagle** is common throughout the southeast Panhandle, especially near salmon streams and tidal areas. Alaska's state bird, the ptarmigan, can be seen in alpine meadows and in shrubby flatlands. **Crows** and **ravens** are common and noisily make their presence known to all. The varied **thrush, kinglets sparrows** and **warblers** may also be encountered on your hike through the forest. For a more comprehensive checklist of birds, contact the Alaska Department of Fish and Game or Forest Service office in your area.

Ground squirrels and marmots are only two of the many species of wildlife found in Alaska's National Forests.

Flora

The plants found in the Tongass National Forest are many. Here are a few of the major varieties you'll find:

Sitka spruce. Comprises about 20 percent of the Tongass Forest. It is easily recognized by the stiff, sharp-tipped needles that are round to square in cross section. Most of the spruce cut in the Tongass is sawn into large timbers for shipment to Japan. Other uses include airplane construction, piano sounding boards and oars.

Western hemlock. Covers about 75 percent of the forest in southeast Alaska. Recognize it by its short, round-tipped needles that appear flattened. Hemlock is economically important as one of the best sources for producing high-grade dissolving pulp for the manufacture of cellophane and rayon. It is also used for lumber, marine pilings and plywood.

Alaska cedar and western red cedar. Cedars are easily recognized by scale-like, flattened needles that grow in an overlapping manner. Western red cedar is the most widely used wood for shingles. The Indians used it for totem poles and canoes. Alaska cedar is valuable for window frames, exterior doors and boat construction. Both woods are highly aromatic.

Lodgepole or shorepine is found in muskegs and areas with poorly drained soils. The pines growing in southeast do not have major commercial value as wood fiber. Their value is in providing habitat for wild animals and birds. The pines are easily recognized by their needles, which exceed one inch in length and are borne in pairs enclosed in a bundle at the twig.

Red alder is the most abundant broadleaf found in this area. All alders are easily recognized by their smooth, gray bark with horizontal lines and a deep green, wide-toothed leaf which greatly resembles a birch leaf. Alders are common along streams, beach fringes and in areas where the soil has been disturbed by landslides, glaciers or logging. Alder makes valuable firewood, and is also used for smoking meat or fish.

Berry bushes are found throughout the region, and all but a few are edible. Depending on the location and elevation, ripe berries are found from July through October. Some of the berries to enjoy are the bright red or orange salmonberry, red and blue varieties of delicious huckleberries, the familiar blueberry, the thimbleberry and high bush cranberry.

Skunk cabbage is common throughout the Tongass and Chugach forests in May and June. The flowers are the first to emerge, and resemble a cupped yellow spearhead with a thick green stem arising from its center. This stem bears the young, edible emerging leaves. Boil them, with several water changes, and eat them like cabbage. When grown, the leaves can reach over two feet in length. The Indians wrapped salmon in the leaves and baked the fish in their firepits. Brown and black bears relish the stalk.

Wildflowers are everywhere, but you may have to hunker close to the ground to see them. In forested areas, the hiker may encounter wood violets, yellow monkey flower, white ground dogwood, pink lousewort or abundant varieties of berries from late summer through fall. The muskegs of southeast Alaska even offer a carnivorous plant, the sundew.

Irritant plants are few, but you should be able to recognize and avoid them. The scientific name for **devil's club** is Opolopanax horridus, and horridus explains how many people feel about this shrub. It grows to 10 feet in height, and the huge maple-shaped leaves and stems are covered with sharp, barbed spines. When a spine touches your skin, it produces the same irritation as a bee or nettle sting. Expect some swelling. Because of the barbs, the spines are difficult to remove. Wear gloves and long-sleeved shirts in areas where devil's club is abundant.

Poisonous plants occur in Alaska, but illness from them is uncommon and reports of deaths are rare. With proper precautions there is little danger. Poisoning can occur through eating (ingestion) and external poisoning. Severe allergic reactions may occur from touching plants. The most serious danger is to children, who may eat plants out of curiosity or because the plant, or its flowers or berries look tasty.

The best advice is to learn to recognize and avoid the uncommon poisonous plants in Alaska. The most dangerous include **water hemlock, death camos and certain species of mushrooms**. In addition, some individuals develop severe allergic reactions from coming in contact with such plants as **Indian rhubarb and nettles**.

Poisonous berries are rare, but one you should become familiar with is the baneberry. It has either white or red berries and is commonly found in forests and thickets. A perennial that grows from two to three feet high, **baneberry** has large, lobed and coarsely toothed leaves. A plant guide to southeast Alaska will make your stay more enjoyable. Consider purchasing, *"Wild and Edible and Poisonous Plants of Alaska"* at your bookstore or from the University of Alaska Cooperative Extension Service. Being able to identify and harvest salmonberries and currants will make a delightful experience, especially when the berries are used in a sauce to baste freshly caught cutthroat or to added to a crouton stuffing of a soon-to-be baked blue grouse.

Alaska's abundant flora attract naturalists from around the world who collect as well as study marine coastal plantlife.

Other Recreational Opportunities

Many Forest Service cabins serve as a base for other activities. Incredibly beautiful waterfalls, glaciers, fiords, islands, lush greenery and an abundance of wildlife, birds and waterfowl provide the setting for a **photo safari** or just plain **sight-seeing**.

Kayaking or **boating** may be your main pasttime in an area that seems to be more water than land. Thousands of miles of coastline offer **beachcombers** Japanese glass-ball commercial fishing floats (which are coveted collector's items), a variety of seashells and unexpected treasures brought in by the tide. **Hiking** trails of all degrees of difficulty will lead you on new adventures and challenges. **Rock hounding** is a popular avocation on national forest lands, and we list a few productive spots in the cabin description pages.

Many of the cabins make perfect retreats in the winter. Trails and wide open meadows become snow-covered playgrounds for **cross-country skiers** and **snow-shoers**. Cabins near the road system host **snowmachiners**, who have thousands of acres of national forest lands to explore. In the Juneau area, local residents gather at USFS cabins for weekends of fun and camaraderie while they **downhill ski**.

Recreational gold panning is your chance to share some of the excitement the early goldseekers felt as they arrived in Alaska and tamed the wilderness. Bring your gold pan, shovel and a glass vial to store your hard-earned flakes. If you're lucky and find a nugget, put it in your pocket—just make sure the pocket doesn't have a hole!

Use of recreational gold pans, manual-feed sluice boxes and 4-inch suction dredges are permitted in active waterway channels of the national forests, but excavating or digging in stream banks is prohibited. The Forest Service publishes guidelines meant to protect the environment, the resources and the rights of other visitors. Obtain the guidelines from the region you plan to visit, and follow them in good faith.

Whatever your choice of recreation, you should have no trouble finding it in Alaska's National Forests.

The Kenai Peninsula hosts a variety of gold mining operations, which hikers and anglers should avoid. Recreationists can pan for gold in designated areas.

Additional Questions?

For more information, contact the following agencies:

Alaska Fishing and Hunting Books, Periodicals and Information
Alaska Angler/Alaska Hunter Publications
P.O. Box 83550
Fairbanks, Alaska 99708
(907) 455-8000

Fishing and Hunting Licenses
Alaska Department of Fish and Game Headquarters
P.O. Box 25526
Juneau, Alaska 99802
(907) 465-4112

Ferry Information
Alaska Marine Highway System
P.O. Box R
1591 Glacier Avenue
Juneau, Alaska 99811
(907) 465-3940

Tourism Information
Alaska Division of Tourism
P.O. Box E
Juneau, Alaska 99811
(907) 465-2010

Nautical and Topographic Maps and Charts
U.S. Geological Survey
Map Sales
Box 12, Federal Building
101 12th Ave
Fairbanks, Alaska 99701
(907) 456-0244

Alaska Chambers of Commerce
State Chamber of Commerce
217 Second Street, Suite 201
Juneau, Alaska 99801
(907) 278-2722

1 Gateway Ketchikan
Fishing the TONGASS National Forest

About the Gateway

Ketchikan is Alaska's port of entry. This fishing town was established when a saltery and a salmon cannery were built near the mouth of Ketchikan Creek in 1887. Timbering is one of the chief industries in Ketchikan today. The city is built on a narrow ledge of land between the ocean and mountains of Revillagigedo Island. Many of the streets and buildings in town are built on pilings, docks or trestles.

The road system on nearby Prince of Wales Island is the most extensive in southeast Alaska. Over 700 miles of gravel roads lead to villages, prime fishing locations, and a variety of resource and fisheries-rich areas. The island hosts a large logging industry, as well as mining and construction.

Population: 14,000
Annual Precipitation: 162 inches
Average summer high temperature: 65 degrees F.

Fishing the Ketchikan Area

The best angling opportunities for Ketchikan anglers are at remote, fly-in and off-road sites, with the USFS cabin waters being the most popular. Due to restricted access, saltwater shoreline fishing is limited. However, local anglers favor Herring Bay for coho salmon, and Settlers Cove and Mountain Point for pink salmon. The best freshwater angling spot accessible by road is the Ward Cove Lake drainage, which offers Dollies, coho, steelhead and cutthroat trout.

About 50 percent of eastern Behm Canal is closed to salmon fishing year round and 75 percent is closed from May 1 to August 15. While Ketchikan supports an active sportfishery, over 80 percent of the angling effort occurs in salt water, with nearly all this effort concentrated in the area between Mountain Point and Clover Pass. However, anglers with their own boats take extended fishing trips around Revillagigedo Island. Several USFS cabins are located along the Behm Canal, which serve as convenient stopover locations and protected anchorages.

The most popular species among non-residents are salmon and halibut. The bulk of the halibut fishing occurs in Clarence Strait, just south of Kasaan Point, along the 20 Fathom Bank. Another popular hotspot is the Naha River and Lake system, located on western Revillagigedo Island. Four species of salmon, fall and spring-run steelhead and trophy-sized cutthroat trout (up to 3.5 pounds) await the angler. According to ADF&G, Orton and Snow lakes offer grayling fishing that receives relatively light pressure.

A good choice for trophy cutthroat trout, (fish to 21 inches and weighing over three pounds) is Wilson Lake. However, the area receives moderate to heavy angling pressure.

Prince of Wales Island offers numerous fishing opportunities for do-it-yourself anglers thanks to the recently extended road system. The most sought-after species are coho, steelhead and cutthroat trout, however, the Luck and Sarkar systems are becoming increasingly popular among sockeye salmon anglers. In the Ketchikan region, lake populations of cutthroat range from two to 11 catchable fish per acre.

There are over 140 lakes that offer good cutthroat trout fisheries. Many more contain cutthroats that are presently unexploited. Over 60 streams in the area contain healthy populations of anadromous trout. Over 14,000 trout are taken from this region annually, with the majority coming from freshwater systems. Nearly half of the total annual harvest occurs near the city of Ketchikan.

Southern southeast Alaska hosts about 269 steelhead streams (compared to 62 in northern southeast Alaska). Fall fish are most common throughout this region, especially on Prince of Wales Island. Size and extent of steelhead runs in this region is vague at best. ADF&G estimates there are at least eight runs having more than 500 fish. These include: Naha River on Revillagigedo Island; Eagle, Staney and Klawak creeks and the Thorne River on Prince of Wales Island; Kadake Creek on Kuiu Island; and Petersburg Creek and Hamilton and Castle rivers on Kupreanof Island. Most offer USFS cabins for anglers, but the cabins are often booked solid during the peak of the runs.

Consensus is that many of these and other systems have greater numbers. For instance, according to Schwan (1984), the Karta River prior to 1983 had an estimated run size of 200 to 500 adult steelhead. A weir count in 1983 established that there were more than 1,021 adult steelhead in the river that spring. Only 50 were taken by sport anglers. Fishing pressure today is much greater. (NOTE: For steelhead fishing in this region, spring is usually listed as the best time for catching fish, due to the number of fish available, and the fact that many have completed spawning. Anglers should keep in mind that these southern southeastern streams often offer good steelheading in the fall).

In southern southeast, about half of the rainbow sport harvest is taken from streams. Many of these fish are reportedly rearing steelhead. On the average, a rainbow here takes four years to grow eight inches and six to eight years to grow 16 inches.

Most of the annual harvest of Dolly Varden are taken in the Kake-Wrangell-Petersburg area. Ketchikan provides the fewest fish taken. One reason is the abundance of other freshwater angling species available to anglers.

In southern southeast, brook trout lakes include Whitman, Perseverance, Ketchikan, Grace and Claude in the Ketchikan area; Crystal Lake near Petersburg; Bugge near Craig; and Nellie in the Bradfield Canal area.

Southeast Alaska has 17 lakes known to contain reproducing populations of grayling, although not all plants have been evaluated.

In southern southeast Alaska, all of the 14 grayling lakes are remote, and provide a harvest of about 250 fish per year. On the average, grayling take two to three years to grow 10 inches, and in watersheds with good forage, grayling can attain lengths of up to 16 inches. Little else is known about this species in southeast Alaska.

In the Ketchikan area, anglers harvest around 20,000 pinks per year, however this harvest fluctuates from 8,000 to 24,000 fish, depending on the size and strength of the annual runs. About 20 percent of this catch is from salt water.

For information on recreational cabins in this area, contact:

Ketchikan Area Office, Federal Building, Mill & Stedman Streets, Ketchikan, Alaska 99901, (907) 225-3101

Ketchikan Ranger District, 3031 Tongass, Ketchikan, Alaska 99901, (907) 225-2148

Prince of Wales Island, Contact: Tongass National Forest, Federal Building, Ketchikan, Alaska 99901, (907) 225-3101

Fishing Index

Forest Service cabins in this gateway are listed below. The types of fish available in the vicinity of the cabin are indicated. You can cross-reference the cabin by the F.S. #, a number assigned to each cabin by the Forest Service. A description of the cabin and its facilities can be found on the page listed on the chart, and the page number of the map showing the exact cabin location is listed in the last column.

Gateway 1 — Ketchikan

Cabin	F.S. #	Page	Cutthroat Trout	Dolly Varden	Grayling	Rainbow Trout	Steelhead	Chinook Salmon	Coho Salmon	Chum Salmon	Pink Salmon	Sockeye Salmon	Halibut	Rockfish	Map pg.
Anchor Pass Cabin	K-1	65							•	•			•	•	61
Barnes Lake Cabin	T-1	66								•		•			64
Black Bear Lake Cabin	KC-1	67	•	•				•	•						57
Blind Pass Cabin	K-2	68						•	•	•			•	•	61
Blue Lake Shelter	K-21	69													60
Control Lake Cabin	T-2	70	•	•					•	•	•	•			57
Deer Mountain Shelter	K-22	71													60
Essowah Lake Cabin	KC-2	72	•	•					•	•	•	•			59
Fish Creek Cabin	K-3	73	•	•				•	•	•	•	•			62
Fisheries Cabin	K-4	75	•	•				•	•	•	•	•			61
Grindall Island Cabin	T-3	74							•	•		•			56
Heckman Lake Cabin	K-5	75	•	•				•	•	•	•	•			61
Helm Bay Cabin	K-6	76	•					•	•	•		•	•	•	61
Helm Creek Cabin	K-16	76	•					•	•	•		•	•	•	61
Honker Lake Cabin	T-4	77	•	•				•	•	•	•	•			57
Jordan Lake Cabin	K-7	78	•	•					•	•	•	•			61
Josephine Lake Cabin	KC-3	79			•										56
Karta Lake Cabin	T-5	80	•	•				•	•	•	•	•			58
Karta River Cabin	T-6	83	•	•				•	•	•	•	•			58
Kegan Cove Cabin	KC-4	84	•	•				•	•	•	•	•	•		56
Kegan Creek Cabin	KC-5	85	•	•				•	•	•	•	•			56
Lake Shelokum Shelter	K-23	86	•												61
Long Lake Shelter	K-24	87	•	•					•						61
McDonald Lake Shelter	K-25	89	•	•				•	•	•	•	•			61
McGilvery Creek Cabin	T-7	97	•	•				•	•	•	•	•			58
Orchard Lake Cabin	K-10	103	•	•											62
Patching Lake Cabin	K-11	90	•	•	•			•	•	•	•	•			61
Phocena Bay Cabin	K-9	91							•	•	•	•	•	•	60
Plenty Cutthroat Cabin	K-12	103	•	•											61
Point Amargura Cabin	KC-6	92							•	•	•	•	•	•	57
Portage Cabin	K-13	90	•	•	•			•	•	•	•	•			61
Rainbow Lake Cabin	K-14	93	•						•		•	•	•		58
Red Bay Lake Cabin	T-8	94	•	•				•	•	•	•	•			63

Gateway 1
Ketchikan

Cabin	F.S. #	Page	Cutthroat Trout	Dolly Varden	Grayling	Rainbow Trout	Steelhead	Chinook Salmon	Coho Salmon	Chum Salmon	Pink Salmon	Sockeye Salmon	Halibut	Rockfish	Map pg.
Reflection Lake Cabin	K-15	95	•	•		•	•		•		•	•			55
Reflection Lake Shelter	K-26	95	•	•		•	•		•		•	•			55
Salmon Bay Lake Cabin	T-9	96	•	•		•	•		•	•	•	•			63
Salmon Lake Cabin	T-10	97	•	•		•	•		•	•	•	•			58
Sarkar Lake Cabin	T-11	98	•	•		•	•		•	•	•	•			57
Shipley Bay Cabin	T-12	99	•	•		•	•		•	•	•	•			63
Staney Creek Cabin	T-13	100	•	•		•	•		•	•	•	•			57
Sweetwater Lake Cabin	T-14	101	•	•		•	•		•	•	•	•			57
Trollers Cove Cabin	KC-7	102	•					•	•					•	56
Wolf Lake Shelter	K-27	104	•			•									61
Wolverine Island Cabin	K-8	89	•	•		•			•		•	•			61

In both the Tongass and Chugach National Forests, anglers catch grayling on stonefly, mayfly and caddisfly patterns, as well as tiny spoons, spinners and plastic baits.

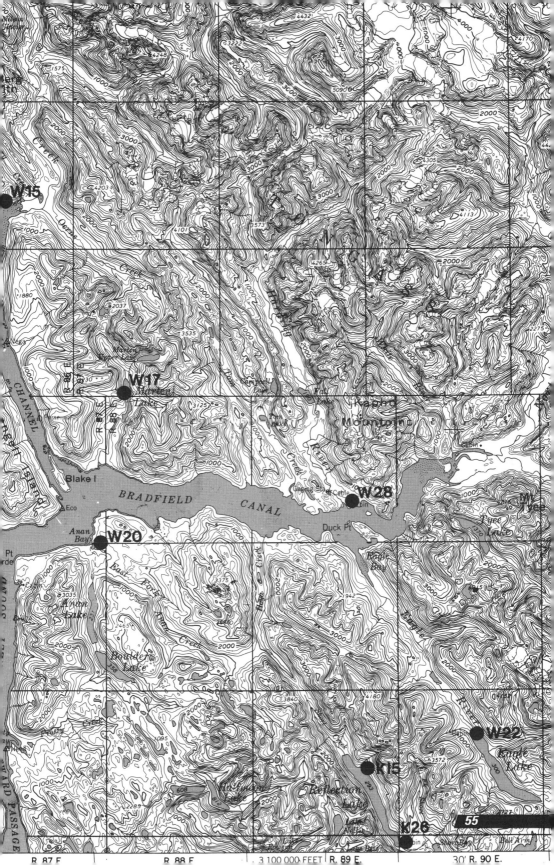

W15

W17

W28

W20

W22

K16

K26

CHANNEL

BRADFIELD CANAL

Kashid Mountain

Anan Bay

Eagle Lake

Mt Tyee

Tyee Lake

Reflection Lake

55

R. 87 E.
R. 88 E.
3 100 000 FEET
R. 89 E.
30′ R. 90 E.

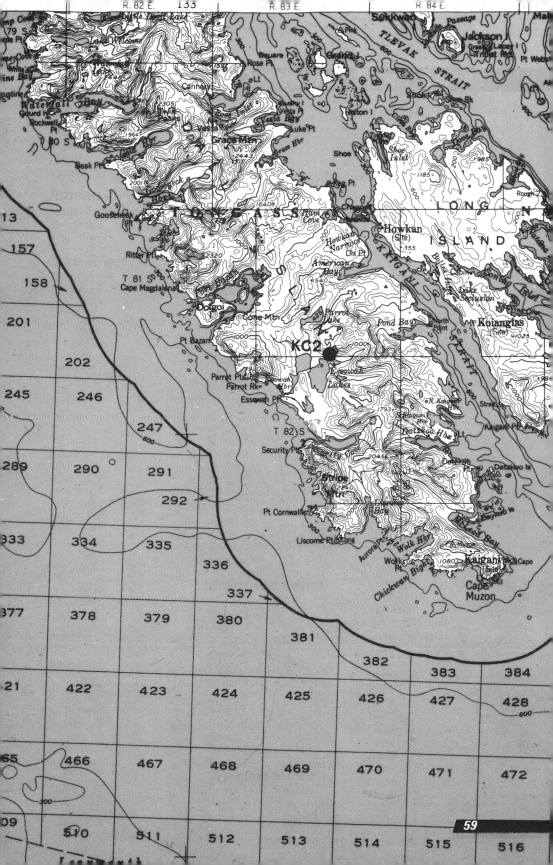

61

Anchor Pass is on the mainland, across from the east end of Bell Island, about 60 air miles north of Ketchikan. Access is by air or water. Minimum round-trip flight time charged from Ketchikan is two hours; three hours by water. (USGS Quad Map Ketchikan D-5)

Fishing

Saltwater fishing and sightseeing are the major attractions of this area. Silver and king salmon, in addition to a variety of bottomfish and halibut, are available. Check state fishing regs for salmon fishing closures in salt water. For the experienced saltwater angler who has a boat, this cabin is a good choice.

Hunting

In areas adjacent to the cabin, hunters pursue Sitka blacktail deer, black bear, brown bear and some distance away, mountain goat.

Other Activities

Numerous opportunities for sightseeing, beachcombing, photography and hiking.

Cabin

Anchor Pass Cabin (K-1)

Anchor Pass cabin is a 12' x 14' Pan Abode, cedar log cabin constructed in 1975. It offers a scenic view of Anchor Pass and Bell Island. The cabin, located at sea level, sleeps six and has a wood-burning stove for heating and cooking. An anchor buoy is provided for boats.

Water source: stream near cabin
Facilities:

- wooden bunks
- outhouse
- wood shed
- wood stove
- ax
- maul
- table
- bench
- no boat

Anchor Pass Cabin.
Photo by USDA
Forest Service.

Barnes Lake

Barnes Lake is in northeast Prince of Wales Island, directly southeast of Stevenson Island. It is 70 air miles from Ketchikan, and 38 air miles from Craig. Minimum round-trip flight time charged from Ketchikan is 2.8 hours. Seaplane anchorage available. Marine travelers can access the lake at high slack tide. (USGS Quad Map Petersburg A-3)

Fishing

Barnes Lake is an intertidal area, and offers good fishing for silver salmon from mid-August through late September. Best fishing is at the narrows where the lake empties into Lake Bay, or in select areas where fish are stranded at low tide. Both flies and spinning lures work well in taking fish here, however, spinning and casting tackle, especially fluorescent spoons and spinners in 1/2- to one-ounce are most effective at high tide. You'll find a small run of pink salmon in a tributary at the western narrows.

Hunting

According to reports, more hunters than anglers use Barnes Lake cabin. Blacktail deer and black bear hunting is good, as well as hunting for puddlers, sea and diving ducks.

Precautions

Use caution when accessing the area by boat. High slack tide is best. Also, the skiff is a heavy-duty model, with a 550-pound capacity. Use a minimum of a 4.5-hp motor, preferably a 7.5-hp.

Cabin
Barnes Lake Cabin (T-1)

Constructed in 1963, the 12' x 12' cedar log Barnes Lake cabin accommodates six people and has a wood-burning stove for heating and cooking. A delightful cabin located in a pristine intertidal area.

Water source: creek
Facilities:
- wooden bunks
- wood stove
- outhouse
- table
- bench
- cooking counter
- shelves
- wood supply
- ax
- maul
- 14-foot aluminum skiff
- oars

Black Bear Lake is in the middle of Prince of Wales Island, 50 air miles from Ketchikan and 12 miles from Craig. Minimum round-trip flight time charged from Ketchikan is two hours. Due to its 1,700-foot elevation, good flying weather is a must to reach the lake. Expect delays flying in and out. (USGS Quad Map Craig C-3)

Fishing

Black Bear Lake offers good fishing for rainbow trout. Fishing is slow during the day, and anglers must resort to deepwater jigging tactics that include drifting with the wind and jigging a spoon or lure at various depths. In early morning and late evening, fish will move into the shallows to feed. Anchor, and cast along the structural breakline, and occasionally into shore with forage fish fly or lure patterns that include sculpins, stickleback or salmon fry. Available in the nearby Black Lake watershed are cutthroat, Dolly Varden and steelhead.

Hunting

Sitka blacktail deer and black bear hunting is good in this area. Glass the hillsides from the lake, and plan your stalk accordingly. Often, stalks can be made from base camp. In late season, the decreasing amount of daylight will restrict how far you can hunt on the mountains behind the cabin. If hunting from a spike camp, severe weather can keep you stranded on the mountains for several days.

Other Activities

An excellent location for hikers or those wishing to explore wilderness areas. Outdoor photographic opportunities are bountiful and excellent.

Cabin
Black Bear Lake Cabin (KC-1)

Reconstructed in 1979, the 12' x 12' Black Bear Lake cabin accommodates six people and offers a wood-burning stove for heating and cooking. Excellent scenery and semi-wilderness environment provide a complete, get-away-from-it-all vacation. Stunted trees and alpine country surround the cabin. Nearby Pin Peak and other mountains rise to nearly 4,000 feet. Ice seldom leaves the lake until June. Few visitors. Construction activity is underway at Black Bear Lake in conjunction with a hydroelectric project. Most activity is at the opposite end of the lake from the cabin. If the dam is constructed, the cabin will have to be relocated.

Water source: lake
Facilities:

- wooden bunks
- outhouse
- wood stove
- wood supply
- table
- bench
- cooking counter
- shelves
- ax
- maul
- 12-foot skiff
- oars

User Comments

8/29-9/5: ''Tell people how difficult access is by plane during most of the summer. Delays in and out. Otherwise a great place.''

Blind Pass is on the northwest side of Hassler Island, off Behm Canal, approximately 40 air miles from Ketchikan. Access is by air or boat. Minimum round-trip flight time charged from Ketchikan is 1.6 hours. It is a two-hour journey by boat. (USGS Quad Map D-5)

Fishing

Hassler Island offers excellent trout fishing a half-mile east by southeast of the cabin. No trail, so take a compass and map. Saltwater fishing for king and silver salmon, plus excellent bottomfishing for rockfish, cod and halibut is in Hassler Pass and Behm Canal. Marine waters also offer good crabbing and shrimping.

Hunting

Deer and black bear are widespread throughout the area.

Other Activities

Sightseeing is a main attraction in this area. There are a myriad of opportunities for beachcombing and photography.

Cabin

Blind Pass Cabin (K-2)

A 12' x 14' Pan Abode cedar log cabin constructed in 1975. Accessible at both high and low tides. Cabin sleeps six, and receives year-round use. Wood stove for heating and cooking. An anchor buoy is provided for boats. Elevation, sea level.

Water source: stream near cabin.
Facilities:

- wooden bunks
- outhouse
- table
- bench
- no boat
- ax
- maul
- woodshed
- wood

User Comments

7/12: ''Excellent upkeep. Sorry to see (that) the cookstove (with oven) which was there in 1980 and '81 is gone, but I'm sure chunk stoves are generally better for the public.''

Blind Pass cabin. Photo courtesy USDA Forest Service.

Blue Lake is above timberline at 2,700 feet elevation on Revillagigedo Island. Accessible via Deer Mountain Trail, 5.3 miles from Ketchikan. (USGS Quad Map Ketchikan B-5)

Hunting

Sitka blacktail deer available in season.

Cabin
Blue Lake Shelter (K-21)

An A-frame that sleeps four. Adirondack shelters are free to the public on a first-come, first-served basis. No reservations are accepted. The area is very scenic.

Water source: lake
Facilities:
* two wooden bunks
* no stove

Blacktail deer track and a 30-06 cartridge.

Control Lake is on northcentral Prince of Wales Island, near Control Lake Junction, about 45 miles from Ketchikan. Minimum round-trip flight time charged from Ketchikan is 1.8 hours. The lake is also accessible by taking Forest Service Road No. 20 from Klawock or Naukati. (USGS Quad Map Craig C-3)

Fishing

Fishing is generally poor in Control Lake, however, there is sometimes fair fishing for a few Dolly Varden in the lake and outlet stream. Use a vehicle to access the Dolly Varden and cutthroat trout fishing that's available in other nearby lakes and streams which connect to the fisheries-rich Thorne watershed. Also expect to catch humpback, coho and sockeye salmon and steelhead in nearby rivers and saltwater.

Hunting

Hunters book the cabin during bear and deer seasons in the fall.

Cabin
Control Lake Cabin (T-2)

Constructed in 1960, this 33' x 27' Pan Abode log cabin is unlike the other Forest Service cabins. It comes furnished with a spring mattress cot, couch and wooden bunks, and accommodates up to eight people. There is a kitchen and a bathroom, but no working plumbing. Use the outhouse. A woodstove is provided for heating and cooking. A 12-foot skiff with oars is located at the dock on the road side of the lake. Use the skiff to reach the cabin. Please leave it at the dock for the next users when you leave the area. Elevation, 300 feet. Year-round use.

Water source: lake and stream
Facilities:

• wooden bunks	• wood stove	• woodshed
• kitchen	• outhouse	• wood supply
• bathroom	• table	• ax
• spring mattress	• chairs	• maul
• cot	• counter	• 12-foot skiff
• couch	• shelves	• oars

Deer Mountain is above timberline, about three miles from Ketchikan on Revillagigedo Island. Accessible via trail. (USGS Quad Map Ketchikan B-5)

Hunting

Blacktail deer in season.

Cabin

Deer Mountain Shelter (K-22)

Deer Mountain shelter is an A-frame Adirondack shelter that sleeps up to four people. It is free to the public on a first-come, first-serve basis. No reservations are accepted. Wood stove for heating.

Water source: ground seepage near the cabin.
Facilities:
* wood stove
* wooden bunks

Even though most cabins are equipped with either an oil or wood-burning stove, take along a Coleman or similar stove for cooking and boiling water.

Essowah Lake is on Dall Island, near Essowah Harbor, immediately adjacent to Prince of Wales Island. The lake is 65 air miles from Ketchikan and 50 miles from Craig. Minimum round-trip flight time charged is 2.9 hours from Ketchikan. (USGS Quad Map Dixon Entrance D-3)

Fishing

Essowah Lake offers cutthroat trout, Dolly Varden, and silver, pink, chum and red salmon. The salmon spawn in either the lake or the harbor. Fishing is good in either location. Parrot Lake outlet offers good fishing for sockeye salmon. The stream beside the cabin offers exceptional cutthroat trout fishing year round. Don't pass up the tiny pools that appear too small to hold fish. As many as five or six cutthroat or Dollies can be caught from these holding areas. Use a size 8 Black Marabou Flash.

Hunting

Black bear and deer hunting is available, and is best in and around the harbor and along the Pacific coast.

Other Activities

Beachcombing is very good. Use caution when walking the beach at low tide, and avoid becoming trapped in an area on an incoming tide. The outer coast is accessible via skiff through the lake system, with a short trail to Essowah Harbor.

Cabin
Essowah Lake Cabin (KC-2)

Built in 1979, the 12' x 12' Essowah Lake cabin accommodates six people and has a wood-burning stove for heating and cooking. The cabin is located on the north side of Essowah Lake. Elevation, 10 feet. Peak season is May through October.

Water source: lake
Facilities:

- wooden bunks
- outhouse
- table
- bench
- cooking counter
- shelves
- wood stove
- woodshed
- wood supply
- ax
- maul
- 14-foot skiff
- oars

User Comments

8/25: "Fishing is limited in north Essowah. Much better in south Essowah. Lots of wolf tracks and bear sign. Be very careful passing from Essowah Lake to the harbor. Slack high (tide) is best."

Fish Creek is at the head of Thorne Arm, 18 air miles from Ketchikan. Year-round access by boat or air. Minimum, round-trip flight time charged from Ketchikan is 1.2 hours. (USGS Quad Map Ketchikan B-4)

Fishing

Cutthroat and rainbow trout and Dolly Varden fishing is good in Fish Creek and Low Lake. A hiking trail leads from salt water to Low Lake.

Casting for Dollies on an incoming tide in July and August is especially productive. Sockeye salmon also available at this time. Fish the creek during the in-migration of silver salmon starting in late August and ending in September. Use a fly rod and salmon egg-colored Glo-bugs for best success in catching Dollies. Use a larger fly rod or spin tackle for silvers. Fluorescent orange is my most productive color in both spoons and spinners. Steelhead available in fall and spring.

Trails across the bay lead to excellent fishing at Granite and Star lakes. Gokachin Creek offers good fishing for coho, pink and chum salmon, and steelheading. Gokachin Creek is roughly two miles by trail from the cabin.

Hunting

Hunting is fair for Sitka blacktails and black bear.

Other Activities

Beaver, mink and marten are commonly sighted along the trail to Low and Mirror lakes. Near salt water you'll find a scenic waterfall.

Cabin
Fish Creek Cabin (K-3)

This 12' x 14' cabin was built in 1978 near Low Lake, near Pop Point. It sleeps six, and has an oil-burning stove for heating and cooking. It can be reached at both high and low tides. An anchor buoy is provided for boats.

Water source: creek
Facilities:
* wooden bunks
* outhouse
* table
* oil stove
* bench
* no boat

Grindall Passage

Grindall Passage is off the tip of the Kasaan Peninsula, on the eastern coast of Prince of Wales Island. The passage is 1.2 hours from Ketchikan via Clarence Strait or Kasaan Bay. There is no aircraft access to the cabin due to submerged rocks, however, some commercial operators do land there at high tide. (USGS Quad Map Craig B-1)

Fishing

Grindall Island and Passage is famous for its excellent king salmon saltwater trolling. Mooching and downrigger techniques using herring, spoons and plugs are most effective. Fish incoming tides in and around the island and Grindall Passage. Check ADF&G regulations for season closures and openings on king salmon fishing in this region. Surf casting for pink and coho salmon is fair to good, depending on timing and size of run. Use level-wind gear to obtain the most distance. One-ounce spoons in silver and fluorescent pink, orange, and chartreuse are good choices.

Other Activities

Beachcombing is excellent in this area for shells as well as fishing floats.

Cabin

Grindall Island Cabin (T-3)

Built in 1969, the 12' x 14' Grindall Island cabin sleeps six people, and has a wood-burning stove for heating and cooking. During stormy weather, the island and cabin offer a protected holdover spot for small boats venturing across Clarence Straight. The cabin is nestled in a wonderfully scenic coastal marine environment and receives year-round use. A boat is a must for fishing, and this cabin has none, so bring your own. Elevation, sea level.

Water source: stream
Facilities:

- wooden bunks
- outhouse
- table
- bench
- cooking counter
- shelves
- wood stove
- woodshed
- wood supply
- ax
- maul
- no boat

Heckman Lake is on northcentral Revillagigedo Island, between Jordan and Patching lakes, about 18 miles north of Ketchikan. Access is by plane or via a 6.3-mile trail from Naha Bay. Minimum round-trip flight time charged from Ketchikan is 1.2 hours. (USGS Quad Map Ketchikan C-5)

Fishing

The Heckman Lake area offers good fishing for rainbow and cutthroat trout and Dolly Varden up to 22 inches. Steelhead fishing is good in the Naha River and lake inlet both spring and winter. Also try the upper headwaters below Jordan Lake. Sockeyes start hitting in July, and cohos in late August and September. Fish for both species in the creek at the lake's outlet. Cutthroat fishing is best along the lake's southern shoreline, and at the inlet to the east. Pink and chum salmon are available in the outlet stream.

Hunting

The area offers good to excellent hunting for Sitka blacktail deer and black bear.

Cabins
Fisheries Cabin (K-4)
Heckman Lake Cabin (K-5)

Heckman Lake cabin is a 12' x 14' Pan Abode structure capable of sleeping six people. The 12' x 12' Fisheries cabin at the southeast end of Heckman Lake, however, is cozier than the larger Heckman Lake cabin. Each cabin is furnished with a wood-burning stove for heating and cooking. They are surrounded by old growth Sitka spruce and western hemlock rainforest. Season runs April through October. Elevation, 139 feet.

Water source: lake
Facilities (both cabins):

- wooden bunks
- wood stove
- woodshed
- outhouse
- 14-foot boat
- oars
- table
- bench
- ax
- maul

Helm Bay is adjacent to the Cleveland Peninsula, about 24 air miles northwest of Ketchikan. The area and cabin are readily accessible by boat or air. Minimum round-trip flight time charged is 1.2 hours. Access time by boat from Ketchikan is 1.5 hours, one way. Year-round use. (USGS Quad Map Ketchikan B-6, C-6)

Fishing

Helm Creek offers fishing for pink, sockeye and coho salmon, cutthroat trout and steelhead. Helm Lake has a good population of cutthroat trout. Bugge Lake offers fishing for western brook trout and cutthroat. Fishing for yelloweye rockfish (red snapper) and rockfish is good at the mouth and along rocky points of Helm Bay. Halibut fishing is good to excellent. The head of Helm Bay offers good crab fishing in 20 fathoms of water.

Hunting

Fair to good hunting for Sitka blacktail deer, mountain goat, brown and black bear. The head of the bay is good for spring brown bear.

Cabins
Helm Creek Cabin (K-16)
Helm Bay Cabin (K-6)

Built in 1985, the 12' x 14' Helm Creek cabin sleeps six, and is furnished with a wood-burning stove for heating and cooking. There's a mooring buoy at salt water for boats 30 feet and smaller. Or, land your boat on the moderately steep, sloping sand beach.

One mile to the south is the Helm Bay cabin, a 16' x 20' structure with two sleeping rooms that can accommodate eight. A state-maintained, floating dock is provided. Nearby is a large tidal flat. Elevation, 20 feet.

Water source: creek at both, two 50-gallon rainwater barrels at Helm Creek cabin.
Facilities (both cabins):

* wooden bunks
* ax
* maul

* broom
* wood stove
* woodshed

* wood supply
* no boat

User Comments

7/26-7/29 (Helm Bay):
"Beautiful cabin in a great location. We were impressed."

*Helm Bay Cabin. Photo by
USDA Forest Service.*

Honker Lake (formerly known as Lake Galea) is on northcentral Prince of Wales Island, 54 air miles from Ketchikan and 27 air miles from Craig. Minimum round-trip flight time charged from Ketchikan is 2.7 hours. Access is also possible via the Honker Divide Canoe Trail. (USGS Quad Map Craig D-3)

Fishing

Honker Lake offers good fishing for cutthroat and rainbow trout and Dolly Varden. In streams connecting Sweetwater Lake to Honker Lake, expect to find steelhead in late fall and spring. Fishing is also fair to good for sockeye and silver salmon at the lake outlet and all along the Honker Divide Canoe Trail. Pink and chum salmon are best pursued in the lower tributaries. Best fishing for cutthroat and rainbow trout is near the lily pads around the lake.

In the summer, the best fishing is at the inlet stream. In the spring, try the creek emptying into Honker Lake and the lake outlet. Occasionally, fish can be caught while trolling along the bank opposite the cabin. The three-mile-long lake also offers the opportunity to enjoy boating in isolated surroundings.

Hunting

Deer and black bear hunting is good.

Cabin
Honker Lake Cabin (T-4)

The cabin is on the eastern shore of Honker Lake. Constructed in 1965, this 12' x 12' structure sleeps six and has a wood-burning stove for heating and cooking. Peak season is May through October, but cabin enjoys year-round use. Elevation, 250 feet.

Water source: lake
Facilities:

- wooden bunks
- outhouse
- table
- bench
- cooking counter
- shelves
- wood stove
- woodshed
- wood supply
- ax
- maul
- 14-foot aluminum boat
- oars

User Comments

7/6: "Everything was clean and beautiful, and we left it clean and beautiful. Our stay was incredible. Thank you."

Jordan Lake is on Revillagigedo Island east of Naha Bay, about 20 miles north of Ketchikan. Access is by air and foot. Minimum round-trip flight time charged is 1.2 hours. Pilots will not land on Jordan Lake due to its small size. Drop-offs are made at either Roosevelt Lagoon or Heckman Lake. Trails lead from both locations to Jordan Lake. (USGS Quad Map Ketchikan C-5)

Fishing

Jordan Lake watershed offers excellent fishing for Dolly Varden, rainbow and cutthroat trout. Sockeye and coho salmon are available in July and September, respectively. Sockeyes are best caught in Jordan Creek, where they are most susceptible to brightly-colored flies. In Roosevelt Lagoon, catch silver salmon on streamer flies, spinners or spoons. An incoming tide offers the best success, especially if you're fishing at the mouth of Jordan Creek. However, casting from a boat or from shore is also productive. Fish for steelhead in the Naha River in the fall and spring. Fishing can be spotty in late spring due to heavy rains which muddy up the water. In the lower drainages, use fly tackle to catch pink and chum salmon.

Hunting

Spring black bear hunting in this area is very good. Use an inflatable boat and 9.9-hp outboard and cruise the shore of Naha Bay. Take a stand near the many bear trails running the length of Roosevelt Lagoon for a chance at black bear, and when in season, blacktail deer. Keep the inflatable at Roosevelt Lagoon, and hike the trail to the cabin each night. A full-frame pack is a must for spring and fall hunting.

Cabin
Jordan Lake Cabin (K-7)

The cabin on Jordan Lake is a 12' x 12' cedar log structure constructed in 1965. It sleeps six, and has a wood-burning stove for heating and cooking. Season runs from April through November. Elevation is 66 feet.

Water source: lake and stream
Facilities:

- wooden bunks
- wood stove
- woodshed
- ax

- maul
- outhouse
- table
- bench

- 12-foot aluminum boat
- oars

User Comments

7/19: "A perfect, highly recommended cabin. Divine."
9/3-9/4: "Lots of cutthroat and rainbow trout in streams."
9/2: "(Cabin is in) beautiful shape. Suggest raise price to $20 per day."

Josephine Lake is east of Hetta Inlet on south Prince of Wales Island, about 38 air miles from Ketchikan. Air access only. Minimum round-trip flight time charged from Ketchikan is two hours. (USGS Quad Map Craig A-2, B-2)

Fishing

Josephine Lake has few or no fish, however, nearby Summit and Marge lakes offer fair fishing for arctic grayling. Grayling are not endemic to this lake, but were planted during the 1950s. The grayling were taken from Tolsona Lake near Glennallen, although earliest introductions were from Canada. Summit Lake grayling are reproducing, and the current stock consists of wild fish. Grayling here are not choosy about lure or fly offerings. Because the fish are small, however, it's necessary to use light fly gear and 6X leaders or 2- to 4-pound mono on ultralight spinning tackle. Standard patterns produce well.

Hunting

Sitka blacktail deer hunting is good in this area. Hunt the alpine slopes near timberline in August and September. October storms can delay scheduled pickup time for days.

Other Activities

The surrounding area is noted for its fine epidote and quartz crystals, especially in and around gullies and atop mountain peaks. Obtain permission to explore or prospect private land in the vicinity of Josephine Lake.

Cabin
Josephine Lake Cabin (KC-3)

Constructed in 1964, the 12' x 12' cedar-log Josephine Lake cabin accommodates six people and has an oil-burning stove for heating. Bring your own No. 1 fuel. Situated at 1,800 feet, this cabin offers some of the best scenery on Prince of Wales Island. Bordering the lake are several mountains that tower to 4,000 feet. Stunted trees and alpine vegetation are nearby. Ice on the lake seldom melts until mid-to-late June.

Water source: lake
Facilities:
- wooden bunks
- outhouse
- table
- bench
- cooking counter
- shelves
- oil stove
- 14-foot aluminum skiff
- oars

Karta Lake

Karta Lake is on central Prince of Wales Island between Salmon Lake and Karta Bay. Air access is 34 miles from Ketchikan and 22 miles from Craig. Minimum round-trip flight time charged from Ketchikan is 1.6 hours. From Karta Bay, marine travelers can moor their boat at the beach, then walk to the lake by a 1.5-mile trail. (USGS Quad Map Craig C-2)

Fishing

Karta Lake offers excellent fishing in several locations for Dollies, cutthroat and rainbow trout. Try fishing directly in front of the cabin, especially in summer when four species of salmon start migrating into the lake. Throughout the various runs, trout feed on salmon eggs, and they can be found in and around schools of in-migrating salmon. If salmon runs are particularly heavy, trout will move into the lake. Catch trout by using egg patterns or fluorescent red/orange spoons or lures.

In the spring, Salmon Lake outlet is an excellent place to fish. Cutthroat feed on out-migrating smolt, and this is an ideal time to catch a trophy cutt up to 25 inches. The Karta is one of the most productive watersheds on Prince of Wales Island, if not all of southeast Alaska. Steelhead are present throughout the watershed. (For stream fishing information, see Karta River, on the page 82.)

Hunting

Good black bear hunting opportunities in the spring. Try the alpine areas on Granite Mountain and nearby intertidal areas. Hunt the mountain in August for blacktail deer, and in the fall (if it's a good year for berries) for black bear. Spruce grouse numbers are low. Blue grouse are absent.

Cabin
Karta Lake Cabin (T-5)

Constructed in 1965, the 12' x 12' cedar log Karta Lake cabin accommodates six people and has a wood-burning stove for heating and cooking. Granite Mountain looms across the lake from the cabin. With the aid of a spotting scope, it's possible to see deer and bear in the alpine country. Elevation, 100 feet. Year-round use. Lottery drawing for cabin use from June through September.

Water source: lake
Facilities:

- wooden bunks
- outhouse
- table
- bench
- cooking counter
- shelves
- wood stove
- woodshed
- wood supply
- ax
- maul
- 14-foot aluminum boat
- oars

Spruce grouse hunting can be successfully combined with a deer hunting or fishing trip to create a diverse outing.

Karta River

Karta River is on east-central Prince of Wales Island, 34 air miles from Ketchikan and 22 air miles from Craig. Minimum round-trip flight time charged from Ketchikan is 1.6 hours. Marine travelers can reach the river via Karta Bay. A 1.5-mile trail connects the bay with the upper river. (USGS Quad Map Craig C-2)

Fishing

The Karta River is one of the most productive watersheds on Prince of Wales Island. Steelhead fishing is world class, with annual runs exceeding a thousand fish. Steelhead average 28.9 inches and 12.1 pounds, with fish up to 23 pounds available. In one year, of 375 steelhead sampled, the average weight for males was 11.4 pounds and 12.3 pounds for females.

The Karta steelhead catch ratio has fluctuated from a low of 36 steelhead in 1981 to a high of 292 in 1980. In mild-winter years, steelhead begin entering the Karta in November and December, and continue throughout the winter. Adults can be in freshwater as early as mid-February. Yet harsh winters and springs may delay entry until April.

Catch efforts generally start in mid-February, and remain low until mid-April. Most of the in-migration takes place from April 25 through May 15. The out-migration of fish takes place around April 27 and peaks from May 9 through May 22, continuing until late June.

Historically, the peak week for anglers has been April 25 through May 1, but it can fluctuate several days each year. If planning a trip, it is best to go a week or two early rather than late, as the runs preceding this time frame are slightly better than those following.

The Karta is a wide stream, and offers both easy and difficult areas from which to fish. Most anglers wade the shoreline. The system also offers good runs of silver, pink, chum and red salmon during the summer and Dolly Varden year-round.

Dolly Varden in Karta Lake are caught near spawning salmon. A red-bladed spinner or egg patterns catch the most fish.

Hunting

Sitka blacktail deer, black bear, waterfowl and grouse are available in the immediate vicinity.

Other Activities

Opportunities to photograph hair seal, otter, mink and marten abound. A five-mile trail leading from salt water to Salmon Lake cabin makes a good day's hike.

Cabin

Karta River Cabin (T-6)

The cabin is on a bluff at the mouth of the Karta River where it flows into Karta Bay. Built in 1968, this cedar log structure is 12' x 14' and accommodates six people. An oil-burning stove is provided for heating, so bring your own No. 1 diesel fuel. Expect to view a variety of scenic wonder from this cabin, from geological structures to marine wildlife. This cabin receives heavy, year-round use. Lottery drawing for dates from June through September. Elevation, 10 feet.

Water source: creek
Facilities:
* wooden bunks
* outhouse
* table
* bench
* cooking counter
* shelves
* no boat

Karta River steelhead average 12 pounds, with the peak of the run taking place from mid-April to mid-May.

Kegan Cove

Kegan Cove is on southern Prince of Wales Island on Moira Sound, 30 air miles from Ketchikan and 51 air miles from Craig. Minimum round-trip flight time charged is 1.6 hours from Ketchikan. Marine travelers can figure 2.5 hours from Ketchikan. (USGS Quad Map Craig A-1)

Fishing

Kegan Cove is an excellent base for catching silver, pink, chum and sockeye salmon starting in mid-July with pinks and ending in late September with silvers. In the spring, a short walk up the creek offers good fishing for steelhead, as well as cutthroat and rainbow trout. The lake, a four-tenths mile hike from the cove, also offers good fishing for cutthroat, rainbow and Dolly Varden. Halibut fishing is excellent.

Hunting

Hunting is good for Sitka blacktail deer, black bear and wolf. Moira Sound and Dickman Bay offer good bear hunting in the spring.

Other Activities

It is common to see hair seal throughout this area.

Cabin

Kegan Cove Cabin (KC-4)

Kegan Cove cabin is a cedar log, Pan Abode, 12' x 14' structure built in 1979. It sleeps six, and comes furnished with a wood-burning stove for heating and cooking. Year-round use. A very popular cabin. Lottery drawing for cabin use dates from June through September. Elevation, 10 feet.

Water source: creek
Facilities:

- wooden bunks
- outhouse
- table
- bench
- cooking counter
- wood stove
- woodshed
- wood supply
- ax
- maul
- no boat

User Comments

8/14-8/21: "Great spot. Enjoyed seeing the bears fishing."

Kegan Creek

Kegan Creek is on southeast Prince of Wales Island, 30 air miles from Ketchikan. Minimum round-trip flight time charged is 1.4 hours. Marine travelers reach the lake via a four-tenths-mile trail from Kegan Cove, located just off Moira Sound. (USGS Quad Map Craig A-1)

Fishing

Kegan Creek and Kegan Lake offer excellent fishing for rainbow trout. Also present are Dolly Varden and anadromous runs of cutthroat trout. Steelhead fishing is fair to good from March through May. Silver, chum, pink and red salmon enter the creek and lake at various times throughout the summer.

The creek offers the best fishing, especially for salmon. White spoons and tail-spinners, when trolled without weight along the lake's shoreline, catch both rainbow and cutthroat trout.

Hunting

Sitka blacktail deer and black bear are available, both near the lake and along the coast to the north of Kegan Cove.

Cabin

Kegan Creek Cabin (KC-5)

Built in 1967, Kegan Creek cabin is a Pan Abode, cedar log structure capable of sleeping six. Located approximately 200 yards downstream from Kegan Lake, the cabin is furnished with a wood-burning stove for heating and cooking and a 12-foot skiff and oars. A nice, cozy structure and location. An excellent trail connects Kegan Lake with Kegan Cove. Peak season is April through November. A very popular cabin. Lottery drawing for cabin use dates from June through September. Make reservations early. Elevation, 50 feet.

Water source: creek
Facilities:

- wooden bunks
- outhouse
- 12-foot skiff
- oars
- table
- bench
- wood stove
- woodshed
- wood supply
- ax
- maul

User Comments

4/23-4/30: "Recommend that only one cabin on Kegan Creek System be rented at a time during steelhead season—too much pressure on fish."

7/14: "A great place. Didn't have a problem with anything. Didn't catch the eight-pound trout in front of the cabin, but we tried. Bring hip boots."

7/17-7/24: "Sockeye run finished on 7/22. Trout available in the lake by trolling. Spent a very enjoyable week and was comfortable in cabin."

Lake Shelokum

Lake Shelokum, on the mainland, is accessible via West Inlet, 50 air miles from Ketchikan or 2.2 miles by water. Tie off at the Bailey Bay buoy and hike two miles to the shelter. Accessible at any tide. (USGS Quad Map Bradfield Canal A-5)

Fishing

Limited cutthroat trout fishing available at Lake Shelokum.

Hunting

Hunting for blacktail deer and goat, in season.

Cabin

Lake Shelokum Shelter (K-23)

This three-sided Adirondack sleeps four and has no stove. It is free to the public on a first-come, first-served basis. No reservations are accepted.

Water source: freshwater stream near shelter
Facilities:
- wooden bunks
- no stove

You'll find Long Lake on the north end of Revilla Island. Access by air is 55 miles from Ketchikan, or three hours by water before taking a one-mile trail to the lake. (USGS Quad Map Ketchikan D-5)

Fishing

Cutthroat, rainbow and Dolly Varden fishing available.

Hunting

Hunting for blacktail deer and black bear, in season.

Cabin

Long Lake Shelter (K-24)

This three-sided Adirondack cabin is capable of sleeping four. Shelter is located at the west end of the lake. Free to the public on a first-come, first-served basis. No reservations accepted.

Water source: stream near cabin

Fly fishermen after rainbow trout should carry a variety of stonefly and mayfly patterns, Odonata and black nymph, as well as Bivisible, scud, leech and Black Gnat patterns.

McDonald Lake is on the mainland east of Yes Bay, about 50 miles northwest of Ketchikan. Air or water access. A hike from Yes Bay to the lake over a 1.5-mile trail is necessary if accessing the area by water. Boats can be moored at Yes Bay Lodge dock (boaters should first obtain permission from the resort operators since this is a private dock). Minimum round-trip flight time charged from Ketchikan is two hours. (USGS Quad Map Ketchikan D-6)

Fishing

McDonald Lake is perhaps one of the richest fisheries in the area. Fishing for rainbow and cutthroat trout; pink, sockeye and silver salmon; Dolly Varden and steelhead is excellent in Wolverine Creek. Rainbow and cutthroat trout fishing is good to excellent in the lake. Closer to tidewater, fishing for pink salmon is excellent.

Fly fishermen do well at catching sockeyes in the creek, while spin fishermen are most successful at triggering strikes once the salmon enter the lake and establish spawning areas. The creek can be difficult to fish, due to a fast current and slick bottom. Use wading shoes with felt bottoms and carry a wading staff. On many stretches of Wolverine Creek, roll casting is a must.

Hunting

Hunters pursue Sitka blacktail deer, black bear and brown bear in this area.

Wolverine Island Cabin. Photo courtesy USDA Forest Service.

Cabin
Wolverine Island Cabin (K-8)
McDonald Lake Shelter (K-25)

McDonald Lake cabin measures 12' by 14' and is constructed of cedar log in the Pan Abode style. It is in a uniquely scenic spot on Wolverine Island. It was built in 1967 and sleeps six. From the cabin window, it's possible to see beaver, mink, marten and otter along the shoreline of the lake. Lottery drawing held for dates from June through September. Elevation, 100 feet.

The McDonald Lake shelter is one-half mile from the Wolverine cabin. It is a three-sided shelter that sleeps four. It has no wood stove, so bring a heat source. The shelter is free to the public on a first-come, first-served basis. No reservations are accepted.

Water source: lake at the cabin, river at the shelter
Facilities:

- wooden bunks
- wood stove
- table
- benches
- 12-foot aluminum boat
- oars
- outhouse
- ax
- maul
- woodshed

User Comments

6/9 Wolverine cabin: "Thanks, USFS. Nice cabin! Skylights are a real plus over other cabins. Bench another plus. Stove is great for heating."

Wolverine Creek offers excellent fishing for Dolly Varden, like this prize.

Patching Lake is near Naha Bay on central Revillagigedo Island, 20 air miles from Ketchikan. Air access only from April through October. Minimum round-trip flight time charged from Ketchikan is 1.2 hours. (USGS Quad Map Ketchikan C-5)

Fishing

Patching Lake offers good cutthroat trout fishing. Grayling are occasionally caught from the lake, and are probably migrants from Snow and Orton lakes, located at the headwaters of the Naha system.

Fishing is good in several areas on Patching: to the north, in the stream near Patching Lake cabin; across from the cabin, along the western lakeshore; the narrows at mid-lake; and the outlet stream that empties into Heckman Lake. Because of the brush along the outlet creek, use ultralight outfits or short, 3-weight fly rods. Grayling are caught on black gnats, woolly worms, tiny leech and shrimp patterns, and chironomid patterns.

Spin anglers should try tiny Dardevles, size 00 spinners in black or gold, and salmon eggs for best results. Cast in a systematic pattern while drifting, or anchor and fish the deepwater areas near an inlet stream. Also try trolling weighted flies in late evening. Spin anglers use a spin bubble with good success. In the lower drainages, expect to catch Dolly Varden, sockeye, silver, pink and chum salmon, as well as steelhead and rainbow trout.

Take the opportunity to explore a variety of waters that seldom get heavily fished. Cutthroat trout seldom get fished in the two major streams, offering unique angling opportunities. Lots of bushwhacking, but worth the effort.

Hunting

Hunting for Sitka blacktail deer and black bear is fair.

Cabins
Patching Lake Cabin (K-11)
Portage Cabin (K-13)

Portage cabin is a 12' x 14' Pan Abode cedar log structure constructed in 1976. Patching Lake cabin, located on the northern end of the lake, is a 12' x 14' cedar log cabin built in 1976. Each cabin comfortably sleeps six people, and has a wood-burning stove for heating and cooking. Elevation, 650 feet.

Water source: lake
Facilities:

- wooden bunks
- wood stove
- woodshed
- ax
- maul
- table
- bench
- outhouse
- 14-foot aluminum boat
- outhouse

User Comments

(no date): "Cabin is in excellent shape. Wish they all were like this. Go for it. Sure could use a trail to Chamberlain."

Phocena Bay is 15 air miles from Ketchikan on the western side of Gravina Island. Access is by floatplane or boat. (USGS Quad Map Ketchikan A-6)

Fishing

Fishing for rockfish, ling cod, kelp greenling, and silver and king salmon is excellent along the western coast of Gravina Island coast. White Mister Twister tails fished with one- to six-ounce leadheads are extremely effective, as are yellow, fluorescent red and chartreuse.

Catch halibut from flat, sandy areas and underwater plateaus. Mooch or long-line herring or squid for silvers and kings.

Hunting

The area offers good hunting for black bear and Sitka blacktail deer. Starting in October, waterfowling is good in both freshwater and saltwater areas.

Cabin

Phocena Bay Cabin (K-9)

Phocena Bay cabin is a 12' x 14' Pan Abode structure constructed in 1973 and moved to this location in 1985. A wood-burning stove is provided for cooking and heating. Enjoy an excellent view of the Puppet Mountains. At low tide, explore the tidal flats directly in front of the cabin. Elevation, sea level. Year-round access.

Water source: creeks and two 50-gallon water drums that collect rainwater from the cabin roof

Facilities:
- wooden bunks
- table
- bench
- outhouse
- wood stove
- woodshed
- ax
- maul
- no boat
- mooring buoy

Silver and blue Gibbs Koho spoons are extremely effective in catching Gravina Island silver salmon.

Point Amargura is on the southern tip of San Fernando Island, west of Prince of Wales Island, 70 air miles from Ketchikan and eight air miles from Craig. Minimum round-trip flight time charged from Ketchikan is three hours. Marine anglers from Craig can reach the area within 20 minutes. (USGS Quad Map Craig B-5)

Fishing

Trolling for salmon is excellent in this area, as is jigging for bottomfish and halibut. Anglers also do well surf casting for migrating pinks and cohos. Concentrate efforts near the mouth of freshwater creeks, off rocky points and at the heads of bays.

Hunting

Hunting is good for brown and black bear, and Sitka blacktail deer.

Cabin
Point Amargura Cabin (KC-6)

Point Amargura cabin is a 16' x 16' A-frame that was built in 1963. It sleeps six, and has a wood-burning stove for heating and cooking. The shoreline offers plenty of driftwood for burning. Look for the cabin about 220 yards from the shoreline. The surrounding vegetation is windswept Sitka spruce and western hemlock, with blueberry and salal and other major understory species. The cabin, which enjoys year-round use, has an excellent view of Portillo and Ursua channels. Elevation, 30 feet.

Water source: creek
Facilities:
- wooden bunks
- loft
- outhouse
- table
- bench
- cooking counter
- wood stove
- woodshed
- wood supply
- ax
- maul
- no boat

Many U.S.F.S. cabins have a woodshed filled with cut spruce, which provides the means for a quick warm-up fire in the wood-burning stove after a long day on the lake or stream.

Rainbow Lake is on the south end of the Cleveland Peninsula, 27 air miles northwest of Ketchikan. Minimum round-trip flight time charged from Ketchikan is 1.2 hours. (USGS Quad Map Craig C-1)

Fishing

Fishing for rainbow trout is fair to good, however, deepwater trolling techniques are often necessary for success. Use one or more portable downriggers with C-clamps that attach to the boat's gunwales. A four-pound weight allows precise trolling of flutter spoons and floating plugs. I prefer flutter spoons with rainbow prism tape, or with a finish of pearlescent white with colored dots, because they best resemble a trout parr. A portable LCR fish finder can pinpoint exact locations of fish. For ease of use, attach a suction-cup mount to the transducer before leaving town. Fly fishermen should look for rainbow trout in nearby streams in late spring and early summer. Angling reports indicate cutthroat fishing is good in the lower creek, but not in the lake. West of the lake, along the coast, silver salmon fishing is good. Pink and chum salmon also available in season.

Hunting

The area offers good to excellent deer and black bear hunting, along with fair hunting for mountain goat and brown bear.

Cabin
Rainbow Lake Cabin (K-14)

A 12' x 14' Pan Abode built in 1968, Rainbow Lake cabin comfortably sleeps six adults. Peak season is April through October. Elevation, 650 feet.

Water source: lake.
Facilities:
- wooden bunks
- wood stove
- outhouse
- woodshed
- ax
- maul
- 12-foot boat
- oars

At Rainbow Lake, the best fishing is often within the first 30 feet of water around shoreline structure. Flutter spoons work well, or when 'bows are holding near submergent aquatic vegetation, use damsel fly nymphs fished on a sink-tip line and 5X tippet.

Red Bay Lake

Red Bay Lake is south of Red Bay on north Prince of Wales Island, 84 air miles from Ketchikan or 55 air miles from Craig. Minimum round-trip flight time charged from Ketchikan is four hours. Access is also by Forest Service Road #5600. (USGS Quad Map Petersburg A-4, B-4)

Fishing

In the spring and late fall, steelhead fishing is fair to good for fish up to 12 pounds. Cutthroat and rainbow trout fishing is excellent in the lake and stream, with fish reaching 3.5 pounds, but averaging one to two pounds. Dolly Varden fishing is good. Silver, pink, sockeye and chum salmon are also available at various times throughout the summer.

Red Bay is a good choice for the angler who wants variety. Silver fishing is excellent in the many tributaries that empty into the lake. Expect this area to receive more fishing pressure as fishermen discover the ample fishing opportunities available along the Prince of Wales Island road system.

Hunting

Hunt black bear and Sitka blacktail deer along Red Bay, and in the alpine country near the lake.

Cabin

Red Bay Lake Cabin (T-8)

Located on the northeast side of Red Bay Lake, this plywood cabin accommodates three people. There is a wood-burning stove for heating and cooking. One skiff is at the cabin and the other is at the north end of the lake to be used for easy access from the road.

Beginning at Red Bridge, a one-mile trail connects the boat to the cabin site. Be sure to wear rubber boots, because this unmaintained trail winds through a floodplain created by beaver activity.

This area offers exceptional scenery. Peak season is May through October. Elevation, 50 feet.

Water source: lake
Facilities:
- wooden bunks
- outhouse
- wood stove
- table
- benches
- counter
- two boats
- oars

Reflection Lake is on the Cleveland Peninsula, north of Bell Island and 50 air miles north of Ketchikan. Access by boat is to Short Bay, followed by a two-mile hike to the lake. By air, a minimum round-trip flight time charged is 2.2 hours from Ketchikan. (USGS Quad Map Bradfield Canal A-5)

Fishing

In April and May, fishing is excellent for cutthroat, rainbow trout and steelhead. Silver salmon fishing is best in late August through early October, and sockeye fishing in early July. Kokanee fishing is good in the lake year-round, while Dolly Varden fishing is good to excellent in the streams and lake from April through October. Pink salmon concentrate in the outlet creek. To the southwest, Lake Nellie offers eastern brook trout fishing. Reflection Lake is a choice location for that spring black bear hunting/steelhead fishing trip, or deer hunting/silver salmon fishing adventure.

Hunting

Big game hunted in this region include mountain goat, Sitka blacktail deer, brown bear and black bear. Because the Adirondack cabin is available on a first-come, first-served basis, plan on bringing your own shelter as a backup or to use as a spike camp. Use the shelter as a base camp if necessary.

Cabins
Reflection Lake Cabin (K-15)
Reflection Lake Shelter (K-26)

Reflection Lake cabin is a 12' x 14' cedar log cabin constructed in 1967. It sleeps six people and has a wood-burning stove for heating and cooking. The lake is in a very scenic location, surrounded by mountains. Lottery drawing for reservations June through September.

Reflection Lake shelter is a 12' x 14' Adirondack (three-sided) structure that is available free to the public on a first-come, first-served basis. No boat or stove provided.

Water source: lake
Facilities (cabin) :

- wooden bunks
- outhouse
- table
- bench
- wood-burning stove
- 14-foot skiff
- oars

Many lakes in Southeast Alaska offer good rainbow trout/steelhead fishing in a scenic coastal setting.

Salmon Bay Lake

Salmon Bay Lake is on north Prince of Wales Island, 84 air miles from Ketchikan or 55 miles from Craig. Minimum round-trip flight time charged from Ketchikan is 3.7 hours. Marine travelers can reach the lake by mooring their boat at the beach and walking a 1.8-mile trail from Salmon Bay. Caution: This route is not recommended as the trail end is high in the intertidal flat and accessible by boat only during the highest tides. (USGS Quad Map Petersburg A-4, B-4)

Fishing

Fishing for cutthroat and rainbow trout and Dolly Varden is good in spring and fall. You'll find good steelhead fishing in the outlet stream in late fall, April and May. Silver, chum and pink salmon are available in season in the lower stretches of the creek, with sockeye present throughout the watershed.

Salmon Bay Lake is a good choice for a fishing/hunting adventure or remote getaway. In April, May and October, expect inclement weather that could delay pickup and departure times. One of this cabin's nicest attractions is the wildlife you can see along the trail to the fishing holes. You may encounter black bear, mink, eagles and deer along the stream banks. Bear protection is advisable during the heaviest salmon runs in July and August.

Hunting

Sitka blacktail deer and black bear hunting is not as popular here as in some areas, probably due to the lake's remote location.

Other Activities

Mink, marten and otter are commonly seen. Trumpeter swans winter on this lake.

Cabin

Salmon Bay Lake Cabin (T-9)

The 12' x 14' cabin is at the southwest end of the lake. Built in 1969, it sleeps six, and comes with a wood-burning stove for heating and some cooking. A sandy beach in front of the cabin permits swimming and related beach activities during the summer months. There are two 14-foot aluminum skiffs with oars. A boat ramp and winch have been added at the trailhead. Peak season is April through November. Elevation, 50 feet.

Water source: lake
Facilities:

- wooden bunks
- outhouse
- table
- bench
- cooking counter
- wood stove
- woodshed
- wood supply
- ax
- maul
- two 14-foot boats
- oars

Salmon Lake is in the east central part of Prince of Wales Island, 36 air miles from Ketchikan and 20 air miles from Craig. Minimum round-trip flight time charged from Ketchikan is 1.6 hours. Marine travelers can reach the lake via a four-mile trail from Karta Bay. (USGS Quad Map Craig C-3)

Fishing

The Salmon Lake system offers good to excellent fishing for cutthroat, rainbow and Dolly Varden in both the lake and streams. In the river, pink and chum salmon are available in July and early August (they are predominant in the lower watershed), sockeyes in July, and silvers starting in late August. While salmon can be caught at the upper lake, fish the water between Karta Lake and Karta Bay for the best results. Steelhead migrate through Salmon Lake to spawn in McGilvery and Andersen creeks. The Karta system is well known for its spring steelhead fishing, and excellent trout and salmon fishing. See Karta River (page 82) for more information.

Hunting

Sitka blacktails and black bear are common in the area and offer good hunting opportunities.

Cabins

McGilvery Creek Cabin (T-7)
Salmon Lake Cabin (T-10)

Salmon Lake cabin is on the north shore of Salmon Lake. Built in the 1800s and renovated in 1964, this cedar shake cabin sleeps six, and has a wood-burning stove for heating and cooking. The unique cabin has hand-hewn beams, wooden door hinges, shake floor and additional woodworking, all of which make this an attractive wilderness cabin. Lottery drawing for cabin use dates from June through September. Elevation, 118 feet.

Built in 1964, McGilvery Creek cabin is 12' x 12' and located on the western end of Salmon Lake. It can accommodate six people, and is furnished with a wood-burning stove and an aluminum skiff with oars. Wear hip boots on your flight to the cabin, as the terrain near the drop-off spot is marshy.

Water source: lake and creek
Facilities (both cabins):

- wooden bunks
- aluminum skiff
- oars
- outhouse
- table
- bench
- cooking counter
- wood stove
- woodshed
- wood supply
- ax
- maul

User Comments

7/31-8/7: ''Keep up the good work. Cabin clean, lots of wood, good fishing. Had a wonderful vacation.''

Sarkar Lake

Sarkar Lake is on northwest Prince of Wales Island, 76 air miles from Ketchikan and 34 air miles from Craig. Minimum round-trip flight time charged is 3.3 hours from Ketchikan. Access is also by road and boat. Take Forest Development Road No. 20 and use the boat at the lake (no oars, so bring your own 7.5 hp or smaller outboard). From Sarkar Cove, marine travelers can reach the lake via trail and Road No. 20. (USGS Quad Map Craig D-4)

Fishing

From April through May, cutthroat and rainbow trout and Dolly Varden fishing is very good at Sarkar Creek. Silver dart patterns work exceptionally well, especially when fished with a tiny strip of pork rind.

Four species of salmon (coho, pink, chum and sockeye) are also taken from this stream from mid-summer through early fall. Use chartreuse flies and tiny flutter spoons for pinks and sockeye. Try spinners, attractor flies and large wobblers for chum and coho. The best fishing structure occurs in a short stretch of water located between the cove and the lake, directly below the bridge.

In season, steelhead are present in the tributaries emptying into Sarkar Lake.

Hunting

Good goose and waterfowl hunting in Sarkar Cove. Set up blinds on points for best success on sea ducks. Puddlers and geese are frequently taken in and near the cove by pass shooters. The area offers good hunting for Sitka blacktails, wolf and black bear.

Precautions

If accessing the cabin via road, users need to bring a 7.5-hp outboard and a marine chart. The cabin is three miles from the launch, and many large protruding rocks in the lake make travel through these waters hazardous.

Cabin

Sarkar Lake Cabin (T-11)

The cabin is on the northeast shore of Sarkar Lake. Built in 1965, the 12' x 12' structure sleeps six, and has a wood-burning stove for heating and cooking. Available are two 14-foot aluminum skiffs with oars; one at the cabin and one near Road No. 20 pullout. Elevation, 25 feet.

Water source: lake
Facilities:
- wooden bunks
- outhouse
- two skiffs
- one set of oars
- table
- benches
- wood stove

Shipley Bay is on northwest Prince of Wales Island adjacent to Sumner Strait. This extremely beautiful site is 85 miles from Ketchikan or 46 miles from Craig. Minimum round-trip flight time charged from Ketchikan is 3.7 hours. Accessible by boat. (USGS Quad Map Petersburg A-5)

Fishing

From April through June, Shipley Creek and Shipley Lake offer good to excellent fishing for cutthroat trout, rainbow, Dolly Varden and steelhead. From late fall through spring, steelhead fishermen hit the many holding pools and runs along the creek's length.

Throughout the summer, spin fishermen with light tackle do extremely well in catching cutthroat and rainbow trout and Dolly Varden. Fish often concentrate in or near the logjams in the creek. Shipley is a good choice for the fly angler due to the variety of fish and fishing conditions. Wading the shoreline shallows is the best way to fish this creek. Take both a floating line and a sink tip. The stream also supports pink, coho, chum and sockeye salmon. Hotspots are the mouth of the creek on an incoming tide, in the Shipley Bay intertidal area, or in the lower creek.

Hunting

Good black bear hunting and fair deer hunting can be had within walking distance of the cabin. The south shore of Shipley Bay is very good for goose and duck hunting, and deer hunting is fair.

Cabin
Shipley Bay Cabin (T-12)

This 12' x 14' cedar log cabin was built in 1967. It enjoys year-round use at an elevation of 15 feet above sea level. Reach the lake by taking a three-quarter-mile trail along Shipley Creek to the cabin. At the outlet of Shipley Lake you'll find a 14-foot boat with oars. The cabin sleeps six, and has a wood-burning stove for cooking and heating. Peak season is from May through September.

Water source: creek
Facilities:
• wooden bunks
• table
• benches
• outhouse
• cooking counter
• wood stove
• no boat

Staney Creek

Staney Creek is on west-central Prince of Wales Island, approximately 68 air miles from Ketchikan or 24 miles from Craig. Minimum round-trip flight time charged from Ketchikan is 2.9 hours. Due to the shallow intertidal zone near the cabin, access by boat can be difficult and should be attempted with a twenty-foot or smaller boat. To reach the cabin, you'll need an 8-foot or greater tide. By auto, take Forest Development Road #2059-300 and a short trail to the cabin. (USGS Quad Map Craig D-4)

Fishing
Saltwater and stream fishing is excellent. Four species of salmon (coho, pink, chum and sockeye), rainbow, cutthroat, Dolly Varden and steelhead are in the stream and nearby salt water. An excellent choice for a spring black bear/steelhead fishing trip. During the summer months, anglers can easily spend a week here and not become bored. A boat will add to your enjoyment of the area.

Hunting
Goose and duck hunting is the prime attraction of this cabin, followed closely by good deer and black bear hunting. Wolves roam the stream banks and ridges, especially in late summer during the salmon spawning season.

Precautions
User should have knowledge of waterways in this area. No buoy or ramp provided. Pull boat onto cobble/gravel beach.

Cabin
Staney Creek Cabin (T-13)
The 12' x 12' Pan Abode cedar log cabin was built in 1964 and renovated in 1986. Oil stove available for heating only. Bring your own fuel supply and cookstove. Cabin sleeps six. Nearby Lester Creek is accessible by trail, as is the Tuxekan Passage. Peak season is April through December. Elevation, 30 feet.

Water source: creek
Facilities:
- wooden bunks
- outhouse
- oil stove
- table
- bench
- no boat

User Comments
7/5-7/7: "Beautiful setting. Cabin could use window on view side."

Sweetwater Lake is on northeast Price of Wales Island, 64 air miles from Ketchikan or 34 air miles from Craig. Minimum round-trip flight time charged from Ketchikan is 2.7 hours. Road anglers should take Forest Development Road #3030 to Coffman Cove. (USGS Quad Map Craig D-3)

Fishing

Dolly Varden and cutthroat trout are the predominant species in Sweetwater Lake. Fishing is good around the islands and in the bays north of the cabin. For best success, use leech or muddler patterns fished at mid-depth. For cutts holding in dense cover, twitch popper bugs through the lily pads.

In late August, coho and sockeye salmon fishing is good in area streams, bays and lake outlets. You'll find pink salmon in Logjam Creek, and chum salmon in its tributaries. At the mouth of the Sweetwater lies Indian Creek, a good steelhead stream that receives minimal angling pressure. Best fishing is in April and May. Steelhead are also present throughout the Sweetwater system, from tidewater to Lake Galea.

Hunting

Migratory waterfowl hunting is excellent prior to fall freeze-up. Hunting for Sitka blacktail deer and black bear is good.

Other Activities

Wildlife viewing in the area is excellent, with marten, mink, otter, beaver and hair seal common in this area.

Cabin

Sweetwater Lake Cabin (T-14)

The 12' x 14' Sweetwater Lake cabin was constructed in 1965. Two 14-foot aluminum skiffs are maintained at the lake: one for use by fly-in anglers; the other for people arriving by road. The second is near the road pullout for easy access. The cabin is a half-mile from the road and boat launch. It sleeps six, and is equipped with a wood-burning stove for heating and cooking. Season is from April through October. Elevation, 25 feet.

Water source: lake
Facilities:
- wooden bunks
- outhouse
- table
- bench
- two 14-foot aluminum boats
- wood supply
- woodshed
- ax
- maul

Trollers Cove

Trollers Cove is on the east coast of central Prince of Wales Island, at the entrance to Kasaan Bay, 21 air miles from Craig and 38 air miles from Ketchikan. Access is by float plane or boat. Minimum round-trip flight time is 1.3 hours. (USGS Quad Map Craig B-1)

Fishing

Fishing is good near 20-Fathom Bank for rockfish and cod; the upper depths are good for king and silver salmon. In the hills behind the cabin, numerous lakes provide fishing for cutthroat trout.

Hunting

Excellent blacktail deer and black bear hunting. Try early spring for black bears, motoring along the coast at low tide.

Other Activities

Nearby coves and waterfalls offer unique photographic and exploration opportunities. To the north, visit Spiral Cove for good sightseeing.

Cabin

Trollers Cove Cabin (KC-7)

Trollers Cove cabin is a 14' x 14' Pan Abode structure constructed in 1986. The cabin sleeps up to four people and is furnished with a wood-burning stove for heating and cooking. An anchor buoy is provided for boaters. Elevation, 10 feet.

Water source: stream near cabin
Facilities:
- wooden bunks
- outhouse
- table
- bench
- woodshed
- ax
- maul
- no boat

User Comments

9/5-9/6: "One of the nicest cabins we've stayed in in Alaska. Really in nice shape."

West Orchard Lake is east of Shrimp Bay on northern Revillagigedo Island, 34 miles from Ketchikan. Access is by air or water. The lake is two-and-a-half hours by boat from Ketchikan, followed by a half-mile hike by trail from Shrimp Bay to the lake. Minimum round-trip flight time charged from Ketchikan is 1.6 hours. (USGS Quad Map Ketchikan D-5)

Fishing

Fishing is good to excellent for Dolly Varden and cutthroat trout that range from 10 to 24 inches. Orchard Creek lies southeast of the cabin. Fish it by walking the bank, casting upstream into pools and under logjams. Cutthroats and Dollies, along with fair numbers of kokanee, are caught along the numerous feeder streams emptying into the lake. Here, an Alaska Mary Ann works well on deepwater cutthroats. Spin anglers should either troll or cast kokanee-imitating spoons for the larger cutts. Watch for surface activity in the western portion of the bay, where big cutts regularly feed on kokanee.

Hunting

The area offers blacktail deer and black bear. Best time for bear hunting is in May, right after ice-out, and again in fall, especially during years with a good berry crop. Look for deer along the lakeshore or eating kelp on the beaches of Shrimp Bay.

Other Activities

A trail leads to Shrimp Bay, which offers beachcombing and abundant marine wildlife for viewing.

Cabins
Orchard Lake Cabin (K-10)
Plenty Cutthroat Cabin (K-12)

Plenty Cutthroat cabin is a 12' x 12' Pan Abode constructed in 1964. It sleeps six people, and is furnished with an oil-burning stove for heating.

Orchard Lake cabin is identical to Plenty Cutthroat cabin. An oil stove is available for heating, so be sure to bring No. 1 heating oil. Elevation, 140 feet. Peak season is April through October.

Water source: lake and stream near cabins
Facilities:
- wooden bunks
- outhouse
- table bench
- oil stove
- woodshed
- ax
- maul
- 14-foot aluminum boat
- oars

Wolf Lake

Wolf Lake is in central Revillagigedo Island, about 18 miles from Ketchikan. You can also access this lake via a 2.6-mile trail from Moser Bay. (USGS Quad Map Bradfield Canal A-5)

Fishing
Fishing is good for cutthroat and rainbow trout.

Hunting
Hunting for Sitka blacktail and black bear available, in season.

Cabin
Wolf Lake Shelter (K-27)
This three-sided shelter sleeps four. It is free to the public on a first-come, first-served basis. No reservations are accepted.

Water source: lake

Ultralight fishing gear, 4-pound monofilament, tiny spoons and spinners are effective in catching Revillagigedo-area rainbows. In late evening, fish cruise the shoreline, providing good action until dark.

2 Gateway Misty Fiords
Fishing the TONGASS National Forest

About the Gateway

The Misty Fiords National Monument is near the Canadian Border in the southern-most part of southeast Alaska. Rivers, sheer rock walls, glaciers and volcanic lava flows make the Monument a must-see attraction. It spans 2,285,000 acres, of which the wilderness portion occupies 2,136,000 acres, making it the largest wilderness of the National Forests of Alaska, and the second largest in the National Forest System.

The monument is accessible by plane or boat. The Forest Service provides a variety of recreational cabins and shelters in the area. Fishing is good to excellent.

For more information on recreational cabins in this area, contact: Misty Fiords National Monument, 3031 Tongass Ave., Ketchikan, Alaska 99901, (907) 225-2148.

Fishing Index

Forest Service cabins in this gateway are listed below. The types of fish available in the vicinity of the cabin are indicated. You can cross-reference the cabin by the F.S. #, a number assigned to each cabin by the Forest Service. A description of the cabin and its facilities can be found on the page listed on the chart, and the page number of the map showing the exact cabin location is listed in the last column.

Gateway 2 Misty Fiords

Cabin	F.S.#	Page	Cutthroat Trout	Dolly Varden	Grayling	Rainbow Trout	Steelhead	Chinook Salmon	Coho Salmon	Chum Salmon	Pink Salmon	Sockeye Salmon	Halibut	Rockfish	Map pg.
Alava Bay Cabin	M-1	111						•	•	•	•	•	•	•	108
Bakewell Lake Cabin	M-2	112	•	•				•		•	•	•	•		109
Beaver Camp Cabin	M-3	119	•	•				•		•					108
Big Goat Lake Cabin	M-4	113				•									110
Checats Lake Cabin	M-5	114						•	•	•	•	•			110
Ella Narrows Cabin	M-6	115	•	•						•	•	•			108
Hugh Smith Lake Cabin	M-7	116	•	•				•	•	•	•	•	•		109
Humpback Lake Cabin	M-8	117	•	•				•	•	•	•	•			109
Manzanita Bay Shelter	M-20	118	•	•						•	•	•	•		107
Manzanita Lake Cabin	M-9	118	•	•						•	•	•	•		107
Nooya Lake Shelter	M-21	120													110
Red Alders Cabin	M-10	115	•	•						•	•	•			108
Wilson Narrows Cabin	M-11	121	•	•											110
Wilson Overflow Shelter	M-23	121	•	•											110
Wilson View Cabin	M-12	121	•	•											110
Winstanley Island Cabin	M-13	122								•		•	•	•	110
Winstanley Lake Cabin	M-14	124	•	•		•	•			•	•	•	•		110
Winstanley Lake Shelter	M-22	124	•	•		•	•			•	•	•	•		110

Alava Bay is near the southern tip of Revillagigedo Island, about 20 air miles south of Ketchikan. Minimum round-trip flight time charged is one hour. From Ketchikan, access by boat takes about 1.5 hours. (USGS Quad Map Ketchikan A-4)

Fishing

Saltwater fishing for halibut, bottomfish and salmon are the main attractions of this cabin. Coho and pink salmon are present in all the streams emptying into the bay. Small runs of chum salmon. Steelhead and rainbow fishing at the head of the bay, and in a stream between Ape and Fox points. Numerous opportunities exist for freshwater fishing at Winstanley and Checat lakes to the north, and Bakewell Arm and Creek to the east. See these entries for specific details.

Hunting

Hunting is fair for black bear and deer. Waterfowl hunting is excellent. Set up decoys off one of the outer points. During minus tides in fall, hunters can find bear or deer feeding in the intertidal areas.

Other Activities

Hiking and beachcombing opportunities abound at this site.

Cabin
Alava Bay Cabin (M-1)

Constructed in 1974, this 12' x 14' cedar log cabin accommodates six people and has a wood-burning stove for heating and cooking. A cook range was installed in 1980. The cabin is nestled in Alava Bay, home to myriad types of marine life. Alava Bay also serves as a protected anchorage for small boats venturing into Revillagigedo Channel. A buoy is provided. Elevation, sea level. Year-round use.

Water source: nearby stream
Facilities:

- wooden bunks
- outhouse
- table
- bench
- cooking counter
- shelves
- wood stove
- wood supply
- no boat
- ax
- maul

User Comments

7/22-7/23: ''Delighted to find this little cookstove to replace the big one that was here in 1981 and 1983. This is a beauty. The oven bakes very well when the back right damper handle is vertical, thereby allowing heat to flow around the oven.''

Bakewell Lake

Bakewell Lake is on mainland Alaska south of Bakewell Arm, about 40 air miles east of Ketchikan. Minimum round-trip flight time is two hours. Access is also by a one-mile trail from Bakewell Bay. (USGS Quad Map Ketchikan B-2)

Fishing

Bakewell Lake offers one of the better cutthroat trout fisheries in the region. Nearby Bakewell Creek is famous for fly fishing for anadromous cutthroats up to 24 inches and Dolly Varden char. Sockeye and coho salmon are also available in the creek and in various sections of the lake throughout the summer months. Pink and chum salmon fishing is best at the head of Bakewell Arm. For best success, fish the creek or surf cast into the tidewater near the creek mouth. Bakewell is also known for its good steelhead fishing. The lower creek beyond the tidal influence offers good holes and runs for fish ranging from six to 12 pounds, often larger.

Hunting

Hunting is chiefly for blacktail deer and black bear. Some brown bear and goat hunting is done from this cabin in and around Smeaton Arm and Wilson Arm. There is sea duck hunting in the Bakewell area, and fair grouse hunting.

Cabin
Bakewell Lake Cabin (M-2)

Built in 1978, this 12'x 14' cedar log cabin sleeps six and has a wood-burning stove for heating and cooking. Two 14-foot skiffs are available; one at the cabin and one at the trailhead. Elevation, 168 feet. Peak season is May through October.

Water source: nearby stream
Facilities:

- wooden bunks
- outhouse
- table
- bench
- cooking counter
- shelves
- wood stove
- wood supply
- ax
- maul
- two 14-foot skiffs
- oars

User Comments

8/12: "Very clean and comfortable cabin. Your maintenance field people deserve credit on this one. Thank you for a nice stay."

Big Goat Lake is on mainland Alaska east of Rudyerd Bay. The lake is 45 air miles from Ketchikan. Minimum round-trip flight time charged is 2.4 hours. Air access only. The lake can be difficult to reach at times due to inclement weather. (USGS Quad Map Ketchikan C-2)

Fishing

Grayling were stocked in Big Goat Lake in 1965. The population has taken hold and fishing is considered good in and around the feeder streams and creeks that empty into the lake, especially the eastern end. There is a sand dropoff nearby that produces good catches of fish during the evening hours. A 4-weight fly rod, floating line and sub-surface nymphs work best in this lake. Dry flies also work well in the smooth side currents opposite the inlet. Try skittering the dry across the surface for aggressive strikes.

Hunting

The area offers goat hunting for those willing to rough it a few days in the mountains. Nearby peaks rise to 4,580 feet, making a long climb to the top, often through dense timber. Hunting for Sitka blacktails and black bear is done on the lower hillsides and near Little Goat Lake.

Other Activities

The area offers exquisite opportunities for remote, wilderness adventures that feature solitude, hiking, boating and scenic photography. Excellent examples of glacially carved mountain peaks.

Cabin
Big Goat Lake Cabin (M-4)

Constructed in 1964, the 12' x 12' cedar log cabin accommodates six people and has an oil stove for heating. Because of the 1,775-foot elevation, it can get chilly, even during the summer months, so take plenty of fuel with you. The scenery is spectacular. The outlet consists of a huge waterfall which makes a spectacular drop to the forest floor below. This is one of my most favorite lakes in this region. The boat can handle five people. Because of its heavy construction, rowing is a chore. Bring at least a 3-hp outboard and save your back. Peak season is June through October.

Water source: lake
Facilities:

- wooden bunks
- outhouse
- table
- bench
- cooking counter
- shelves
- oil stove
- 14-foot boat
- oars

Checats Lake is on mainland Alaska south of Punchbowl Cove, about 35 air miles from Ketchikan. Minimum round-trip flight time charged from Ketchikan is 1.6 hours. (USGS Quad Map Ketchikan B-3)

Fishing

Fishing for rainbow trout up to 24 inches is good in Checats Lake. During the day, fishing is good to the south of the cabin along the deepwater breakline. Fish hide in the lily pads during the summer months, and a belly boat can be most effective in putting a fish into your hand. Also, at various times throughout the day rainbows migrate in and around the islands at mid-lake, searching for forage fish, leeches and crustaceans. Anchor off these islands and fan cast, or drift with the wind and jig off the bottom with black or gold spoons. Many anglers have good success using a slip-sinker rig and salmon eggs fished on the bottom. Between Checats Cove and lower Checats Lake you'll find a small run of steelhead. The outlet creek offers pink, chum and coho salmon action.

Hunting

Hunting in the area is fair to good for mountain goat, deer and black and brown bear. There are several mountain ranges to choose from, but the group of peaks south of the lake offer the best opportunities for a variety of species.

Cabin
Checats Lake Cabin (M-5)

Constructed in 1964, the 12' x 12' cedar log Checats Lake cabin accommodates six people and has a wood-burning stove for heating and cooking. Mountains surrounding the lake offer scenic beauty and isolation. Peak season, May through October. Elevation, 710 feet.

Water source: lake and stream
Facilities:

- wooden bunks
- wood stove
- wood supply
- ax
- maul
- outhouse
- table
- bench
- cooking counter
- shelves
- 14-foot skiff
- oars

User Comments

8/5-8/9: "Fishing is good."

Ella Lake is on eastern Revillagigedo Island near the Behm Canal, about 24 air miles from Ketchikan. Minimum round-trip flight time charged from Ketchikan is 1.2 hours. There is a 2.5-mile trail that extends from Ella Bay to the lake, however, it does not continue to the cabin. (USGS Quad Map Ketchikan C-4 and B-4)

Fishing

Ella Lake offers excellent fishing for cutthroat trout, Dolly Varden and kokanee salmon. Cutthroat fishing is good in the narrows itself, especially during early morning and late evening. Flies work best here, with leech, stonefly, sculpin, kokanee and scud patterns most effective. During midday try fishing off the point stretching out into the lake. Start at the 15-foot depth and work your fly or lure from shallow to deep while fishing horizontally along the breakline for 200 yards or more. Fair to good runs of coho, pink and chum salmon in the lower stretches of Ella Creek. Fish an incoming tide for best results, moving upstream after fish as the tide recedes.

Hunting

The area offers excellent hunting for Sitka blacktail deer. The marshes near the cabin and the alpine areas directly above the cabin offer the best chances for success.

Cabins
Ella Narrows Cabin (M-6)
Red Alders Cabin (M-10)

Constructed in 1966, the 12' x 14' cedar log Ella Narrows cabin accommodates six people and has a wood-burning stove for heating and cooking. The cabin has two 14-foot skiffs, one at the cabin and one at the trailhead for marine travelers to use. Peak season is May through November. Elevation, 255 feet.

Located on the northwest arm of Ella Lake, Red Alders cabin is a 12' x 12' cedar log structure with a wood-burning stove. It can sleep six people. A skiff is available for fishing and exploring the area.

Water source for both cabins: lake
Facilities:

- wooden bunks
- outhouse
- table
- bench
- cooking counter
- shelves
- wood stove
- wood supply
- ax
- maul
- three 14-foot skiffs

Hugh Smith Lake is on the mainland south of Martin Arm, 55 air miles from Ketchikan. Minimum round-trip flight time charged is 2.6 hours. Air access only. (USGS Quad Map Ketchikan A-3)

Fishing

Fish for rainbow and cutthroat trout, Dolly Varden and steelhead throughout the Hugh Smith watershed. Sockeye Creek, which drains Hugh Smith Lake, offers the best steelheading and pink, chum, silver and sockeye salmon fishing. Silvers, sockeyes and pinks spawn in the headwaters of Hugh Smith Lake. Additional steelheading opportunities in nearby creeks.

Hunting

Sitka blacktail deer, black and brown bear hunting available in season.

Cabin

Hugh Smith Lake Cabin (M-7)

This Pan abode cabin sleeps six. A wood-burning stove is available for heating and cooking. Peak season is May through October. Scenic location. Excellent get-away.

Water source: lake
Facilities:

- wooden bunks
- outhouse
- table
- benches
- counter
- shelves
- wood stove
- ax
- maul
- boat
- oars

User Comments

8/25-8/26: "Fish put on a wonderful display, jumping in tandem. But we had trouble catching them."

The Misty Fiords National Monument is a perfect choice for anglers desiring world-class fishing in a scenic wilderness environment.

Humpback Lake

Humpback Lake is on the mainland east of Mink Bay, about 48 air miles from Ketchikan. Air access only. Minimum round-trip flight time charged from Ketchikan is 2.6 hours. (USGS Quad Map Ketchikan A-2)

Fishing

Anadromous cutthroat trout and Dolly Varden fishing is excellent, with fish in Humpback Creek reaching lengths of up to 28 inches. Best times to fish are from April through June, and again in the fall. Steelhead fishing is very good in the Marten River, seven miles from the lake. No trail or boat access from Humpback Lake to Marten River. Overland route is via bushwhacking, and advisable only for the experienced outdoorsman. Very difficult route.

Dollies and cutthroat congregate at select feeder creeks emptying into Humpback Lake. Choose those creeks with fan-shaped gravel bottoms, where the cutts feed on drifting forage food items. Also good are the weedbeds and shallow shoreline areas near the northcentral section of the lake, and the inlet end of the lake. Look for fish feeding here late in the evening and on cloudy days. When you find a school of cutts, a fish a cast is common for 10 to 15 minutes. Fish for pink, coho and chum salmon in the lower outlet creek, within one mile of salt water. Good area for the fly fisherman.

Hunting

The area offers fair hunting for brown bear, black bear and mountain goats, in season. Try the areas south of Billy Goat Creek, and the Stripe Mountain area.

Cabin
Humpback Lake Cabin (M-8)

Constructed in 1979, this 12' x 14' cedar cabin accommodates six people and has a wood-burning stove for heating and some cooking. It is located in a wonderfully scenic, mountainous setting and provides ample opportunities for wilderness solitude. Elevation, 272 feet, with mountain peaks rising to 3,400 feet near the lake. Peak season is May through October.

Water source: lake and creek
Facilities:

- wooden bunks
- outhouse
- table
- bench
- aluminum boat
- shelves
- cooking counter
- wood supply
- wood stove
- ax
- maul

Manzanita Lake

Manzanita Lake is located on Revillagigedo Island near the Behm Canal, 28 air miles from Ketchikan. Minimum, round-trip flight time charged is 1.6 hours. Marine travelers can reach the lake via a 3.5-mile trail from Manzanita Bay. (USGS Quad Map Ketchikan C-4).

Fishing

Manzanita Lake is noted for its excellent fishing for cutthroat trout, kokanee salmon and Dolly Varden. For best success, fish the lily pads and weed beds in the southern arm of the bay. Best fishing is during evening and morning. Fish the outlet and inlet streams during mid-day or troll the western shoreline in 10 to 40 feet of water. Find the breakline with the forage food items, and you'll find fish. Better yet, watch for cutthroat activity in and around the shoreline. Cast or jig a silver/orange spoon in nearby deeper water where big cutts cruise.

Excellent fishing for cutthroat trout is also available in Manzanita Creek. Take a four-weight or smaller fly rod, weighted nymphs and floating fly line. Pack a shooting head for the deeper runs and holes near the undercut banks. Use nymphs and terrestrials in spring and summer, and salmon egg patterns during the fall. Silver salmon fishing is good in the Manzanita Creek intertidal area. Five miles to the north, Grace Creek provides an excellent late-fall/spring steelhead fishery.

Hunting

Hunting for Sitka blacktails and black bear is considered fair in this region.

To catch Manzanita Creek Dolly Varden, work fluorescent red or orange spinners and streamer flies along undercut banks and through deep holes.

Other Activities

Beaver, mink and marten are commonly seen in this area.

Cabins

Beaver Camp Cabin (M-3)
Manzanita Lake Cabin (M-9)
Manzanita Bay Shelter (M-20)

Constructed in 1965, the 12' x 14' Beaver Camp cabin accommodates six people and has a wood-burning stove for heating and cooking.

Manzanita cabin is 12' x 14', constructed in 1973, and accommodates six. It has an oil stove for heating only, so bring at least five gallons of oil for a weekend stay, more during fall and spring.

Each cabin has one 14-foot skiff; a third is located at the lake outlet for trail/boat access. Elevation, 239 feet. Peak season May through October.

Manzanita Bay offers a three-sided, Adirondack shelter on a first-come, first-serve basis. No payment required, or reservations accepted. There is no stove or boat. Year-round use.

Water source: lake
Facilities:

* wooden bunks
* outhouse
* table
* bench
* cooking counter
* shelves
* wood stove (M-3)
* oil stove (M-9)
* skiffs
* oars

User Comments

8/26-8/28: "Great cabin. Had a very pleasant time."

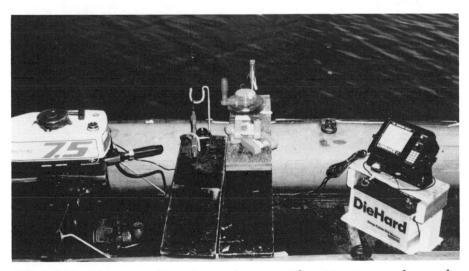

When fishing deepwater lakes for rainbow or cutthroat trout, a graph recorder, downrigger and rod holder will greatly increase your chances of success.

Nooya Lake

Nooya Lake is on mainland Alaska on the north side of Rudyerd Bay. The lake is 42 air miles from Ketchikan; also accessible by boat to Rudyerd Bay, then taking a 1.1-mile trail to the lake. (USGS Quad Map Ketchikan C-3)

Fishing

Dolly Varden are present throughout the Nooya Lake system, which provides a major overwintering habitat for this species. In nearby Nooya Creek, expect to catch humpback, chum and coho salmon. The best fishing takes place where the creek empties into salt water. Bright attractor flies with plenty of tinsel are best, as are silver-plated spoons and spinners. Take a sink-tip or mini lead head for fly fishing this watershed, and use it when fishing the upper headwaters and lake.

A tidebook is a must to properly plan the best fishing times. Halibut fishing is good in offshore waters.

Hunting

Sitka blacktail deer, brown and black bear available throughout the area, in season.

Cabin
Nooya Lake Shelter (M-21)

This three-sided shelter sleeps six. There is no stove for heating, so bring both a heat source and cooking stove. Peak season, June through October. This shelter is free to the public on a first-come, first-served basis. No reservations are accepted.
Water source: lake
Facilities:
- outhouse
- wooden bunks
- skiff

Wilson Lake is immediately north of Wilson Arm, 44 air miles from Ketchikan. Minimum round-trip flight time charged is two hours. Air access only. (USGS Quad Map B-2, C-2)

Fishing

Cutthroat, Dolly Varden and kokanee fishing is good to excellent. Due to a diet of kokanee, Wilson Lake cutthroats can reach lengths of up to 24 inches. I prefer to troll kokanee-type plugs in a zig-zag pattern in late evening at the inlet end. During mid-day, jig a slab spoon in deep water along the steep-banked shore to the north. In the spring, the Wilson River receives a strong run of anadromous cutthroat trout. When fishing for cutthroat and Dollies during periods of sunny weather, concentrate on lily pads and deepwater weedlines.

Hunting

Wilson Lake and Narrows is a common base camp for hunters pursuing mountain goat, Sitka blacktail deer, and black and brown bear. Expect a rugged hunt—a spike camp is advised for best success.

Cabins
Wilson Narrows Cabin (M-11)
Wilson View Cabin (M-12)
Wilson Overflow Shelter (M-23)

Constructed in 1978, the 12'x 14' cedar-log, Wilson View cabin is located at the north end of Wilson Lake. It can accommodate six people, and has a wood-burning stove for heating and cooking. Wilson Narrows cabin is nearly identical, and located at the south end of Wilson Lake. The cabins are nestled in a scenic area surrounded by a chain of mountains rising to 5,000 feet. An overflow shelter is located at mid-lake, and is available on a first-come, first-served basis. There is no charge for using this shelter. Each cabin (shelter excluded) has a 14-foot aluminum boat with oars. Elevation, 256 feet. Peak season late May through October.

Water source: lake and creek
Facilities:

- wooden bunks
- outhouse
- table
- bench
- cooking counter
- shelves
- woodstove
- wood supply
- ax
- maul
- aluminum boat
- oars

User Comments

6/10-6/12: "Great cabin. Beware of bear that frequently visits."

Winstanley Island is 30 air miles from Ketchikan in east Behm Canal between Rudyerd Bay and Smeaton Bay. Minimum round-trip flight time charged is 1.8 hours. Access by boat from Ketchikan takes about three hours. (USGS Map Ketchikan B-3)

Fishing

No freshwater fishing opportunities exist on the island. However, boat-equipped anglers use this cabin as a base to work the numerous salmon, trout and steelhead systems nearby. These include Winstanley, Checats, Ella, Manzanita and Bakewell lakes and their subsequent feeder and outlet creeks.

Halibut fishing, as well as crabbing, shrimping and rockfish fishing is excellent in and around the island. Saltwater salmon fishing is good to excellent during the migratory runs.

Hunting

Black bear, Sitka blacktail deer and brown bear hunting is available along the mainland coast, along with excellent sea duck hunting and puddle duck hunting in the coves and lagoons.

Other Activities

The island offers an excellent base to sightsee and fish Rudyerd Bay, Walker Cove, Chickamin River, Smeaton Bay and the entire Behm Canal.

Cabin

Winstanley Island Cabin (M-13)

Constructed in 1972, the 12' x 14' cedar-log Winstanley Island cabin can accommodate six people and has a wood-burning stove for cooking and heating. It is on the north end of Winstanley Island facing Shoalwater Pass. A mooring buoy is provided. Very scenic area, with great potential for exploration if you have your own boat. Elevation, sea level. Year-round use.

Water source: nearby stream
Facilities:

- wooden bunks
- outhouse
- table
- bench
- cooking counter
- shelves
- wood stove
- wood supply
- ax
- maul
- no boat

User Comments

5/24-5/27: ''Beautiful. Great cedar smell throughout. Ten black bear sightings, loons, harlequins, seals, crabs. Wonderful!''

6/1: ''Condition of cabin excellent. Weather, perfect. We did not fish. Kayaked around island and along shore north four miles and saw three black bears, several seals, three eagles and ducks. Wish we had known there were no docking facilities. Would have packed differently. Made four trips with our gear from adjacent small island because cruiser couldn't land on shore near cabin. Left via plane.''

7/30: ''An excellent use of taxpayers' money.''

Winstanley Lake is on the mainland east of Winstanley Island about 32 air miles from Ketchikan. Minimum round-trip flight time charged is 1.8 hours. Marine travelers can reach the lake by taking a 2.3-mile trail, starting at East Behm Canal at Winstanley Creek and ending at a three-sided shelter at the lake outlet. There, a boat is available to reach the cabin. (USGS Quad Map Ketchikan B-3)

Fishing

One of the finer fisheries in the area, Winstanley Lake offers cutthroat trout to 27 inches and kokanee to 10 inches. Kokanee here prefer red rooster tails with gold blades. Dolly Varden are present, but are small and infrequent. Three-inch Storm plugs are also very effective when trolled along shoreline structure. Winstanley Creek offers steelhead, pink, chum and coho salmon fishing near the outlet and at the mouth of the creek where it empties into Shoalwater Pass. Try the inlet creek for cutthroat, and the entire length of the outlet creek for rainbow and steelhead. Best steelhead fishing is in April and May. Drift lures and attractor patterns work best. Steelies here tend to hold in deep channels and pools. Be prepared to add a shot of lead to get your fly to the bottom.

Hunting

Good to excellent hunting for Sitka blacktail, black and brown bear and mountain goats, especially in the mountains directly behind the cabin. Various parts of the mountain range can be reached by taking a skiff to the end of the lake and taking Winstanley Creek to the south. Ducks raft on the lake on their southward migration and offer fair wingshooting opportunities. Grouse hunting is fair.

For anglers with a boat, Winstanley Island offers a premier base camp to fish for steelhead, salmon and trout in several nearby watersheds. For silver salmon like this, plan a mid- to late-August or September fishing trip.

Other Activities

For the wildlife viewer, mink, marten, beaver and otter are common in the area.

Cabin

Winstanley Lake Cabin (M-14)
Winstanley Lake Shelter (M-22)

Constructed in 1967, the 12' x 14' cedar log Winstanley Lake cabin can accommodate six people, has a wood-burning stove for heating and cooking, and two skiffs. One skiff is at the cabin and one at the trailhead for easy access from salt water.

The three-sided Adirondack-type shelter at the lake outlet can sleep four people. The shelter (M-22) has neither stove nor boat. Adirondack cabins are free to the public on a first-come, first-served basis. No reservations are accepted. Elevation, 400 feet. Mountains rise to nearly 3,800 feet near the lake. Excellent scenery. Peak season May through October.

Water source: lake
Facilities (M-14 cabin):

- wooden bunks
- outhouse
- table
- bench

- cooking counter
- shelves
- wood stove
- wood supply

- ax
- maul
- two aluminum boats
- oars

Pink or humpback salmon are the most abundant of the five species of Pacific salmon. They are most often caught in intertidal areas throughout their range.

3 Gateway Wrangell
Fishing the TONGASS National Forest

About the Gateway

Located on the northern tip of Wrangell Island, the town of Wrangell is the second oldest community in southeast Alaska. It served as an important supply depot for miners and traders beginning with the Stikine Gold Rush in 1877.

The area's major attraction is the Stikine River. Gorgeous scenery and abundant wildlife and fisheries attract visitors from around the world. The Stikine begins as a glacially-fed river in the northwest mountains of British Columbia. It courses for over 400 miles, where it empties into the sea near Wrangell. This region is covered with dense stands of hemlock-spruce rainforest covering the lower mountain slopes. The valley floor is a combination of muskeg, dense alder, willow, and berry thickets and devil's club. Grassy flats, tidal marshes and sand bars make up the nearly 17-mile Stikine Delta. Much of the Stikine River drainage is important fish and wildlife habitat.

Many different varieties of wildlife live in or near the "flats." The region is a major nesting and resting area for migratory waterfowl, and waterfowl hunting is extremely popular and productive there. A number of Forest Service cabins are found throughout the area.

Population: 2,400
Annual Precipitation: 79 inches
Average High Temperature: 42 degrees

Fishing the Wrangell Area

In the Wrangell area, over 70 percent of the fishing takes place in saltwater areas. Marine sport fishing is usually restricted to the Eastern Passage and Zimovia Straight (north of Nemo Point). Marine salmon anglers regularly fish Stikine Straight east of Howe Point. The Wrangell area does not offer an extensive roadside sportfishery. Most areas are fly-out or boat accessible only. The shoreline adjacent to the Zimovia Highway south to Pat Creek offers Dolly Varden, coho and pink salmon. Pat Creek itself offers fair to good fishing for Dollies, cutthroat and coho and pink salmon. Thoms Creek offers steelhead, sockeye and coho salmon, cutthroat and Dollies. Also accessible by road is Fool's Creek where anglers catch cutthroat, Dolly Varden and pink and coho salmon. The best choices for fly-out or boat accessible fisheries include the Virginia Lake watershed, located eight miles from Wrangell. Trophy cutthroat trout, salmon and char are available below the falls. For steelhead, pink and coho salmon, visit Olive Creek. The pink salmon fishery is rated very good.

Goat Lake offers scenic beauty and rainbow trout; the Anan Lake system for salmon, trout and char; and Marten Lake with numerous but small landlocked cutthroats. Areas that receive little to moderate fishing pressure include the Salmon and Red Bay areas, and the Sweetwater Lakes system. If you have several days to spend, journey up the Stikine River tributaries and fish for salmon, char, cutthroat and steelhead. The Eagle Lake watershed offers some of the best angling in the area. Steelhead, cutts, coho and pink salmon are all available, in season.

For information on recreational cabins in this area, contact: Wrangell Ranger District, 525 Bennett St., P.O. Box 51, Wrangell, AK 99929, (907) 874-2323.

Fishing Index

Forest Service cabins in this gateway are listed below. The types of fish available in the vicinity of the cabin are indicated. You can cross-reference the cabin by the F.S. #, a number assigned to each cabin by the Forest Service. A description of the cabin and its facilities can be found on the page listed on the chart, and the page number of the map showing the exact cabin location is listed in the last column.

Gateway 3 Wrangell

Cabin	F.S. #	Page	Cutthroat Trout	Dolly Varden	Grayling	Rainbow Trout	Steelhead Trout	Chinook Salmon	Coho Salmon	Chum Salmon	Pink Salmon	Sockeye Salmon	Halibut	Rockfish	Map pg.
Anan Bay Cabin	W-20	134	•	•		•	•	•	•	•	•	•	•	•	128
Berg Bay Cabin	W-15	136				•	•			•	•	•			128
Binkley Slough Cabin	W-9	137													132
Eagle Lake Cabin	W-22	138	•			•	•			•	•	•			128
Garnet Ledge Cabin	W-12	140					waterfowl hunting								132
Gut Island Cabin No. 1	W-8	141					waterfowl hunting								132
Gut Island Cabin No. 2	W-24	141					waterfowl hunting								132
Harding River Cabin	W-28	142	•	•		•	•			•	•	•			128
Koknuk Cabin	W-10	147					hunting								132
Little Dry Island Cabin	W-7	143					hunting								132
Mallard Slough Cabin	W-23	144					hunting								132
Marten Lake Cabin	W-17	145	•	•		•	•			•	•	•			128
Mount Flemer Cabin	W-6	146	•	•											129
Mount Rydna Cabin	W-5	135	•	•		•	•			•	•	•	•		132
Sergief Island Cabin	W-11	147													132
Shakes Slough No. 1	W-1	148	•					•	•						132
Shakes Slough No. 2	W-2	148	•					•	•						132
Steamer Bay Cabin	W-14	150	•	•						•	•	•	•	•	130
Twin Lakes Cabin	W-3	139	•	•						•	•	•	•		132
Virginia Lake Cabin	W-13	151	•	•								•	•	•	131

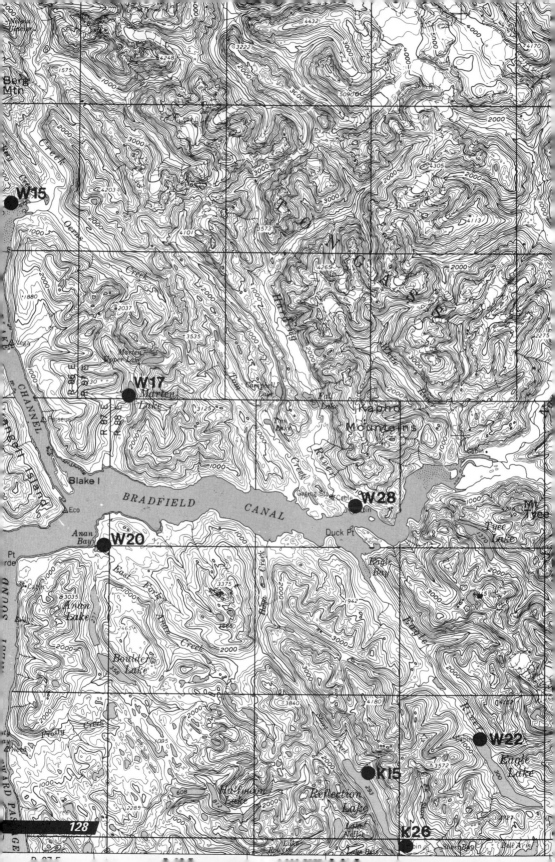

W15

W17

W28

W20

W22

K15

K26

Berg Mtn

CHANNEL

Blake I

BRADFIELD CANAL

Anan Bay

Anan Lake

Boulder Lake

Kvapno Mountains

Duck Pt

Eagle Bay

Mt Tyee

Tyee Lake

Eagle Lake

Reflection Lake

Hole in Wall
Mtn
3015
2500

Darsmith
Creek

Middle
Mtn

Pheno
Mtn

Snowcap
Mtn
3035

Icecap
Mtn

Eagle
Crag

Fowler
Creek

Great
Glacier

2500

RIVER

Mt
Robertson

Big Mtn

5000

The
Knob
4470

Sugarloaf
Mtn

Choquette Gl

Warm Spring
Mtn

Mt
Laura

Glacier

Talbot
Mtn

Glasier
Mtn

Choquette River

Mt
Choquette

2500

Johnson

Surprise
Mtn

Tasaddin

R-85
R-86

Mt
Gallatin

2500

Mt
Turner

Mt
McGrath

River

IKSUT

Elbow
Mtn

STIKINE

Johnson Creek

Iskut
Mt
4710

Snowy
Mtn

Fizzle
Mtn

Barnes
Lake

Guerin   Slough

Katete
Mtn

Katete

Geoffrim

Creek

Fulena

2500

W6

634

Mt
Steiner

Mt
Geoffrich

Mt
Whimple
5740

BRITISH COLUMBIA

River

Mt
Fawcett
5583

Mt
Cote

NATIONAL   FOREST   BOUNDARY

950

West   Fork

3000

Black Cree

5980

Cone Mtn
5855

2000

4000

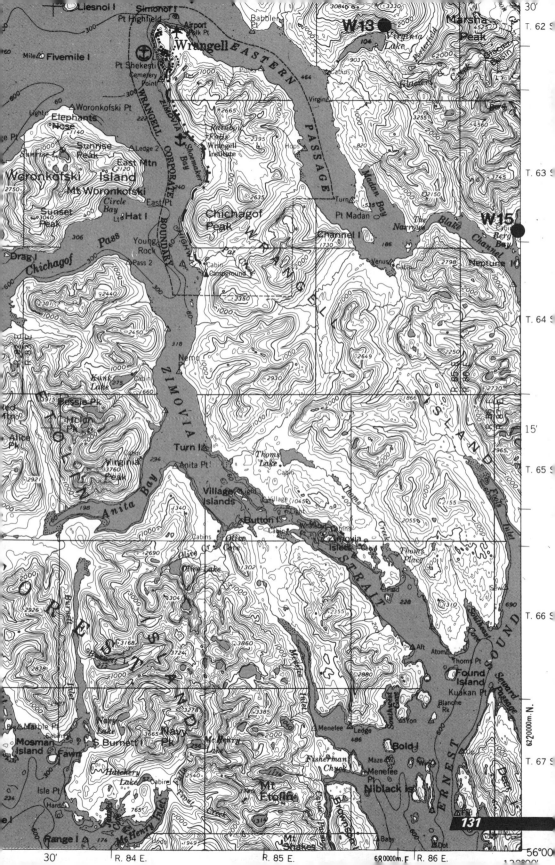

Liesnoi I
Simonof I
Pt Highfield
Airport
Babbler
Pt

Wrangell

EASTERN

Mile
Fivemile I

Pt Shekesti
Cemetery
Point

WRANGELL

W 13

Virginia
Lake

T. 62 S

Marsha
Peak

Lights
Woronkofski Pt
Elephants
Nose
ZIMOVIA

CORPORATE

Punta

Virgin

Ritchie
Fort
Wrangell
Institute

Hope

PASSAGE

Cabus

River

T. 63 S

Sunrise
Peak
East Mtn

Ledge 2

Shoemaker
Bay

Madan Bay

Turn

T. 63 S

Woronkofski
Island

Mt Woronkofski
Circle
Bay
Hat I
East Pt

Chichagof
Peak

Pt Madan

The
Narrows

Blake

W 15

Berg
Bay

Sunset
Peak

BOUNDARY
Young
Rock
Pass 2

WRANGELL

Channel I

Venus I

Cabin

Neptune I

Drag I
Chichagof
Pass

Campground

Cabin

T. 64 S

Kunk
Lake

Cabin

Nemo

ISLAND

T. 64 S

Bessie Pk
Highton

Turn I.
Anita Pt

Thoms
Lake
Cabin

Alice
Pk

Virginia
Peak

Village
Islands

Village

Thoms

15'

T. 65 S

Anita Bay

Button I.

Olive
Cove

Zimovia
Islets

STRAIT

Creek

Thoms
Pines

T. 65 S

Olive
Lake

Cabins

Cabin

T. 66 S

BURNETT

Olive Cr

Aft
Atom

Thoms Pt

SOUND

Found
Island

Mosman
Island
Fawn

Navy
Pk

McHenry

Menefee
Ledge

Kukan Pt

Blanche
Rk

ERNEST

6220000m. N.

T. 67 S

Isle Pt
Hard

Hatchery
Lake
Cabins

S Burnett

Mt
Etolin

Fisherman
Chuck

Menefee
Pt

Bold I

Niblack Is

SEWARD

Range I

McHenry Inlet

Mt
Snakes

Baby

56°00'

From the southeast corner of Wrangell Island, Anan Bay is located on the Alaska mainland, on the south shoreline of the Bradfield Canal. It is 31 miles from Ketchikan and accessible by either boat or plane. A 25-foot mooring float is available. (USGS Quad Map Bradfield Canal, A-6)

Fishing

In April and May, Anan Creek has good runs of steelhead and anadromous cutthroat. Fishing is fair in the lagoon. Dolly Varden are present throughout. For best success, fish the stream below the bear observatory, especially on an incoming tide. However, angling near the fish ladder is prohibited.

Anan Lake, 430 acres, has good cutthroat fishing; bring a 2-man inflatable to reach the best holes. Nearby is 420-acre Boulder Lake. Both Anan and Boulder lakes have received little pressure from anglers.

Saltwater king salmon fishing (May through July) and halibut fishing (year-round) is good three miles from the cabin. Pink salmon are numerous in the lagoon and creek in July and early August, and silver salmon in the bay from August to early September. However, silvers continually enter the system through early November. Sockeye salmon available in early summer.

Hunting

The area is closed to black bear hunting.

Hootchies fished behind a dodger or flasher trigger aggressive strikes from both silver and king salmon. Concentrate efforts along migration routes near shoreline structure in May and June for kings and August for silvers.

Other Activities

A one-mile trail, originally developed as a result of aboriginal use of the area as a summer fish camp, extends from the cabin to the bear observatory at Anan Creek Falls. A fish ladder in a tunnel blasted through bedrock provides salmon with an access route to the upper watershed. Photographs of black and brown bears, eagles and seals feeding on large concentrations of salmon are best taken in July and August. Good crabbing available in Anan Bay.

Precautions

Make your presence known to bears when using the trails in this area. Whistle, talk loudly, wear a bell.

Cabin

Anan Bay Cabin (W-20)

Located on the shore of Anan Bay, the cabin is an A-frame capable of sleeping seven people and is furnished with an oil stove for heating. The surrounding area is rainforest with Alaska yellow cedar and western red cedar present on the wetter slopes. Muskeg is common between Anan Lagoon and Anan Lake. Due to the nearby bear observatory, this area receives heavy use during the summer months. The bear observatory is an open-style, wood-frame shelter without doors or windows. If needed, a ladder is available for emergency access to the roof.

Water source: stream
Facilities:
- wooden bunks
- table
- benches
- outhouse
- cooking counter
- oil stove
- no boat

Andrew Creek is on the south side of the Stikine River near Andrew Slough. It is 18 miles by boat from Wrangell and 15 miles by air. Charged flight time from Wrangell is 40 minutes. When traveling via boat, a 14-foot or higher tide is needed to cross the Stikine River tidal flats to reach the main river channel past Point Rothsay. When the river is low, the cabin is often inaccessible by boat or plane. (USGS Quad Map Petersburg C-1)

Fishing

From June through September, Andrew Creek offers fishing for cutthroat trout and Dolly Varden. Fish for pink salmon during late July and August, and silver salmon during August and September. Chum and sockeye salmon fishing is also good in season. Steelhead fishing is good not only in Andrew Creek, but in nearby tributaries. A boat is necessary for full enjoyment.

Hunting

Hunters use this cabin as a base camp during the moose season.

Other Activities

The creek and slough offer excellent opportunities to photograph eagles, seals and brown and black bears fishing during the salmon runs. The geographic layout of Andrew Creek offers good scenic photography and exploration.

Cabin
Mount Rydna Cabin (W-5)

This cabin is at the Andrew Creek/Andrew Slough confluence. Its A-frame structure with loft can sleep seven people, and there's an oil stove for heating and cooking. The slopes adjacent to the cabin are gentle to moderate. The surrounding forest is Sitka spruce, with western hemlock and cedar. Peak season is May through October.

Water source: creek
Facilities:

- three bunks
- loft
- table
- benches
- oil stove
- cooler box
- outhouse
- no boat
- cooking counter

Berg Bay is on the east side of Blake Channel, 22 miles by boat from Wrangell. A 25-foot mooring float is available near the cabin. (USGS Quad Map Petersburg B-1 and Bradfield B-6)

Fishing

Steelhead and rainbow trout fishing is good in nearby Oerns and Aaron creeks. From July through September expect chum, pink and silver salmon action in these watersheds, intertidal areas and nearby streams. A boat is necessary for optimum fishing enjoyment and exploration of surrounding watersheds.

Hunting

From September through December, waterfowl hunting on the Aaron Creek tideflats is excellent. Expect fair to good brown bear and black bear hunting away from the beaten path. Moose hunting is best in the north. Mountain goats are available on nearby ridges. Exactly where they are depends on time of year and weather conditions. Goats in this region are often difficult and hazardous to reach. Take overnight and emergency gear. Grouse hunting is fair to good in the forest.

Cabin
Berg Bay Cabin (W-15)

Berg Bay cabin is an A-frame structure with sleeping loft. Capable of sleeping seven people, the cabin is furnished with an oil-burning stove. A four-tenths-mile planked trail leads from the cabin to the Aaron Creek tidal grass flats. The trail from the cabin to Berg Creek is four miles long, and beyond that is four miles of unmaintained trail that leads to Berg Basin. The area is surrounded by muskeg and dense rain forest. Expect gentle slopes near the cabin, while distant slopes are steep and hazardous.

Water source: creek
Facilities:
• three bunks
• sleeping loft
• table
• benches
• mooring float
• oil stove
• outhouse
• no boat
• cooking counter

Binkley Slough is on the southwest side of Farm Island on the Stikine River tidal flats. The island is 12 miles by boat from Wrangell and nine miles by boat from Banana Point boat ramp on the south end of Mitkof Island. Boat access requires a tide of 15 feet or higher. (USGS Quad Map Petersburg C-2)

Hunting

The area has fair moose hunting in season, however, a boat is required to reach the best areas. Waterfowl hunting is good and can be enjoyed within walking distance of the cabin.

Other Activities

In May and June, the island is blooming with wildflowers. In spring and fall, bird-watchers congregate here to observe annual migrations.

Cabin

Binkley Slough Cabin (W-9)

This hunter-style cabin accommodates six people, and is furnished with an oil stove for heating. The cabin is in a small group of spruce trees surrounded by tidal flats.

Water source: catchment
Facilities:
- oil stove
- four wooden bunks
- table
- benches
- outhouse
- cooking counter
- cooler box
- no boat

Eagle Lake

Eagle Lake is on mainland Alaska, south of the Bradfield Canal. It is accessible only by floatplane and is 44 air miles from Wrangell. (USGS Quad Map Bradfield Canal A-5)

Fishing

The lake is known for its excellent anadromous cutthroat trout fishing, with trophies taken in the 20-inch class. In the spring, fishing is excellent in the river, after spring run-off has subsided. The lake offers good fishing year-round.

Eagle Lake is perhaps the most scenic lake in the area and a good choice for a weekend get-away. Take a portable downrigger, trolling spoons and trolling motor for best success. The outlet of Eagle River, several miles away, offers steelhead, silver, pink and chum salmon fishing. Access is via extremely difficult brush-busting.

Hunting

The immediate area offers fair to good hunting for goat, black bear and brown bear. Goat hunting is tough, and requires extensive hiking through timber to reach the alpine area.

Cabin

Eagle Lake Cabin (W-22)

Located on the east shore of Eagle Lake, this hunter-style cabin sleeps six. The cabin and lake are surrounded by steep hills covered by a dense rainforest of hemlock, spruce and cedar. There is a wood-burning stove for cooking and heating. Elevation, 300 feet.

Water source: stream
Facilities:
- four bunks
- table
- benches
- outhouse
- cooking counter
- wood stove
- maul
- cooler box
- skiff
- oars

Figure Eight Lake (Twin Lakes) is adjacent to the Stikine River about 14 air miles north of Wrangell. Minimum flight time charged is 45 minutes. From Wrangell, the distance by boat is 18 miles. A 14-foot or higher tide is generally required for a boat to cross the Stikine River tideflats and reach the main river channel past Point Rothsay. (USGS Quad Map Petersburg C-1)

Fishing

Figure Eight Lake offers fair to good fishing for cutthroat trout. In North Arm Creek, fishing for silver salmon is good in August and September; pink salmon are in the intertidal areas and Andrew Creek from mid-July to mid-August; some chum salmon in August. Sockeye salmon are available in June, but difficult to catch. Fishing for Dolly Varden, cutthroat and whitefish is tops late in the season. A boat is necessary to reach the best fishing.

Hunting

This is a good base camp for moose hunters. Ptarmigan hunting is good in late summer and fall.

Other Activities

The area is popular with swimmers and water skiers. There is a warm springs on the north side of the first lake. A portage is available for canoe/kayakers.

Cabin
Twin Lakes Cabin (W-3)

The Twin Lakes cabin is on the north arm of the Stikine River at the mouth of Twin Lakes Slough. It is an A-frame structure with a second-floor loft; it can sleep eight people. It has an oil stove for heating. Bring your own fuel for the stove. The area has an elevation of less than 100 feet, with surrounding vegetation consisting primarily of Sitka spruce and western hemlock rainforest with scattered stands of cedar. Steep mountains, crowned by numerous glaciers, rise behind the cabin. Meadows are scattered throughout the area. Peak use is May through October. A short trail leads from the cabin to the south shore of Figure Eight Lake.

Water source: lake or slough
Facilities:

- three bunks
- loft
- oil stove
- table
- benches
- outhouse
- table
- cooking counter
- no boat

Garnet Ledge

Granite Ledge is on the mainland at the mouth of the Stikine River south of Point Rothsay. The area is eight miles from Wrangell and accessible by boat. There is no access to the area at low tide. To reach the ledge you must have a 15-foot or higher tide. (USGS Quad Map Petersburg C-2)

Hunting

During the fall hunting season, Garnet Ledge cabin serves as a base for moose and bear hunters. There is some pass shooting for waterfowl.

Other Activities

The special attraction of this area is the garnet outcropping located on nearby private land. For information on collecting garnets here, contact Southeast Alaska Council, Boy Scouts of America, P.O. Box 510, Juneau, Alaska 99802 or stop by the Wrangell Museum.

During the April eulachon (hooligan) run, this area boasts the state's second largest concentration of eagles. Also sea gulls, sea lions and seals concentrate on the tidal flats during the hooligan run.

Cabin
Garnet Ledge Cabin (W-12)

Garnet Ledge is an A-frame with loft that sleeps seven people. A wood-burning stove is furnished for heating and cooking. The cabin window and door face the massive Stikine tidal flats. The surrounding terrain is spruce and hemlock rainforest with scattered cedar. While the immediate area near the cabin is nearly flat, various slopes behind the cabin range from moderate to very steep.

Water source: stream behind cabin
Facilities:

- bunks
- table
- benches
- wood stove
- wood supply
- cooking counter
- no boat
- loft
- outhouse
- ax
- maul

Gut Island is at the western tip of Farm Island on the Stikine River tidal flats. It is accessible by boat from Wrangell (12 miles) or from the Banana Point boat ramp on the south end of Mitkof Island (seven miles). Distance by floatplane from Wrangell is 11 miles. A tide of 17 feet or higher is required for floatplane access, and 15 feet for boat access. (USGS Quad Map Petersburg C-2)

Hunting

Same as Little Dry Island. Excellent waterfowl and ptarmigan hunting. Sea and diving ducks and geese will decoy into either shell, full-bodied or silhouette decoys. Use floating decoys during high tide, and shell decoys at low tide. After watching the birds' movements for a day, start working your decoys the second day. Right in front of the cabin is good hunting. Hunt birds from September through the season closure.

Cabins
Gut Island Cabin No. 1 (W-8)
Gut Island Cabin No. 2 (W-24)

Gut Island has two hunter-style cabins located within a few hundred feet of each other. Both cabins are furnished with oil stoves; be sure to bring your own fuel. The surrounding area is tidal marsh, and snow-capped mountains can be seen in the distance.

Water source: catchment, bring your own
Facilities:
- wooden bunks
- outhouse
- table
- bench
- oil stove
- cooking counter
- cooler box
- no boats

Waders and a boat are two prerequisites for successful goose hunting on the Stikine River Flats.

Harding River

Harding River is on the north side of Bradfield Canal, 31 air miles or 40 boat miles from Wrangell. (USGS Quad Map Bradfield Canal A-5)

Fishing

The Harding River has a healthy run of big chum salmon. Fish can exceed 20 pounds, and are caught in August and September. Coho and pink salmon are also plentiful. Steelhead fishing is good in April and May. A boat is necessary for best success. Plugs are especially effective in this river, with productive colors depending on water color and temperature. A good choice would include fluorescent colors, metallic shades, and blacks and whites. Best success is at the mouth of the river, or in holes immediately upriver. Cutthroat trout and Dolly Varden char are also available in good numbers in spring and during the salmon runs. Good crabbing near the river mouth.

Hunting

Waterfowl hunting is good at the head of Bradfield Canal, Eagle River and along various points and sloughs. The area offers good opportunities for black and brown bear hunting.

Other Activities

Area supports a good concentration of eagles and seals during the salmon runs. Kayakers can get quite close for observation or photography.

Cabin

Harding River Cabin (W-28)

Located at the mouth of the Harding River, this hunter-style cabin sleeps six people and has an oil stove for heating. It is surrounded by rainforest and muskeg. Geography consists of gentle and steep slopes; however, the immediate area near the cabin is flat.

Water source: river
Facilities:
- four bunks
- table
- benches
- oil stove
- outhouse
- cooking counter
- cooler box
- no boat

Little Dry Island

Little Dry Island is on the tidal flats of the Stikine-LeConte Wilderness Area. Access is 12 miles by boat from Wrangell or seven miles by boat from Banana Point boat ramp (south end of Mitkof Island). By air, the distance is 12 miles. To reach the island by plane, a tide of 17 feet or higher is necessary; by boat, 15 feet. (USGS Quad Map Petersburg C-2)

Hunting
Excellent waterfowl hunting in the area. Sea ducks, diving ducks and geese readily decoy into shell, full-bodied or silhouette decoys. Use floaters during high tide, and shells at low tide. Watch bird movements for the first day, and work birds second day. Hunting is often good in front of the cabin. Best time is from September through the season closure.

Cabin
Little Dry Island Cabin (W-7)
Located on the south side of Little Dry Island, this modified A-frame cabin is on a low rock outcrop at the transition zone between tidal flat and rainforest. With the loft, the cabin can sleep seven people and it is furnished with a wood-burning stove. Firewood is readily available. The cabin offers an excellent view of the surrounding area.

Water source: catchment, bring your own

Facilities:
- three bunks
- loft
- table
- wood stove
- wood supply
- benches
- outhouse
- cooking counter
- ax
- maul

Hunting for harlequin and game ducks is best done by setting out several decoys off points of land, and establishing a blind in nearby shoreline cover.

Mallard Slough

Mallard Slough is on the mainland between LeConte Bay and the North Arm of the Stikine River. The area is accessible by boat, 22 miles from Wrangell, 20 miles from Petersburg. Distance by floatplane from Wrangell and Petersburg is 18 miles. A tide of 16 feet or greater is required for floatplane landing; 14 feet for boat access. (USGS Quad Map Petersburg C-2)

Hunting

The area offers excellent waterfowl hunting. A good base camp for moose hunting. Goat and bear hunting is good to excellent in the adjacent Wilkes Range. Ptarmigan hunting is fair to good. A boat is a prerequisite for reaching the best hunting areas.

Other Activities

LeConte Bay and Glacier are within easy boating distance and offer excellent sightseeing and photographic opportunities. Icebergs are frequently encountered at the mouth of the bay and along the Horn Cliffs. Use caution near the icebergs as they can roll over and swamp a boat. The area is profuse with wildflowers in June and July. Kayaking opportunities are excellent.

Cabin

Mallard Slough Cabin (W-23)

Mallard Slough cabin is a modified A-frame structure in a grassy, shrubby area of tidal flat. It can sleep seven people, and has a wood-burning stove for heating and cooking. A dense spruce and hemlock rainforest is a short hike from the cabin. A half-mile trail leads from the cabin to LeConte Bay.

Water source: stream
Facilities:

- three bunks
- loft
- table
- benches

- counter
- wood stove
- outhouse
- maul

- cooler box
- no boat

Marten Lake is on the mainland near Bradfield Canal, 25 air miles from Wrangell. Air access only. Lake is usually ice-free from May through November. (USGS Quad Map Bradfield Canal B-6).

Fishing

Marten Creek receives good runs of anadromous cutthroat trout and Dolly Varden char, making this a prime location for anglers wishing good fly fishing away from the crowds. It also receives a run of steelhead in the lower section of the creek below Clay Lake. Going can be rough, with lots of brush busting. Follow game and bear trails that wind along the creek.

There is good fishing directly across from the cabin near the inlet stream draining Upper Marten Lake. The outlet offers good fishing in mid-summer, when cutts cruise the weedbeds searching for forage-food items. After periods of heavy rain, the fish often go off the bite for two or three days; however, fishing remains fair in the lake.

In the lower section of outlet stream expect to catch silver, pink and chum salmon. Carry bear protection during the salmon runs, especially when walking along Marten Creek.

When water level is normal or low, you can dock your boat easily on a sandy beach area near the cabin.

Hunting

The area offers good brown and black bear hunting. The bears den in the upper mountains, and come down to the creek and tidal area to feed on new grasses in the spring. May is the best time for large boars. Fair to good goat hunting in the area. Depending on the weather, grouse and ptarmigan hunting is fair to good.

Precautions

After heavy rains, expect the lake to rise and flood the cabin floor.

Cabin

Marten Lake Cabin (W-17)

This cedar log cabin on Marten Lake is capable of sleeping four people. It is furnished with a wood-burning stove for cooking and heating. The area around the cabin is flat, covered with Sitka spruce and western hemlock rain forest interspersed with some cedar. Steep mountains rise from the lake's edge. Wonderfully scenic location. Elevation, 178 feet.

Water source: lake
Facilities:

- four bunks
- table
- benches
- 14-foot skiff
- oars
- wood stove
- wood supply
- outhouse
- cooler box
- ax
- maul
- cooking counter

Red Slough is on the south shore of the Stikine River near the U.S./Canada border. From Wrangell the slough is 32 miles by water and 22 miles by air. Charged flight time from Wrangell is 55 minutes. A 14-foot or higher tide is needed before a boat can cross the Stikine River tideflats and access to the main river past Point Rothsay. (USGS Quad Map Bradfield C-6)

Fishing

A boat is necessary to pursue cutthroat and Dolly Varden char in the clearwater streams and lakes along the edges of this steep, mountainous country. There is silver and chum salmon fishing in streams directly to the east.

Hunting

This cabin is used as a base camp for moose hunters in the fall. Brown and black bear hunting is also fair to good. A boat is required for best success.

Cabin

Mount Flemer Cabin (W-6)

Mount Flemer cabin is an A-frame with a loft, and is capable of sleeping seven people. It is furnished with an oil stove for heating. Located at the mouth of Red Slough, the cabin is surrounded by spruce and hemlock rainforest with scattered cedar at the foot of the valley wall. Nearby slopes are very steep and rugged. Spectacular scenery.

Water source: small stream 30 yards from cabin
Facilities:
- three bunks
- table
- benches
- cooler box
- oil stove
- outhouse
- cooking counter
- no boat

Stikine River chum salmon can be caught in the clearwater feeder streams to the east of Red Slough. Chartreuse and silver Mepps, sizes 4 and 5, produce the most strikes.

Sergief Island is in the Stikine tidal flats approximately ten miles by boat from Wrangell or eight miles from Banana Point boat ramp on Mitkof Island. An 18-foot or greater tide is necessary to reach Koknuk cabin by boat; plane access is not recommended. A 15-foot or greater tide is necessary to reach Sergief cabin by boat, and a 17-foot or greater tide is necessary for floatplane access. (USGS Quad Map Petersburg C-2)

Hunting

Waterfowl hunting is good from September through December. Moose hunting is fair.

Cabins
Koknuk Cabin (W-10)
Sergief Island Cabin (W-11)

You'll find Koknuk cabin on the western side of Sergief Island. This cabin sleeps four, and has an oil stove for heating.

Sergief Island cabin is on the north side of the island. There is no boat at either cabin. The surrounding area is marshy with grass, shrubs and willows.

Water source: catchment
Facilities:
- four bunks
- table
- benches
- cooking counter
- oil stove
- cooler box
- outhouse
- no boat

Shakes Slough

You'll find Shakes Slough on the Stikine River east of Elbow Mountain. From Wrangell, the slough is 25 miles by boat or 20 miles by air. Minimum flight time charged is 50 minutes. Usually a 14-foot or higher tide is required for a boat to cross the Stikine River tideflats and reach the main river channel at Point Rothsay. (USGS Quad Map Petersburg C-1)

Fishing

Cutthroat trout fishing is available from June through October in Shakes Lake and Slough. A boat with an outboard is a must to fish this watershed as the lake is three miles to the north. King and coho salmon mill around the mouth of the slough before continuing their spawning migration up the Stikine. Angling in nearby Andrew Creek for steelhead, rainbow trout and whitefish is good. Success depends on water clarity, time of year and available structure to hold and concentrate fish.

Hunting

Moose hunting in the area is fair. A heavy frost in September can cause leaves to drop early, creating good visibility for hunting and increasing chances of success. In this area most hunters use riverboats for transportation. Also available is brown bear and black bear hunting, as well as mountain goat hunting, which is fair to good. Rugged terrain keeps many herds from receiving heavy hunting pressure, while those herds easily reached are subject to heavy hunting pressure. Weather and snowfall influence the timing of a goat hunt. Ptarmigan hunting is good.

Other Activities

Shakes Glacier, located at the head of Shakes Lake, is a must-see attraction. Chief Shakes Hot Springs is located by Hot Springs Slough off Ketili Slough. Access depends on river level. Numerous wildlife and scenic opportunities in this region.

Cabins
Shakes Slough No. 1 (W-1)
Shakes Slough No. 2 (W-2)

These cabins are within 100 yards of each other on the north side of the Stikine River at the mouth of Shakes Slough. Nestled in the Stikine-LeConte Wilderness Area, the cabins are surrounded by a rain forest of Sitka spruce and western hemlock, with scattered cedar in the valley bottoms. Meadows are interspersed throughout the area. Snow and ice-covered peaks can be seen directly across from the cabins. Shakes Slough cabin No. 1 is a Pan abode structure with a sleeping capacity of four. The No. 2 cabin is an A-frame with a loft that can sleep seven. Peak use is June through October.

Water source: slough
Facilities (both cabins):

- table
- benches
- oil stove
- cooler box
- cooking counter
- outhouse
- no boat
- **No. 1:** four bunks
- **No. 2:** three bunks, sleeping loft

Andrew Creek offers good steelheading in the spring and fair rainbow fishing during the summer months. Water levels and turbidity greatly influence angler success.

Steamer Bay is in the northwest corner of Etolin Island, about 27 miles by boat or 25 miles by air from Wrangell. (USGS Quad Map Petersburg A-3)

Fishing

King salmon fishing (trolling) is good from May through the first of July. Check regulations for opening dates. Silver salmon action picks up in late July and lasts until September. The head of Steamer Bay is a popular silver hotspot; pinks and chums are also available. In nearby Porcupine Creek, expect good fishing for cutthroat trout. Halibut fishing is excellent from May through September.

Excellent abalone, clamming and crabbing nearby. Many people say Steamer Bay is the best place region-wide to gather seafood.

Hunting

Deer and bear hunting is good in and around Steamer Bay. Waterfowl hunting can be excellent when storms push birds into the bay.

Other Activities

Beachcombing opportunities abound in this area. A small gravel beach near the cabin allows swimming, docking or sunning. Abundant marine life.

Cabin

Steamer Bay Cabin (W-14)

The cabin is an A-frame located on the east shore of Steamer Bay. Equipped with a loft to sleep five people, the cabin has an oil-burning stove for heating. Muskeg and dense rainforest blanket this mountainous area.

Water source: lake
Facilities:
- oil stove
- two bunks
- table
- benches
- cooler box
- outhouse
- cooking counter
- no boat

Virginia Lake is on the Alaska mainland about 10 air miles from Wrangell. It is nine miles by boat to the trailhead in Eastern Passage. Once there, marine travelers can walk to the lake by taking the one-mile trail to the Virginia Lake outlet. (USGS Quad Map Petersburg B-1)

Fishing

From May through October, this 580-acre lake offers excellent fishing for trophy cutthroats up to 22 inches. In warm, sunny weather big cutts like to hold near drop-offs at the head of the lake. Then, deepwater jigging or nymphing is very productive.

Near an inlet south-by-southwest of the cabin, deep-diving plugs and silver-plated spoons produce big fish in 10 to 20 feet of water. Also try herring strips trolled in a zig-zag pattern. Some anglers are successful using cowbells and trolling spoons fished with "poor man" downriggers. In the fall, Dolly Varden action is excellent. In the outlet creek, catch pink and sockeye salmon on size four attractor patterns.

Hunting

Hunting is fair for moose and grouse. Scout meadows for sign and build a tree stand nearby for optimum success. Excellent opportunity to combine trophy fishing with a big-game hunting trip.

Precaution

Surrounding mountains contain old and new mining activity.

Cabin
Virginia Lake Cabin (W-13)

Virginia Lake cabin is a Pan Abode structure that sleeps four. It is furnished with an oil stove for heating, and comes with a 14-foot skiff with oars. The cabin is surrounded by rain forest. Steep mountains near the lake create a grand, majestic setting. People wishing to rent the cabin during the first week of moose season must participate in a lottery.

Water source: lake
Facilities:
- four bunks
- table
- benches
- cooking counter
- cooler box
- oil stove
- outhouse
- 14-foot skiff
- oars

4 Gateway Petersburg
Fishing the TONGASS National Forest

About the Gateway

Petersburg was named after Norwegian Peter Buschmann, who built a salmon cannery and sawmill on the present townsite in 1897. Buschmann chose the site because of its fine harbor, abundant fish and a ready supply of ice from the nearby LeConte Glacier. The cannery, now known as Petersburg Fisheries, has operated continuously since its founding. The city has the largest home-based halibut fleet in Alaska and the chief occupation is fishing.

The state fish hatchery at Crystal Lake is used for fish enhancement projects throughout southeast Alaska. It has the capacity to raise one million king and coho salmon and 48,000 steelhead trout. A 30-mile system of roads on Mitkof Island allows anglers, hunters and recreationists to explore the local attractions.

Petersburg Creek-Duncan Salt Chuck Wilderness and Tebenkof Bay Wilderness are in this region. Both areas host geological sights, marine wilderness and excellent fishing.

Population: 3,200
Annual Precipitation: 105 inches
Average High Temperature: 63.7 degrees

Fishing the Petersburg Area

Petersburg, like Wrangell, offers a variety of remote, scenic fishing locations for a variety of species. From April through June, chinooks are the favorite with trollers concentrating their efforts in the Point Frederick-Farragut Bay area. Wrangell Narrows to Scow Bay is another popular area.

Petersburg Creek, Falls Creek and Blind Slough have historically been popular with anglers trolling for cohos. Blind Slough and Wrangell Narrows, as well as lower Duncan Canal, offer good coho fishing. In August and September, stream fishing for coho is good in Petersburg Creek and all streams in Duncan Canal.

When it comes to halibut, Petersburg anglers know where to fish. One hotspot is a sand/gravel bar at the mouth of Thomas Bay. Biologists say this bar is likely a terminal moraine from an earlier advanced stage of the Baird Glacier. Similar structure can also be found near Vandeput Point, Cape Strait, drop-offs near Sukoi Islands, McDonald Island and the Wrangell Narrows when halibut are moving through in early spring and late fall. Sukoi Island offers fair fishing for rockfish and ling cod, but populations are not overly abundant. One popular roadside fishery is off the beaches adjacent to the Wrangell Narrows. Fishing is good throughout the summer, with most action taking place at the northern end between the cannery and Hungry Point. Migrating coho, pinks and anadromous cutthroat are taken with spoons and spinners.

Blind Slough and Wilson Beach on the south end of Mitkof Island offer good fishing for Dollies, with bonus coho, pink and chinook salmon a possibility. Excellent fishing for anadromous cutthroat trout can be had at the upper intertidal end of Duncan Canal. If weather keeps you stranded in town, try fishing off one of the downtown floats. Anglers catch small herring, flounder and cod on a regular basis, with an occasional bonus halibut.

Locals target Ohmer, Bear and Falls creeks, "Sumner" Creek, Blind Slough and "Dry Straight" Creek for cutthroat and Dollies year-round, and pinks and cohos from July through September. These streams are also good in April and May for steelhead. Petersburg Creek, located across the Narrows from Petersburg, can be reached via charter or rental boat. It offers excellent sportfishing year-round, but expect crowds during the peak of the various runs. Cutthroat and Dolly Varden fishing is available year-round, and good to excellent steelheading is available in April and May. All four species of salmon can be caught in season. Also good are Dry Bay Creek, Kah Sheets Creek, Castle River and the mouth of Blind Slough for cutts, Dollies and salmon. On northern Prince of Wales Island, Red Lake and Salmon Bay Lake offer Petersburg residents and visitors good fishing for cutthroat, steelhead and salmon. The Most Scenic Location Award in this district goes to Swan Lake, about 15 minutes by plane from Petersburg. Excellent rainbow fishing, scenic waterfalls and a high alpine environment make this an excellent get-away choice.

For information on cabins in this area, contact: Petersburg Ranger District, Post Office Building, P.O. Box 1328, Petersburg, AK 99833, (907) 772-3871

Fishing Index

Forest Service cabins in this gateway are listed below. The types of fish available in the vicinity of the cabin are indicated. You can cross-reference the cabin by the F.S. #, a number assigned to each cabin by the Forest Service. A description of the cabin and its facilities can be found on the page listed on the chart, and the page number of the map showing the exact cabin location is listed in the last column.

Gateway 4 Petersburg

Cabin	F.S. #	Page	Cutthroat Trout	Dolly Varden	Grayling	Rainbow Trout	Steelhead	Chinook Salmon	Coho Salmon	Chum Salmon	Pink Salmon	Sockeye Salmon	Halibut	Rockfish	Map pg.
Beecher Pass Cabin	P-23	157							•	•			•		154
Big John Bay Cabin	P-15	158													155
Breiland Slough Cabin	P-12	159							•	•	•				154
Cascade Creek Cabin	P-21	160				•			•	•			•		156
Castle Flats Cabin	P-10	162	•	•		•	•		•	•	•				154
Castle River Cabin	P-11	162	•	•		•	•		•	•	•				154
DeBoer Lake Cabin	P-1	164				•									156
Devil's Elbow Cabin	P-9	165							•				•	•	155
Harvey Lake Cabin	P-13	166	•	•					•						154
Kadake Bay Cabin	P-8	167	•	•		•	•		•	•	•				155
Kah Sheets Bay Cabin	P-20	168	•	•		•	•		•	•	•	•			154
Kah Sheets Lake Cabin	P-19	168	•	•		•	•		•	•	•	•			154
Petersburg Lake Cabin	P-7	171	•	•		•	•		•	•	•	•			154
Portage Bay Cabin	P-25	172	•	•		•	•		•	•	•		•	•	154
Raven's Roost Cabin	P-22	170													154
Salt Chuck East Cabin	P-4	173	•	•		•	•		•	•	•	•			154
Salt Chuck West Cabin	P-3	173	•	•		•	•		•	•	•	•			154
Spurt Cove Cabin	P-24	174		•					•	•	•	•			156
Swan Lake Cabin	P-16	177				•									156

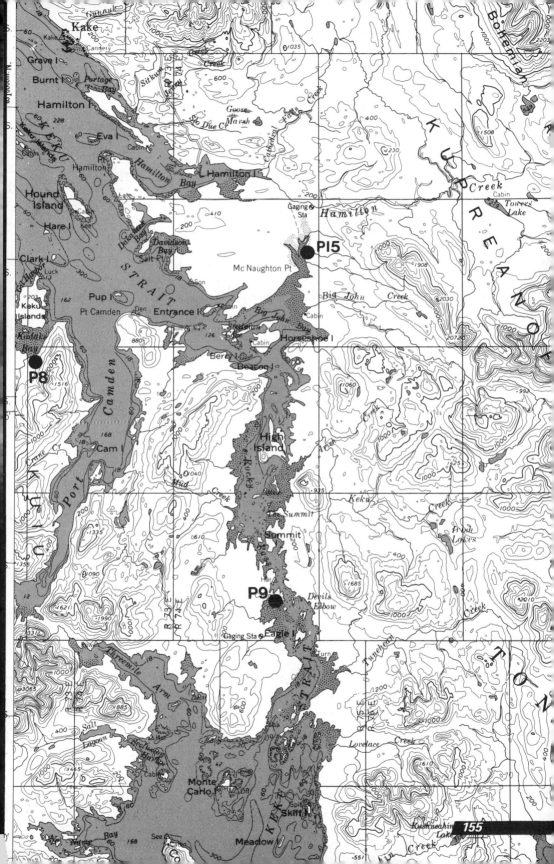

156

Located on Woewodski Island, Beecher Pass is 17 miles by air or 20 miles by water from Petersburg. (USGS Quad Map Petersburg C-4)

Fishing

This is a saltwater fishery, with the major attractions being king salmon in June and July, and silver salmon in August. Halibut fishing is good throughout the summer months near Fair and Grief islands. Anchor and fish bait directly off the bottom or use large Diamond or Sebastes jigs for best success.

Hunting

This location is an excellent choice for the waterfowler who wants a variety of sea and diving ducks. Set up off the point, and hide your skiff with camo netting. Best shooting is in October and November. Grouse hunting is fair at the higher elevations.

Cabin

Beecher Pass Cabin (P-23)

This cabin is on the south side of Beecher Pass, situated in flat terrain but surrounded by fairly steep slopes. It is also surrounded by protected waters and is accessible by small boat during windy weather. This hunter-style cabin sleeps four and has both oil and wood-burning stoves. Access is possible at any tide.

Water source: creek 100 yards east of cabin.
Facilities:
- four bunks
- oil stove
- wood stove
- cooking counter
- table
- ax
- maul
- outhouse
- no boat

Big John Bay

Big John Bay is near Horseshoe Island on Kupreanof Island, 28 air miles from Petersburg and 18 miles by water from Kake. A 15-foot tide is necessary for boat or plane access, or face a one-mile hike through the mud. Access is also possible via a 16-mile drive from Kake, followed by taking a 1.5-mile trail. (USGS Quad Map Petersburg D-6)

Hunting

The cabin offers a base of operations for waterfowl and bear hunters. With a boat, bear hunting is rated as good. Grouse hunting is good in the hills across from the cabin. Waterfowl hunting is excellent, especially after northern flights of birds arrive. Both floating and shell decoys required for best success. A large decoy spread works well here in attracting birds from farther out in the bay.

Cabin
Big John Bay Cabin (P-15)

Located on a small flat island and surrounded by tidal flat at the north end of Big John Bay, this hunter-style cabin was built in 1965 and sleeps four. It has an oil-burning stove for heating. There is no trail access to the cabin during high tide.

Water source: catchment in a small creek a quarter-mile north of cabin.
Facilities:
- four bunks
- cooking counter
- table
- benches
- oil stove
- outhouse
- no boat

Located on the west side of Duncan Canal south of Castle Island, Breiland Slough is 30 minutes by air and 25 miles by boat from Petersburg. (USGS Quad Map Petersburg C-3 and D-4)

Fishing

Beach casting in front of the cabin for silver and pink salmon in late August is excellent. Chum salmon available. Fish are heading for nearby Castle River and their migration route passes directly in front of the cabin. Bring your own boat for best success, especially when fishing the coves and flats. If fishing from shore, use a spoon and flutter and twitch retrieve for best success. I prefer a one-ounce silver or prism-taped spoon with a good wobbling action. A Gibbs Coho is a favorite here for large silvers.

Hunting

Waterfowl hunting is excellent during October and November, and grouse hunting is fair to good across the bay. The cabin is also used as a base camp by bear hunters in both spring and fall. Excellent waterfowling is available by setting up blinds on various points of the Castle Islands. Birds will be in the protected coves, depending on which direction the wind is blowing. Decoys recommended.

Cabin

Breiland Slough Cabin (P-12)

The cabin is an A-frame with loft capable of sleeping seven and furnished with an oil-burning stove. It is on a small spit of land on the edge of a flat stretch of muskeg forest at the base of rolling hills.

Water source: small creek a quarter-mile south of the cabin.
Facilities:
- four bunks
- sleeping loft
- cooking counter
- oil stove
- outhouse
- no boat
- table
- benches

User Comments

7/19: "Crabbing good. Fishing fair. Castle River good for trout, Kah Sheets also good. Halibut fishing fair. Caught four halibut at Red Can across from camp. One went about 50 pounds, the other 60 pounds."

7/28: "Lovely to have a pair of barn swallows nesting by the door. Also saw eight woodpeckers in family group, six Canada geese, song sparrows, Wilson's warbler, white-winged scoter, seals and kingfishers."

Cascade Creek

Located on the mainland in the Thomas Bay area east of Spray Island, Cascade Creek is 14 miles by air and 19 miles by water from Petersburg. Access at any tide. Mooring buoy provided. (USGS Quad Map Petersburg D-3, Sumdum A-13)

Fishing

Cascade Creek is mainly a saltwater fishery. Halibut are caught at the mouth of the bay throughout the summer months. Large herring and 8-ounce Vi-ke jigs work well here. King salmon are caught in the bay throughout the month of June; fishing success fluctuates, depending on size and strength of the run. Better fishing for coho salmon in August. Rainbow trout can be caught in Falls Lake, a three-mile hike from the cabin.

Hunting

Hunters have access to moose, deer, goat, waterfowl and grouse populations from this cabin. A boat is required for moose and waterfowl hunting. Check with ADF&G for applicable seasons and bag limits for this area.

Other Activities

Trail leads from cabin to Swan Lake, an extremely scenic location. Good hiking skills are a must. Cascade Creek Trail to Falls Lake are passable, and worth the hike. Trail beyond Falls Lake impassable at this time.

Cabin

Cascade Creek Cabin (P-21)

This single-level, tongue and groove, hunter-style cabin was built in 1978 and is furnished with wood and oil burning stoves. Sleeps six. Scenic view of Thomas Bay in front. Massive, 4,740-foot Cosmos Peak rises directly behind the cabin. Dense rain forest nearby. This is a very popular cabin. Early reservations are a must.

Water source: creek

Facilities:
- four bunks
- table
- benches
- cooking counter
- wood stove
- oil stove
- ax and maul
- outhouse
- no boat

User Comments

7/8: "A neat place, especially the trail to the falls. View was excellent. Worth it."

7/17-7/19: "Shared the beach with a hungry eagle, a mink, and a persistent heron. Seals on a rock up the way. No fish. Lots of rain. Fantastic location for a cabin; the best on salt water."

8/4-8/9: "Saw big brown bear by outhouse on first day. Ran like hell for boat and gun! Second day went fishing, and caught a 170-pound halibut by mooring log. Fantastic! Also caught two silver salmon; 17 and 13 pounds. Saw three wolves by cabin on the third day. Brown bear back at outhouse. Ate part of the halibut. Wolves back again, kept us up all night. Fourth day, two halibut, 1 black bear, two crabs and 31 shrimp. Wolves back again. Four this time. Wife went on hike, not back yet. Wolves not as hungry? Brown bear back again..."

Throughout southeast Alaska, deepwater bays offer excellent fishing for halibut. Herring or large jigging lures fished near bottom catch the most fish.

Castle River

Castle River is on the west side of the Duncan Canal, 16 air miles and 30 water miles from Petersburg. To reach the mouth of the creek, a 15-foot tide is required for floatplanes and 13-foot tide for boats. A minimum 16-foot tide is required for boat access to the upper creek. (USGS Quad Map Petersburg C-3, C-5 and D-4)

Fishing

Fishing in the Castle River is excellent for both silver salmon and steelhead trout. Steelhead are available in numbers from late April through early June, while cohos are an August and September fish. During low tide look for silvers holding in the side sloughs on the flats, but use caution when traveling over the mud flats. Because of the large runs of salmon, plugging, fly fishing, hardware and bottom-bouncing all work well in this river. The best fishing is done from a boat, however, find and work channels from shore whenever possible.

Storm Wiggle and Wee Warts are effective here as are the brighter attractor flies, such as the Crystal Bullet and Flashabou. Fish for pink and chum salmon in the intertidal area of the lower river. Anadromous cutthroat and Dolly Varden fishing is also excellent. Use egg patterns for the Dollies and cutts in the fall and smolt patterns during the spring months. When water levels are low, switch to black or gray patterns in early summer, changing to white in late fall. This is a popular location, so make your reservations early.

Hunting

Waterfowl, grouse and black bear hunting ranges from fair to excellent, depending on time of year.

Precautions

Black bears are common in this area, so be on the lookout when fishing along the riverbanks.

Cabins
Castle Flats Cabin (P-10)
Castle River Cabin (P-11)

Castle Flats is a hunter-style cabin originally donated to the USFS by a group of sportsmen. It has wood and oil-burning stoves and sleeps five. Unlike other cabins in intertidal areas, a boat is provided for use in the river. Be sure to keep it secured so the tide doesn't carry it away.

Castle River cabin is a modified A-frame furnished with a wood-burning stove. It sleeps seven. There is a half-mile trail to the boat. Keep the boat tightly secured when not in use to prevent the current from sweeping it over the rocks. The only access to this cabin is via a one-mile trail from Castle Flats cabin or by boat on a 16-foot or higher tide.

Water source: river

Facilities:
- wooden bunks
- oil/wood stove (P-10)
- wood stove
- table
- cooking counter
- ax and maul
- outhouse
- skiffs

In addition to excellent silver and pink salmon and steelhead fishing in their upper stretches, many rivers offer good fishing for chum salmon in intertidal areas.

DeBoer Lake is on the mainland three miles above and to the northwest of Thomas Bay. Access is by air, 20 miles from Petersburg. (USGS Quad Map Sumdum A-3)

Fishing

The lake offers rainbow trout averaging 10 to 12 inches, occasionally larger. Tactics include ultralight trolling with hardware, or shotgunning the shoreline with nymph patterns and tiny muddlers. Fish the drop-off directly across the lake from the cabin. At times, the outlet stream offers fair rainbow fishing.

Hunting

The area is popular with mountain goat hunters. The terrain from cabin to peaks is too rough to traverse each day, so take a spike camp, and use the cabin as a base of operations. It is possible to hunt goat and return to the cabin each day, especially when the animals are on Jefferson Peak.

Ptarmigan hunting is also good at the higher elevations in fall, and along the lake in winter.

Precautions

Fog and high winds can prevent scheduled flights into this area for several days at a time. Pack extra food and fuel.

Cabin

DeBoer Lake Cabin (P-1)

The DeBoer Lake cabin is a spacious A-frame that was constructed in 1962. It is situated at the west end of the lake, surrounded by several 4,000-foot peaks. Scenery is spectacular, and the area offers ample opportunities for isolation and seclusion. It is furnished with an oil-burning stove and can sleep six. Elevation, 1,420 feet.

Water source: lake
Facilities:

* two bunks
* loft
* cooking counter

* benches
* table
* skiff

* oil stove
* outhouse

User Comments

8/14-8/18: "Fishing was good. Caught six trout, saw three mountain goats, weather was bad, fogged in and couldn't get to them. All in all a nice trip."

Devil's Elbow is on the east side of Kuiu Island at the east end of Rocky Pass, 40 miles by air or 66 miles by boat from Petersburg, or 26 miles by boat from Kake. Floatplane access requires a 16-foot tide for landing and take-off to cabin area or face a half-mile walk. (USGS Quad Map Petersburg C-6, D-6)

Fishing

Silver salmon can be caught in August while trolling herring, hootchies or lures in the salt water. Also fish in the streams directly across Rocky Pass. There is some rockfish and halibut fishing in and around the reefs and islands.

Hunting

The area is rated as excellent for waterfowl hunting, and fair for bear and grouse. Waterfowl congregate in and around the rock formations, especially during stormy weather. Decoys will add to your enjoyment of the hunt. A boat is required for travel in this area and for retrieving downed birds.

Other Activities

Kayakers will find Rocky Pass to be loaded with interesting rock formations and marine life.

Cabin

Devil's Elbow Cabin (P-9)

The cabin—an A-frame with loft capable of sleeping seven—is located on the west end of Rocky Pass across from Devil's Elbow. It has an oil-burning stove for heating. The cabin is in a relatively flat, intertidal area surrounded by abundant marine life.

Water source: catchment in a small creek one-quarter mile north of the cabin.
Facilities:

- two bunks
- loft
- table
- benches
- cooking counter
- oil stove
- outhouse
- large deck
- no boat

Harvey Lake is on Woewodski Island near Duncan Canal, 30 minutes by air, 21 miles by boat (and a one-mile hike to lake) from Petersburg. (USGS Quad Map Petersburg C-3, C-4)

Fishing

There is fair silver salmon fishing at the saltwater end of the trail in late August. Cutthroat trout and Dolly Varden fishing in the lake and creek is fair from June through September. Fishing in Harvey has a tendency to slack off for indefinite periods of time during mid summer.

At those times, fly fish the stream, using sink tips and nymph patterns. Or hit the weed beds in the lake, using dry flies, leech patterns or popper bugs. Fish the shoreline structure in the early morning and on cloudy days. Teeny nymphs in black and yellow work well here.

Other Activities

There's evidence of old mining activity throughout the area. Also, the Harvey Lake area is an excellent location for August and September blueberry picking.

Cabin

Harvey Lake Cabin (P-13)

The cabin is at the west end of this very picturesque lake and is furnished with a wood-burning stove. Sleeps seven. Lake is surrounded by flat and rolling terrain. Picnic grills, small beach and swimming areas are near the cabin. Usually ice-free from May through November. An especially nice cabin for a family outing. Elevation, 100 feet.

Water source: lake
Facilities:

- two bunks
- wood stove
- boat
- cooking counter
- large deck
- ax
- maul
- table
- loft

Harvey Lake Cabin.
Photo courtesy USDA
Forest Service.

Kadake Bay is on Kuiu Island, immediately adjacent to Port Camden. From Petersburg, the bay is 39 miles by air and 13 water miles from Kadak. An 18-foot tide is required for boat access. At low tide, there is a two-mile walk across a mud flat to reach the cabin. (USGS Quad Map Petersburg D-6, or Port Alexander D-1 or Petersburg C-6)

Fishing

Kadake Creek is noted for its good runs of steelhead trout in late April and May. Best fishing is upstream from the cabin, away from tidal fluctuation. Fishermen often do well with drift lures in front of the cabin. The creek has a good run of pink and chum salmon in July and August, and cohos in late August and September. Of course, April through October offers good fishing for anadromous cutthroat, rainbow trout and Dolly Varden char.

Hunting

Bear and waterfowl hunting is available in season. Look for bears in and around the bays and tidal flats to the north.

Cabin

Kadake Bay Cabin (P-8)

Kadake Bay is a modified hunter cabin capable of sleeping six. It has both oil and wood-burning stoves for heating and cooking. The cabin is nestled in a terrain of gently rolling hills and rain forests. Kadake Creek flows directly in front of the cabin, offering a nice view.

Water source: creek
Facilities:
- four bunks
- oil stove
- wood stove
- table
- benches
- cooking counters
- outhouse
- large deck
- no boat

Kah Sheets Lake

Kah Sheets Lake and Bay are located on the southern end of Kupreanof Island. From Petersburg, the lake is 22 miles by air and 24 miles by water. Marine travelers need to anchor their boat and take a 2.75-mile trail to reach the lake. They also need a 14-foot tide to reach the trailhead by boat. (USGS Quad Map Petersburg C-3, C-4)

Fishing

Good fishing year-round for cutthroat trout and Dolly Varden char in Kah Sheets Creek. Steelhead fishing is good in April and May, fishing for silvers is good from August through September, and chum and pink fishing is best in early August.

The lake offers good fishing for cutthroat trout. Fish the small bay at the far end of the lake, in and around the rocky islands, and the widened outlet of the lake. Drifting or jigging directly off bottom works best. Use egg patterns, Mepps Black Fury lures and other tiny lures for best success.

Fishing for sockeye salmon is good in July, especially at the base of the falls that are three-quarters of a mile up the creek from salt water.

Hunting

The bay offers fair bear and good waterfowl hunting in season. Decoys are not necessary, but increase your chances of success. Set up on outer rocks and islands for pass shooting. A boat is necessary to access prime bear hunting, however, hunters have reported taking bears in and around the creek itself.

Cabins
Kah Sheets Lake Cabin (P-19)
Kah Sheets Bay Cabin (P-20)

Located on a small peninsula jutting out into the east end of the lake, the P-19 cabin is an A-frame with loft that sleeps seven. This cabin was modified during the summer of 1989 to provide wheelchair access with a fishing/floatplane dock, trails to the cabin and outhouse, and a large deck area.

P-20 is a single-level, tongue and groove, hunter-style cabin capable of sleeping four. Located on salt water at the head of Kah Sheets Bay, the cabin has both oil and wood-burning stoves. No boat available; bring your own.

Water source: creek

Facilities (P-19) :
- two bunks
- counter
- table
- boat
- oars
- oil stove
- loft
- outhouse
- benches

(P-20):
- four bunks
- counter
- table
- oil stove
- wood stove
- no boat
- outhouse
- benches

User Comments

Kah Sheets Bay 8/22: "Fishing is great! Caught a 12-pound coho."

8/23: "Creek fishing is great! Catching lots of chums, and humpies. Caught one nice coho. Going up to the lake tomorrow to fish."

Kah Sheets Lake 8/18: "Making lots of trips to the falls and bay. Lake fishing is awful, creek fishing fabulous for humpies, dogs, silvers and Dollies. Having a great time."

9/17: "Caught 14 silvers in seven days. Just a little late on the run. Lots of humpies at lower cabin. Saw a black bear across the river. Caught five small trout also."

Yes folks, its day eight of the "Humpies from Hell" expedition and we are patiently awaiting the plane back to civilization. as the week has progressed we have found our "voice" so to speak, but the problem is no one knows all the words to "Blue Moon". It was a rainy but relaxing sojourn at Lake Alexander and the menfolk finally found a response to the "disposable man" accusations. The three amazons of the group completed the trip with a symbolic paddle/hike to saltwater at Mole Harbor. The group did make one important discovery - instant pudding doesn't taste half bad when you've been out in the woods for a week. and that about sums it up. Happy travels and light portages to all who follow in our path.

Humpies from Hell

Question for the Day - Marti Tom Bonnie
Is there a company Lynn Linda Bob
out there that makes
mosquito netting for boobs
for bare-breasted amazons who only
hike in panties and bare chests?
answer at Big Shaheen.

Most of the Forest Service cabins have log books, where recreationists write on a variety of topics. This entry was taken from Alexander Lake cabin on Admiralty Island.

Raven's Roost is on Mitkof Mountain, behind the Petersburg airport. Access is three air miles from Petersburg by helicopter. The cabin is four miles by trail from the airport. Look for the orange and white tank south of the airport that marks the trailhead. (USGS Quad Map Petersburg D-3, C-3)

Hunting

The surrounding forests offer fair grouse hunting in early fall and late spring. Snowshoers and cross-country skiers also find good sport in the dense timber throughout the winter months. Look for birds perched on the limbs of spruce or on the ground foraging for berries.

Other Activities

The mountain is a popular destination among hikers during the summer months. Middle section of trail is very steep, then flattens considerably near the cabin.

Cabin

Raven's Roost Cabin (P-22)

Built in 1979, the cabin is a custom built alpine structure capable of sleeping eight people. It is furnished with a wood-burning stove for heating and cooking. The cabin offers a scenic view of the Wrangell Narrows and a spectacular view of mainland mountains.

Water source: catchment only
Facilities:
- two wooden bunks
- loft
- wood stove (bring own kindling)
- ax
- maul
- table
- outhouse
- benches

User Comments

4/10: "Feet hurt. Long way down in the drifts."
5/29: "Long hike, but well worth it."
(no date) "Fantastic. Nothing more beautiful than watching 'Sunset Theater' during dinner."

Petersburg Lake is on Kupreanof Island, nine air miles or four water miles from Petersburg. Access is via the 6.5-mile Petersburg Trail, however, a 15-foot tide is required for access. Access is also possible by taking a boat one-half mile from Petersburg to the state dock, then walking the 11.5-mile trail to the lake. Contact the USFS Petersburg office for specific trail information. (USGS Quad Map Petersburg D-4, D-3)

Fishing

Because it is located just across the Narrows from Petersburg, the lake and creek are popular destinations among local residents and tourists. Fishing is excellent throughout the year.

Cutthroat trout and Dolly Varden char are available in the lake and creek year-round. In April and May, steelhead enter the creek in fair to good numbers. Large steelhead up to 21 pounds have been caught from Petersburg Creek. During the summer, four of the five species of Pacific salmon can also be caught there: sockeyes in June, pinks and chums in July and August, and coho in late August through September.

The creek offers the best fishing for cutthroats immediately after ice-out. The intertidal area is a popular place to fish, as is the first 100 yards of lake's outlet.

In the summer look for cutts in backwater areas of the creek, and in the lily pads and other structure along the perimeter of the lake. Light tackle and bulky dry flies (elk-hair caddis, humpy) are best. During the peak of the salmon season, boats will anchor off the mouth of Petersburg Creek to fish for coho salmon.

The lake is a popular ice fishing hotspot. Anglers may want to investigate the trails leading to Portage Bay and Duncan Salt Chuck for additional fishing opportunities.

Hunting

Grouse hunting is available in season.

Cabin
Petersburg Lake (P-7)

This single-level cedar cabin is in a flat area near the lake, surrounded by steep, forested mountains rising to 2,500 feet. Capable of sleeping four, the cabin has both oil and wood-burning stoves for heating and cooking.

Water source: lake
Facilities:

- four bunks
- wood stove
- oil stove
- cooking counter
- skiff
- no motor
- ax
- maul
- table
- outhouse

User Comments

9/5: "Back down for more coho. Caught three at Hogies Hole."
9/27: "Caught salmon by hand. Had a great salmon dinner."

Portage Bay

Portage Bay is on Kupreanof Island due east of Stop Island, 15 air miles or 25 water miles from Petersburg. (USGS Quad Map Petersburg D-4, D-3, Sumdum A-4)

Fishing

Portage Creek is a short one-mile hike from the cabin and offers some of the finest fishing in the area. At the mouth of the bay, halibut fishing is excellent throughout the summer months, along with deepwater snapper (yelloweye rockfish) and some bottomfish. Stick to the main channels, drifting with the current, and avoid the shallow-water flats. Try the flats in early summer, when salmon are entering freshwater tributaries. Halibut often move into these areas to feed on salmon and salmon remains left by seals.

The salmon fisherman will find good fishing for pinks and chums in mid-July and August, with silvers in late August and September.

Steelhead fishing is considered fair to good in April and May, and cutthroat trout and Dolly Varden fishing is good from ice-out in May until late October.

Hunting

The area is popular with waterfowl, black bear and grouse hunters. Waterfowl hunting is best in October and November, however, puddlers can be bagged in and around the freshwater sloughs throughout the season. For the best black bear hunting, base out of the cabin and use an inflatable to cruise the bays and coves.

Cabin
Portage Bay Cabin (P-25)

This single-level, hunter-style cabin is on the eastern shore of Portage Bay. The USFS converted the cabin from administrative to recreational use in 1984. An oil-burning stove is provided for heating. Bring your own fuel. From the cabin there is access to the area's logging roads which provide exploring opportunities, especially for people with mountain bikes or motor bikes. The terrain is hilly along the east shore of Portage Bay and flat and rolling to the south and west.

Water source: creek about 100 feet behind cabin
Facilities:
- four bunks
- table
- oil stove
- outhouse
- cooking counter
- benches
- no boat

Salt Chuck is on Kupreanof Island on the east side of Duncan Salt Chuck, 15 air miles and 40 water miles from Petersburg. The area is located in the Petersburg Creek-Duncan Salt Chuck Wilderness. A 14-foot tide is required to clear rocks in the rapids south of the Salt Chuck when accessing East cabin, and a 17-foot tide is necessary to reach West cabin. Both should only be navigated at high slack tide, preferably three-quarters of an hour before and after high tide. Tides are one hour later than published times. (USGS Quad Map Petersburg C-3, C-4, D-3, D-5)

Fishing

Steelhead fishing in this area is good in fall, best in spring. Nearby Duncan Creek offers good numbers of steelhead. Silver salmon run in August and September. Try the lower slough and upper creek for best success. There is good fishing for anadromous cutthroat trout year-round, but it is best in spring and fall.

At low tide, look for pools and channels that hold fish. Be careful of muddy sections on tidal flat. Fly fishing is excellent on outgoing tide. For silvers and steelhead, use large streamers such as Baker Buster, Thor and Skykomish Sunrise. Use silvery, mylar patterns for cutts and Dollies, size 6. At high tide, spin fishermen have slightly better success with plugs and spoons. If fish refuse to strike, go to smaller lures and move away from holding areas. Use boats whenever possible. An outboard is a plus for this area.

Hunting

Black bear and grouse hunting is available throughout fall and early spring. Waterfowl hunting is good in October and November. Local birds are taken in September.

Other Activities

Evidence of old mining activity can be seen throughout the area. View the remains of an old trestle roadway behind the cabin. Road leads south to Towers Arm.

Cabins
Salt Chuck West Cabin (P-3)
Salt Chuck East Cabin (P-4)

Erected in 1953, Salt Chuck West is a hunter-style cabin located on flat terrain with a 1,000-foot ridge running behind it. It is furnished with a wood-burning stove and it sleeps four.

The Salt Chuck East cabin is a modified A-frame built in 1963 directly across from the West cabin. It is in a flat area with a 300-foot knob behind it. The cabin has a wood-burning stove, and it sleeps seven. Three miles to the east is 3,577-foot Portage Mountain.

Water source: small creek near cabins
Facilities:
- two bunks (East)
- four bunks (West)
- wood stove
- table
- benches
- ax
- maul
- outhouse
- skiffs
- oars

Spurt Cove

Spurt Cove is on the north side of Thomas Bay, 16 air miles and 18 water miles from Petersburg. Because of rocks and shallow-water areas, some pilots will not land in this bay at any tide. Check with your pilot before making cabin reservations. (USGS Quad Map Sumdum A-3, Petersburg A-3)

Fishing

Saltwater trolling for king salmon is fair to good in May and June. Halibut fishing is excellent in the bay throughout the summer months. Saltwater casting for cohos and Dollies also good. Nearby Porter Cove offers coho, pink and chum salmon fishing. Spurt Point Lake has a small population of rainbow trout. Boat required for optimum enjoyment of the area.

Hunting

The cabin is used as a base camp for goat, deer, waterfowl and grouse hunters. A boat is required to reach the best areas. Waterfowlers can expect good success within walking distance of the cabin. Take a dog for retrieving downed birds.

Cabin

Spurt Cove Cabin (P-24)

This single-level, hunter-style, tongue and groove cedar cabin has both wood and oil-burning stoves and can sleep four. Located in a flat clearing surrounded by steep bluffs, this cabin is a favorite among hunters and saltwater anglers.

Water source: small stream near cabin
Facilities:
* four bunks
* wood stove
* oil stove
* cooking counter

* large deck
* ax
* maul
* benches

* table
* outhouse
* no boat

User Comments

5/20: "Gary caught a 35 and a 36 pounder first thing today. Killed a mouse this morning after he ate our bread last night."

6/1: "Have paddled our way here from Seattle, Washington. Headed for Skagway and then the Yukon. Nice, warm, dry cabin.

6/6: "It's so easy when undertaking a long journey to get so preoccupied with 'getting there' that you forget about 'being here.' Fatigued by strong headwinds and a rough crossing, I paddled in here dazed. Had a chance to use the other cabin but I passed it up (too far in and out, I thought). Spent last night around the corner camped near a shipwreck. Realized I needed to take time to be here. Spent today exploring the other end of the bay. If you've got the time, give yourself a day or two off. It's gorgeous back there. Sure wish I had stayed at the other cabin when I had the chance (the other occupants left early and still had it reserved). Glad to have this one tonight! Paddling from Ketchikan to Glacier Bay or maybe Skagway. Then backpacking, hitchhiking and and wilderness hiking parts of the Interior. Alaska is a beautiful place. Well worth taking the time to enjoy what it has to offer."

Fresh-caught salmon grilled over an open fire is a gourmet's delight, especially when it is enjoyed in the scenic Duncan Salt Chuck Wilderness area.

Swan Lake is on the mainland, two miles east of Thomas Bay and 18 air miles from Petersburg. (USGS Quad Map Sumdum A-2 and A-3; or Petersburg D-3)

Fishing

Swan Lake offers excellent angling for rainbow trout up to four pounds. Look for big trout holding at various depths directly off shallow-water shelves. Also look for fish holding near drop-offs near runoff creeks emptying into the lake.

The rest of the lake's shoreline drops immediately into deep water. Trout will suspend from 10 to 40 feet along these drop-offs throughout the day. Try fan casting or jigging while drifting with the wind. In the evening you'll have good success with flies or small lures as the fish move into the shallow-water bays or to the surface to feed. The outlet is good for small fish, but use caution, as the current could carry the boat over the falls.

A Mirro-Lure in a trout and/or silver pattern is a proven producer when trolled slowly in a zig-zag pattern. Also for large trout, try jigging lures off the point to the right of the cabin. Start at 20 feet and work your way deeper. Rainbows will hit the lure while it's dropping, so be ready to set the hook.

Hunting

Goat and ptarmigan hunting are available in season. Check with ADF&G for current season and harvest information.

Swan Lake is one of the most scenic areas to fish in the Petersburg Gateway. Lake fishing for rainbow trout is excellent. Photo courtesy USDA Forest Service.

Other Activities

Swan Lake is a popular destination for anyone seeking seclusion and scenic beauty. For the climber, there are excellent rock, ice and glacier climbing opportunities. The hiker can anticipate hiking the Cascade Creek Trail, which is accessible by boat from the cabin. Destinations are Falls Lake (two miles), Thomas Bay (four miles), and Cascade Creek cabin (five miles). All three trails require good hiking skills. Take care when approaching the trailhead by boat, as the current can possibly carry the boat over the falls. Secure the boat when leaving it unattended. The area also offers good photographic opportunities for the wilderness or outdoor scenic photographer.

Precautions

Fog and high winds can prevent scheduled flights in or pickups for up to several days. Take along extra food, fuel and supplies. Lake may remain frozen until early July, and is subject to October snowfall and icing. And for the third time, take care around the top of the falls.

Cabin

Swan Lake Cabin (P-16)

Located at the east end of the lake, the Swan Lake cabin is an A-frame that was built in 1967. It sleeps seven, and has an oil-burning stove. This is perhaps one of the most scenic locations for a cabin in this ranger district. The surrounding terrain is very steep with exposed rock cliffs and snow-capped mountains around the lakeshore. Elevation, 1,514 feet. Reserve this cabin early, as it is a popular destination among local outdoorsmen.

Water source: small creek near cabin
Facilities:
- two bunks
- sleeping loft
- table
- benches
- skiffs
- oil stove
- cooking counter
- outhouse

5 Gateway Sitka
Fishing the TONGASS National Forest

About the Gateway

Sitka is a Tlingit name meaning, "by the sea." Sitka served as Alaska's capital city until Juneau was given the honor in 1906. The city is rich in Russian and Indian history. Major employers are a pulp mill, federal and state government, commercial fishing and fish processing, and tourism.

Population: 8,500
Annual Precipitation: 100 inches
Average High Summer Temperature: 60 degrees

Fishing the Sitka Area

Marine trolling for salmon is good in Sitka Sound, with the eastern shore of Kruzof Island a popular hotspot. South of town, Biorka Island and Necker Bay are good for chinook and coho salmon. Surf casters fishing Katlian Bay and Nakwasina Sound do extremely well on Dolly Varden and coho salmon. Starrigavan Bay and the breakwaters near Sheldon Jackson support good fishing for pink and coho salmon and Dolly Varden. If you're visiting in the spring, make a few casts for Dolly Varden along the shoreline parallel to Halibut Point Road.

If you're waiting for a flight out or have an extra day or two to spend, rent a car and fish Starrigavan Creek or Indian River for Dollies. Lake fishing is also good. Blue Lake, accessible by road, offers rainbow trout. Thimbleberry and Heart Lakes offer brookies, and Beaver Lake contains arctic grayling. Popular fishing locations with U.S. Forest Service cabins are Sitkoh Lake and Sitkoh Creek, both which offer an excellent steelhead fishery, and Lake Eva, which offers cutthroat and Dolly Varden.

Halibut anglers frequently fish the depths near St. Lazaria, about an hour's run from Sitka.

For information on cabins in this area, contact:

Sitka Ranger District, 204 Siginaka Way, Sitka, Alaska 99835, (907) 747-6671

Fishing Index

Forest Service cabins in this gateway are listed below. The types of fish available in the vicinity of the cabin are indicated. You can cross-reference the cabin by the F.S. #, a number assigned to each cabin by the Forest Service. A description of the cabin and its facilities can be found on the page listed on the chart, and the page number of the map showing the exact cabin location is listed in the last column.

Gateway 5 — Sitka

Cabin	F.S. #	Page	Cutthroat Trout	Dolly Varden	Grayling	Rainbow Trout	Steelhead	Chinook Salmon	Coho Salmon	Chum Salmon	Pink Salmon	Sockeye Salmon	Halibut	Rockfish	Map pg.
Avoss Lake Cabin	S-12	185		•		•									180
Baranof Lake Cabin	S-18	186	•	•											183
Brents' Beach Cabin	S-19	190		•									•	•	182
Davidof Lake Cabin	S-13	191				•									180
Fred's Creek Cabin	S-9	192													182
Goulding Lake Cabin	S-2	193	•									•	•	•	181
Kook Lake Cabin	S-5	194	•	•					•		•	•	•	•	184
Lake Eva Handicap Access Cabin	S-20	196	•	•				•	•		•	•	•	•	183
Plotnikof Lake Cabin	S-14	198						•	•	•					180
Redoubt Lake Cabin	S-11	200	•	•				•	•	•			•		180
Shelikof Cabin	S-8	201											•	•	182
Sitkoh Lake Cabin	S-6	203	•	•				•	•		•	•	•	•	184
Suloia Lake Cabin	S-7	204					•					•			182
White Sulphur Springs Cabin	S-1	188	•					•	•			•	•		181

Chatham

Peninsular Pt

Florence Bay

Pt Hayes
Queen
Morris Reef

Pt Craven

S T R A I T

Pt Benham

Appleton Cove

Saook Pt

Pt Kennedy

2015

Saook Bay

600

Todd

Lindenberg Hbr

Lindenberg Head

Fairway I

Svensen Rk

Eva I

Traders Is

Pt Thatcher

S20

Moses

Cabin

Dead Tree

Long Pt

3450

Hanus

Middle Arm

3279

1000

Kelp Bay

Hoof 2

600

3845

South

3040

Flower Rk

3680

Crow I

Pond

The Basin

1684

3457

South Arm

3066

River

1000

South Pt

1000

3985

4230

3774

Kelp 2
Graystone Cliff

North Pt

Kasnyku Bay
Lt

3180

4152

Round I

Waterfall Cove

White Rk

4667

Takatz Bay

4305

3083

4260

Takatz Islands

1000

4558

4620

3225

Baranof

Warm Spring Bay

Medleyville

4140

2052

S18

4090

4423

Mount

4005

3010

2396

Silver Bay

Cascade Bay

STRAIT

GREATER

SITKA

BOROUGH

Mess 2

False Bay

Square Cove

Whaler

Cube Pt

Quest 2

Cabin

Cube Cove

Pt Hepburn

Freshwater Bay

Gypsum

Flints Point

Iyoukeen Cove

Cabin

Redcliff Is

Cabin

Pleasant Lake

973

L. Kathleen

CH 9

Cedar I

Ward

Iyoukeen

Pavlof

Pavlof Lake

Pavlof Hbr

Jims Cove

Bar 2

North Passage

Washusett Cove

Outer Pt

Tax 2

3662

Lake Florence

WG

135

Cabin

Cabin

East Pt

2756

CH 18

Fishery Pt

WS

Cannery

Springs HO

Grave I

Don Hill Pt

600

Cannery Pt

600

Fishery

Hen

Lt

South Passage Pt

Marble Bluffs

Corner Bay

VABM

Mur 3

2015

2443

2495

Jam 2

Tap 2

Marble Cove

2445

2000

S5

Cabin

Kook L

Basket Bay

2551

Little Basket Bay

600

Basket Lake

2658

2750

600

C H A T H A M

Basket

2845

Parker Pt

Harp

Dip 2

2780

1000

2307

White Rk

2090

Kootznahoo Hea

Lt

Danger Pt

Cen

Angoo

CAA

S6

194

Chatham

Peninsular Pt

Kenasnow Rks

Avoss Lake

Avoss Lake is within the South Baranof Wilderness Area, about five miles northwest of Whale Bay in the southcentral part of Baranof Island. Air access is 30 miles from Sitka. (USGS Quad Map Port Alexander C-3)

Fishing

Fishing in Avoss Lake is often slow, due to the size of the lake and its oligotrophic nature. However, knowledgeable anglers will find fair fishing for rainbow trout and Dolly Varden year-round. Deepwater trolling techniques and casting perpendicular to shoreline with heavy spoons take the most fish.

Other Activities

This cabin is used by hunters in pursuit of blacktail deer and mountain goats.

Precautions

Bears frequent the area in spring and early fall. Also, a long-shaft outboard is needed for the skiff.

Cabin

Avoss Lake Cabin (S-12)

Avoss Lake cabin is a 16' x 16' A-frame nestled in a spectacular wilderness valley on the north shore of the lake. It has an oil-burning stove and sleeping space for eight to 10.

During the spring and summer months, the area has an abundance of wildflowers. Numerous creeks and streamettes flow through the area, fed by underground springs and snowmelt. A five-minute walk northwest of the cabin will have you in sight of unique rock formations. This cabin is an excellent choice for anyone wanting a complete get-away with fishing a secondary pursuit.

Water source: stream
Facilities:

- two double bunks
- loft
- table
- bench
- cooking counter
- outhouse
- oil stove
- skiff
- oars
- screened cooler
- ax
- maul
- broom

Baranof Lake

Baranof Lake is on Baranof Island, approximately 20 miles east of Sitka and just west of Warm Springs Bay and the community of Baranof Warm Springs. (USGS Quad Map Sitka A-3)

Fishing

This crescent-shaped lake is best fished by boat, as thick vegetation along the lake shoreline makes walking difficult. You'll need an anchor: bring a long rope and a small mesh sack to fill with rocks.

Fishing for cutthroat trout and Dolly Varden is available year-round, and is especially good near the inlet stream.

Dry flies, such as an Adams or Grey Wulff, work exceptionally well when dropped lightly amid the lily pads to feeding fish. For larger cutts, use light-colored muddler patterns.

Other Activities

The skiff can be used to reach the east end of Baranof Lake and the half-mile trail to Warm Springs Bay, where a privately-operated hot springs bath is available. It takes approximately one-and-a-half hours to row from the cabin to the east end of the lake. There is a small charge for use of the baths. Also available is a boat dock, ramp and fuel.

Cabin
Baranof Lake Cabin (S-18)

The 12' x 14' Pan Abode cabin is tucked away in a towering stand of lush spruce at the west end of the 2.5-mile-long lake. Ridges gradually rise to over 3,000 feet in elevation on both sides of the lake.

Water source: stream
Facilities:

- two single bunks
- two double bunks
- table
- benches
- counter

- shelves
- ax
- maul
- broom
- wood stove

- wood skiff
- oars
- cooler box

User Comments

7/15-7/17: "Weather fantastic. Temps in high 70s all three days. Scenery: spectacular. Condition of cabin: excellent. Very clean with good supply of dry wood. We'll leave the same way. Fishing: good. Ate 10, took home 39. Caught and released 13 for total of 62 fish. All cutthroat 10 to 15½ inches. Fifteen-inch fish weighed 1 to 1¼ pounds. Etc: Berries ripe at lower end (salmonberries and blueberries). Berries ripe around cabin. Saw one deer on beach by falls, and fresh tracks on beach. No bear sign. Skiff needs one oar lock replaced."

8/5-8/10: "New stove is good. It would have been nice to have a cook stove like the last one. It's hard to use as it's so small. Fishing was poorer than the other years we've been at the lake."

The lakes of the "ABC" islands (Admiralty, Baranof and Chichagof) offer good to excellent fishing for rainbow and cutthroat trout. Action is good year-round.

Bertha Bay is on West Chichagof Island, which is in the Chichagof-Yakobi Wilderness Area. The bay is about 65 miles northwest of Sitka and is accessible via boat or helicopter. Take a 0.2-mile trail to the cabin. Boats can anchor in Mirror Harbor, where a 0.9-mile trail leads to the cabin. (USGS Quad Map Sitka D-7 and D-8)

Fishing

Fishing in Sea Level Slough watershed is good to excellent for pink and chum salmon. Steelhead, rainbow and cutthroat trout are available. Good trout fishing in lake nearest the cabin. Take a float tube or belly boat for best success at this lake. No boat is provided.

Hunting

Blacktail deer, bear and waterfowl hunting are all good at various times in their respective seasons.

Other Activities

The popularity of White Sulphur Springs recreation cabin is due to its scenic location and to the hot spring mineral bath located there.

The bath house is a Pan Abode structure covering a cement and boulder hot spring pool. Cabin users are reminded that they are renting the cabin only—the hot spring is available to any visitor and it does receive a lot of use from commercial fishermen, kayakers and campers. However, no overnight camping is allowed in the bath house.

Because of the easy terrain, consider hiking to various points around White Sulphur cabin. Lake Elfendahl and Lake Morris are only a two-hour hike away. Marked trails to Sea Level Slough and Mirror Harbor are easily followed, too. Note that Sea Level Slough is passable only at low tide: Plan your hike accordingly.

Precautions

There is no fresh water source in the area, although water may be obtained from the lake near the cabin or from two small flows crossing the trail north of the cabin. This water must be boiled or treated. Take extra water, juices and other beverages as the heat of the hot springs has a dehydrating effect on users.

Brown bear are frequently seen in the slough area when salmon are running.

Cabin
White Sulphur Springs Cabin (S-1)

This cabin is on the mixed muskeg and wooded north shore of Bertha Bay. It is a 12' x 14' Pan Abode cabin that receives the most use of any cabin in the Sitka Ranger District. Located near the water's edge, the cabin can sleep six and sports a grand overlook of Bertha Bay. The hot springs bath house is about 50 feet from the recreation cabin.

Water source: bring your own

Facilities:
- two single bunks
- two double bunks
- table
- cooking counter
- outhouse

- ax
- maul
- broom
- wood stove
- wood supply

- cooler box
- cupboard
- hot springs
- mineral bath house

User Comments

(no date): "This place has got to be one of the finest cabins to stay at in southeast—not because of the cabin, but because of the hot springs. We paddled by kayak from Pelican (can be done in one day) but were storm bound for an extra day because of heavy seas (8-to 10-foot seas in Islas Bay). Cabin obviously gets heavy use from passing fishermen. Our only visitors were the helicoptering miners from Lisiansky Strait."

6/22-6/24: "Small lake good for planes. Mirror Harbor is no better, maybe worse. Can anchor boat in front of springs if not too windy. Nice plank trail to Mirror Harbor. Cabin is clean, tight and comfortable. Good wood stove. No good water; springs and muskeg about. Hot springs are wonderful; a little slimy, but not bad. Lots of deer and bear sign about. A few sea birds. Otters are wonderful out in shoal water. Need sign in spring telling people not to use soap."

10/5-10/10: "Cabin and outhouse very clean. No foam mats. Be sure and advise people to bring everything; don't count on anything being there (at cabin). Weather was warm, windy and wet. Fishing usually poor this time of year. Lots of deer, also lots of bear sign. Had a great goose dinner one night. Bird hunting fair. Spent one afternoon observing sea otters. Enjoyed the bath, great as always."

Brent's Beach is on Crab Bay on the east shore of Kruzof Island, about 15 miles southwest of Sitka. Access by boat takes about 35 minutes. Helicopter takes 15 minutes or less. (USGS Quad Map Sitka A-5)

Fishing

Try saltwater casting for pinks and Dolly Varden migrating through the area. Otherwise, there is limited fishing from shore. Go to deeper water for good halibut fishing.

Other Activities

Brent's Beach has a stretch of white sand that's great for beachcombing, sunbathing and digging razor clams. A fishing license is required for razor clam digging. Minus tides are best. For an interesting exploration trip, take a 10-minute hike north of the cabin to visit the lava domes and caves.

Precautions

There have been reports of erratic and abnormally large waves off Kruzof Island at low slack tide. The Coast Guard recommends that you avoid approaching the beach and unloading while the tide is turning. Also, Brent's Beach cabin is extensively used by the local residents of Sitka and although routine maintenance is performed regularly, the cabin is difficult to keep in optimum condition and it does bear the brunt of some vandalism.

Cabin

Brent's Beach Cabin (S-19)

This rustic 16' x 16' A-frame cabin is built from native materials. It was donated by the family of Brent Petty as a memorial to Petty and Billy and Teddy Mossberg after the trio drowned while halibut fishing in the area. Because it's easily accessible by boat from Sitka, this popular cabin receives much local use. An ideal choice for an overnight or weekend family excursion. Sleeps six.

Water source: creek
Facilities:

- double bunk
- loft (sleeps four)
- wood stove
- wood supply
- table
- benches
- outhouse
- ax
- maul
- broom
- cooler box
- no boat

Davidof Lake

Davidof Lake is 40 miles southeast of Sitka and five miles east of Whale Bay in the South Baranof Wilderness Area. Floatplane access only. The lake is surrounded by forested, snow-capped mountains that rise in excess of 2,000 feet. (USGS Quad Map Port Alexander C-3)

Fishing

Davidof Lake's main attraction is good fishing for average-sized rainbow trout. Hotspots include the lake immediately east of the cabin. A leech pattern works well in early evening when fished slowly through the depths.

For the best fishing, however, you'll need to travel the length of the lake and fish the outlet stream. Use non-descript brown and black nymph patterns during the summer months, and fry patterns in early spring. This area has thick, overhanging brush, so a short fly rod is a must. Spin anglers should consider ultralight tackle only.

A 1.2-mile trail starting at Davidof Lake's outlet stream connects to Plotnikof Lake, where you'll find good to excellent fishing for salmon and trout. ADF&G indicates that steelhead are present in the lower watershed, from Plotnikof Lake outlet to salt water.

Other Activities

Deer hunting is available all season long. Brown bear are also available.

Cabin
Davidof Lake Cabin (S-13)

Davidof Lake cabin is a 16' x 16' A-frame with a wood stove and sleeping space for eight to 10. The cabin is on the northeast end of the 1.7 mile-long lake. The cabin offers a good view looking down the lake. A very scenic location.

Water source: lake
Facilities:
* two double bunks
* loft
* wood stove
* wood supply
* cooking shelf
* ax
* maul
* broom
* skiff
* oars
* table
* bench
* outside cooler box
* outhouse

Interior of Davidof Lake Cabin. Photo courtesy of the USDA Forest Service.

Fred's Creek is on the southeastern shore of Kruzof Island, about a half-hour journey by boat from Sitka. (USGS Quad Map Sitka A-5 and Sitka A-6)

Hunting

Deer are plentiful here and the area is popular among deer hunters from August through December. Bear are common from early to late spring.

Other Activities

Easy access, beachcombing and views of the breaking surf make this cabin a popular choice among residents and visitors alike. The Mount Edgecumbe Trail is about six miles in length and leads very gradually up to the summit. Expect to cross miles of muskeg alternating with thick stands of forest. Near the top, the trail becomes very steep. The panoramic view at the top, however, is worth the hike.

Precautions

Exercise caution when unloading and anchoring, as the surf breaks along a pumice rock shoreline. There have been reports of erratic and abnormally large waves off Kruzof Island at low slack tide. The Coast Guard recommends that marine travelers avoid approaching the beach or unloading their craft while the tide is turning. There is no protected anchorage during rough weather.

Cabin

Fred's Creek Cabin (S-9)

This cabin is a popular 16'x 16' A-frame that sleeps six to eight people. It is at the head of the Mount Edgecumbe trail, with a beautiful view of the beach and surf. The terrain surrounding the cabin is flat, with dense stands of spruce and hemlock.

Water source: creek
Facilities:

* two single bunks
* loft
* wood stove
* wood supply
* table
* benches
* cooking shelf
* woodshed
* ax
* broom
* maul
* screened cooler
* outhouse

Fred's Creek Cabin. Photo courtesy USDA Forest Service.

Goulding Lakes

The Goulding Lakes, located on West Chichagof Island about 60 miles northwest of Sitka, are part of the West Chichagof-Yakobi Wilderness Area. Air access from Sitka takes about 30 minutes, one way. (USGS Quad Map Sitka D-7)

Fishing

Cutthroat trout is the main fish here and fishing is good in all four lakes of the chain. The Goulding River also receives a run of anadromous cutthroat.

The best fishing takes place in late April through June for the sea-run variety and year-round for resident fish. Standard cutthroat patterns work well here. Light leaders are a must. Don't pass up the pools below the falls or the breaklines near the freshwater inlets of the lower lake.

In season, pink and chum salmon are found in the system's intertidal area. Sockeye salmon are available throughout the Goulding Lakes chain. Otter and Lower Otter lakes are connected.

There is usually a second skiff at Lower Otter Lake. Find it by taking the trail (near the outhouse) to the lake. The boat is normally stored just inside the trees near where the creek from Otter Lake empties into the lower lake. Bring oars from the cabin. If you take the Otter Lake boat down the creek, plan on getting wet bringing it back up: the current is too strong to row it and the shore is too brushy for walking. You end up wading the creek, which is fairly deep.

Other Activities

For outdoorsmen with plenty of stamina, bushwhacking from the Goulding recreation cabin to Dry Pass Harbor is a possibility. From there the trail to White Sulphur Hot Springs can be taken for an adventurous trek. Hikers should be experienced backpackers and allow at least two days for this trip. A topo map of the area is a must for explorers who want to take advantage of the opportunities in this area.

Precautions

The skiff available at the cabin has a high transom, thus a long-shaft outboard is recommended. Brown bears are abundant. Bear protection is a must for cross-country hikers.

Cabin
Goulding Lake Cabin (S-2)

The Goulding Lake cabin is on the north shore of Otter Lake, one of several larger lakes in the Goulding Lakes chain. It is a 16' x 16' A-frame structure that sleeps six to eight people. It is located in a flat, lightly wooded area next to the lake. The surrounding terrain varies from open muskeg to densely forested slopes.

Water source: stream, lake

Facilities:
- double bunk
- loft
- cooking counter
- table
- benches
- cupboard
- ax and maul
- broom
- wood stove
- wood supply
- cooler
- skiff
- oars
- outhouse

Kook Lake

Kook Lake is about seven miles south of the mouth of Tenakee Inlet on the east side of Chichagof Island, about 13 miles southeast of the town of Tenakee Springs. Floatplane time from Sitka is approximately 30 minutes, one-way. (USGS Quad Map Sitka C-3 and C-4)

Fishing

Anglers at Kook Lake can expect good fishing for cutthroat trout and Dolly Varden throughout the year. Big cutts up to three pounds cruise the lake at various depths throughout the summer months, looking for schools of sockeye fingerlings. It's common to catch cutthroats in the middle of the lake, both right below the surface and at depths of 20 feet or more.

In Kook Creek, sockeye salmon fishing is good in mid-July, and coho salmon fishing in late August. Fishing for pink and chum salmon, steelhead and Dolly Varden is good in the lower outlet creek. Good choice for a fishing vacation.

Other Activities

The Kook Lake area was logged in the 1970s and clearcuts may be seen from the lake. Logging in the immediate vicinity started again in 1989. The nearby logging road will probably be in use for the next five years. Visitors may want to take advantage of the road system in the area to explore. To reach the road, go behind the cabin, and you'll find a quarter-mile trail that leads to the Corner Bay Road system.

Basket Bay is the final destination of the Kook Lake watershed, and is a fun area to explore during a lull in the fishing action. The easiest way to reach Basket Bay is to boat from the recreation cabin to the outlet of Kook Lake. From this point avoid following the creek, as much of the area has been clearcut. It is brushy, and debris left from logging makes some sections difficult to traverse. After hiking approximately 150 yards from the lake outlet, a logging road should be visible. Bushwhack to the road, then follow the road until it ends within sight of Basket Bay. From there, just follow one of the many game trails leading to Basket Bay. The tidal area of Basket Bay is full of shellfish and sometimes salmon before they start their spawning run up Kook Creek.

One of the more exciting features of this area is the terrain where Kook Creek enters into Basket Bay. There the creek disappears, then reappears flowing through a large, naturally formed limestone arch.

Precautions

Brown bear frequently fish for spawning salmon in Kook Creek.

Cabin

Kook Lake Cabin (S-5)

This is a 16'x 16' A-frame cabin nestled in a beautiful stand of hemlock and spruce forest. A sandy beach in front of the cabin allows easy access to the lake. The cabin can sleep eight to 10 people. The terrain immediately surrounding Kook Lake is flat. The north section of the lake is also flat, gradually rising to 1,500 feet. From this point, the mountains ascend sharply to alpine tundra.

The south side of the lake is fairly steep with the mountains rising directly from the lake. Bring your own bow saw for cutting firewood.

Water source: stream
Facilities:

- two double bunks
- loft
- wood stove
- wood supply
- table

- benches
- cooler box
- skiff
- oars
- counter

- ax
- maul
- broom
- outhouse

User Comments

5/22-5/26 "Cabin and outhouse in good condition. Ten to 12 deer seen on shore of lake, no bear sighted in area. Set mouse traps, but no mice in cabin. Take Coleman stove for cooking if more than 2 people. Take coffee pot, one there has seen better days. Watch out for handle of smaller skillet; it twirls around. Lost breakfast before we discovered looseness. You can hike from the southeast end of the lake (300 yards) to south logging road which takes you almost to Basket Bay. Plenty of 6-to 8-foot devil's club. Caught cutthroat up to three pounds and some Dollies also. Fishing only good 3 hours after sunrise and before sunset."

7/25: "The cabin was clean when we arrived. There was plenty of firewood, paper for starting the fire, and even toilet paper. The small stream next to the cabin is perfect for cooling canned or bottled drinks. Fishing was fair in front of the cabin, but better at mouth of the stream south of the cabin and great at the mouth of the larger stream at the southwest corner of lake. We also caught a large stringer full of cutthroat trout at the extreme east end of lake. The weather was great! We watched three brown bear walking the beach around 7 a.m. One walked past the cabin. We hiked back up to the logging road behind the cabin, followed (the bear) around to the southeast until we reached the bridge over the salmon spawning stream where we watched another bear feeding. Also spotted two deer."

Kook Lake cabin. Photo courtesy USDA Forest Service.

Lake Eva

Lake Eva is near the northeast coast of Baranof Island off Peril Strait, about 27 miles from Sitka. Access is by floatplane. (USGS Quad Map Sitka B-4)

Fishing

Steelhead fishing is best in the outlet stream from mid-April through mid-May. Take the boat to the lake's outlet and hike the Lake Eva Trail (–472) to Hanus Bay. Distance is less than one mile.

Sockeye fishing is good from mid-July to mid-August, and coho from late August through September. Pink and chum salmon fishing in the lower outlet stream. Dolly Varden and cutthroat are available in the lake and stream year-round.

Lake Eva is an excellent choice for handicapped or non-handicapped anglers. Fishing from the dock, however, is marginal. Use salmon eggs for best success. Out on the lake and in the creek, forage-fish patterns, muddlers, Glo-bug, caddis, stonefly and Odonata nymph patterns regularly take trout and char.

Hunting

Deer hunting is available from August through December. Brown bear roam throughout the area. There is waterfowl hunting at the lake and intertidal area.

Cabin
Lake Eva Handicap Access Cabin (S-20)

This 12' x 14' Pan Abode cabin is in a small clearing on the north shore of Lake Eva, surrounded by mature stands of spruce and hemlock. Snow-capped mountains can be seen to the southwest. The cabin comfortably sleeps six, and has a wood-burning stove for cooking and heating.

A series of boardwalks allow easy access for people in wheelchairs; and, because of the railings, is a popular choice among elderly visitors or families with young children. The boardwalk leads to a deck area with outdoor firepit, picnic table with wheelchair access, and a fishing platform with guard rail. The outhouse also has a boardwalk leading to it and is handicap accessible.

The cabin conversion took place in 1982. A Forest Service work leader and young laborers from the now-disbanded Young Adult Conservation Corps used on-hand materials to make the conversion less costly. When the cabin was completed, the Sitka District Ranger commented, ''The Lake Eva cabin can now be used in safety and comfort by a wide variety of people. The elderly will find the ramps and railings handy, and people with young children appreciate the railing-enclosed deck. Though the cabin was redesigned with the physically challenged in mind, it provides a wonderful camping experience for almost anyone.''

This particular cabin site was chosen because its central location on northwest Baranof Island makes it accessible to more people. It is 66 air miles from Juneau, Alaska's capital city, 26 miles from historic Sitka, and 50 miles from the small fishing village of Hoonah. The Forest Service does not give preference to physically challenged users, although it will consider doing so if response from these users becomes high.

Water source: stream, lake
Facilities:

- two single bunks
- two double bunks
- wood stove
- wood supply
- table
- bench

- skiff
- oars
- ax
- maul
- broom
- fishing deck

- outdoor firepit
- picnic table
- outdoor benches
- outhouse
- handicap access

User Comments

7/26-7/28: "Cabin and area in excellent condition. We were very impressed with the decking, BBQ pit, and the dock, as I have my own plane! Fishing was great! Mostly Dollies, and a few cutthroats. No wildlife other than loons. Thanks much!"

Lake Eva cabin can be used in safety and comfort by a wide variety of people. A series of boardwalks allow easy access for people in wheelchairs. Because of the railings, Lake Eva cabin is a popular choice among elderly visitors or families with young children. Photo courtesy USDA Forest Service.

Plotnikof Lake is on Baranof Island, within the South Baranof Wilderness Area about four miles east of Whale Bay. It is approximately 45 miles southeast of Sitka. Floatplane charter time out of Sitka is approximately 25 minutes, one way. (Refer to USGS Quad Map Port Alexander C-3)

Fishing

Plotnikof Lake is one of the most scenic on Baranof Island. Steep granite mountains rise sharply from the lake shoreline to snow-capped ridges peaking at 3,000 feet. The lake itself is narrow and fiord-like with numerous waterfalls running its four-mile length.

Rainbow fishing is good in the lake, especially at the narrows and at times, in the shallows near the cabin. Steelhead in the outlet stream are best taken in May and early June. Coho salmon can be caught in fair to good numbers from late August through September.

Hunting

The area has fair deer hunting, but is often too steep for most hunters. Bear hunting is best at the higher elevations late in the season, and at low elevations in spring and early fall.

Precautions

Use caution when fishing the streams. Brown bear frequent the area in spring and early summer, and especially during the coho salmon run.

Cabin
Plotnikof Lake Cabin (S-14)

Plotnikof Lake cabin is situated at the north end of the lake in a small stand of Sitka spruce. It sleeps four to six people and has an oil-burning stove. There's a 1.2-mile trail to Davidof Lake and cabin.

Early in the season, or immediately after a heavy rain, is the best time to enjoy and/or photograph this area. Wear rubber boots, as the area near the cabin is marshy.

Water source: lake and stream
Facilities:

- two double bunks
- two single bunks
- oil stove
- table
- cooler box
- cooking shelf
- skiff
- oars
- shelves
- ax
- maul
- broom
- outhouse

When fishing southeast lakes in the spring and early summer, salmon fry patterns and lures are very effective in taking both rainbow and cutthroat trout.

Redoubt Lake

Redoubt Lake cabin, located on Baranof Island, is approximately 10 miles south of Sitka. It can be reached by taking a six-mile hike from Silver Bay, or a short air charter flight. (USGS Quad Map Port Alexander D-4).

Fishing

A short hike to Salmon Creek, to the north, will reward the angler with steelhead, rainbow and cutthroat trout fishing. According to USFS, Redoubt Lake offers Dolly Varden, rainbow and cutthroat trout. One of the best areas to fish, especially during the summer months, is the inlet stream, located at the head of the lake. Concentrate on the area where the silt bottom of the inlet stream suddenly disappears from view. Both cutthroats and rainbow can be caught there by either trolling or casting ultralight spoons and spinners. Fry patterns (about an inch long) are productive in catching char when cast into the current and allowed to swing out and into the deepwater area. Some anglers use a 1/2-ounce fluorescent red or orange flutter spoon and cowbells and troll along the drop-offs.

Expect sockeyes in mid-July to mid-August, and coho salmon from late August through September. For best fishing, try Redoubt Creek.

Hunting

A popular area for blacktail deer and bear.

Precautions

It's possible to portage small boats or kayaks from Redoubt Bay (at the base of the falls) into Redoubt Lake at the west end of the lake. The tramway is not in operation at the present time. Also, the skiff has a high transom, and a long-shaft outboard is recommended to properly propel the craft.

Cabin
Redoubt Lake Cabin (S-11)

The 16' x 16' A-Frame cabin is nestled in a mature stand of spruce and hemlock on the east end of 9.5-mile-long Redoubt Lake. It has one double bunk and two single bunks downstairs; the loft can accommodate up to six people. The area offers grand scenery: forested mountains rise approximately 3,500 feet to snowfields, alpine meadows and granite cirques. Numerous waterfalls running the length of the lake offer a spectacular backdrop for photos.

Water source: stream
Facilities:

- two single bunks
- one double bunk
- loft (sleeps 4-6)
- cooler box
- cooking shelf
- wood stove
- wood supply
- woodshed
- outhouse
- table
- benches
- ax
- maul
- broom
- skiff/oars

Shelikof Bay is on the west coast of Kruzof Island about 20 miles northwest of Sitka. Reach the bay by taking the Kruzof Trail from Mud Bay for approximately seven miles, or charter a helicopter from Sitka. (USGS Quad Map Sitka A-5 and A-6)

Fishing

Minimal freshwater fishing opportunities. Salmon fishing in a nearby creek can sometimes be good. It's possible to catch Dolly Varden and rockfish by casting off rocky points. Halibut fishing is excellent in deeper water.

Other Activities

The sand beaches are among the nicest in the area, and are easy to walk. This part of the coast is a beachcomber's paradise, with hard-to-find Japanese fishing floats along with numerous sand dollars and shells.

A must-hike is through Iris Meadows, easily reached by following the river upstream for approximately one-quarter of a mile. The trail to Iris Meadows crosses an estuary and may be difficult to cross at high tide. The terrain is relatively flat and easy to explore. Wildlife and flowers are abundant.

Bear and deer are common in the area and are often photographed by cabin guests. The area also offers a myriad of sea life to study, especially at low tide.

Cabin

Shelikof Cabin (S-8)

This 16' x 16' A-frame cabin situated in a dense stand of spruce at Shelikof Bay offers a beautiful view of open ocean and good to excellent beachcombing along a sandy beach. The cabin sleeps eight. Water source is from a spring a quarter-mile from the cabin. This cabin may be replaced or an addition may be made in 1989. Check with the regional Forest Service office for current information.

Water source: spring
Facilities:

- two double bunks
- loft
- wood stove
- wood supply
- table
- benches
- ax
- maul
- broom
- cooking shelf
- outhouse

Sitkoh Lake

Sitkoh Lake is in the southeast portion of Chichagof Island, approximately 35 miles northeast of Sitka. Access is primarily by air. The cabin can also be reached by taking a 4.3-mile trail that starts at Sitkoh Bay near Chatham Cannery. Follow Sitkoh Creek until you reach the lake. (USGS Quad Map Sitka C-4)

Fishing

Sitkoh Lake and Sitkoh Creek are known for their excellent runs of anadromous cutthroat trout and Dolly Varden char. The outlet stream offers good to excellent steelhead fishing in April and May. Sitkoh Bay is the best place to catch pink and chum salmon from July to mid-August. Sockeye are available in the lake and stream from mid-July to mid-August. Coho salmon fishing is good from late August through September.

Because of the forage food base of sockeye, use flies or lures that best imitate kokanee fry or fingerlings when fishing for trout or char. Favorite spoons include silver with orange markings or stripes. Long-lining is effective, or fish the edges of aquatic vegetation during midday.

For char and trout in the creek, use No. 8 salmon egg patterns, especially during the salmon runs. Salmon can be caught on spinning lures and bright attractor flies. This creek is one of the better watersheds in this region for fishing variety.

Hunting

There is good deer hunting in the area during the fall months. Hunt the old logging trails and meadows for best success. Bear and waterfowl hunting also available. Success varies, depending on weather, experience of hunters, and game and bird migrations.

Sitkoh Creek sockeyes will readily take brightly colored attractor patterns such as Sockeye Green, Sherry's Deliverer and Polar Shrimp.

Precautions

Brown bear are abundant along Sitkoh Lake Trail, especially during the salmon season. Make plenty of noise when walking the trail. Some people carry bells, whistles or a loud-playing radio to forewarn bears of their approach. A firearm is recommended.

Cabin
Sitkoh Lake Cabin (S-6)

This 12' x 14' Pan Abode cabin is near the outlet stream at the east end of the 2.5-mile lake. The cabin is nestled in mature, coniferous timber and brush. It sleeps from four to six. A second cabin on the north shore of the lake about half a mile from the Sitkoh cabin is being built. The lake is surrounded by small mountains rising to approximately 2,500 feet.

Water source: lake
Facilities:

- two single bunks
- two double bunks
- wood stove
- wood supply
- ax

- maul
- broom
- skiff
- oars
- outhouse

- table
- cooking counter
- cupboard
- cooler box

User Comments

11/17: ''Cabin in excellent shape. Water table is high. Several bears still roaming. Mixed snow and rain. Many deer. Several old roads which can be very difficult to reach—try the trail behind the cabin.''

The wooden bunks in the USFS cabins require air or foam mattresses, so be sure to pack one or more to suit your needs.

Suloia Lake is near the southern tip of Chichagof Island within the West Chichagof-Yakobi Wilderness Area. It is approximately 30 miles northwest of Sitka. (USGS Quad Map Sitka B-6)

Fishing

As a result of several stockings, Suloia Lake offers fair rainbow trout fishing. A small run of pink salmon spawn from the lake outlet to tidewater.

Hunting

Deer hunting is good to excellent in season.

Precautions

The Suloia Lake Trail leads from Suloia Bay to the lake. The trail which leads from the lake to the old cabin site no longer exists. Because there is little or no beach, and the shoreline is brushy and forested with plenty of downfall, brush busting along the shoreline to reach the new cabin is not recommended. Also, the height of the skiff's transom requires an outboard with a long shaft.

Cabin

Suloia Lake Cabin (S-7)

This 12' x 14' Pan Abode recreational cabin was built and donated in 1984 by the Carl Eurich family in memory of their son. The cabin is located on the northwest shore of two-mile-long Suloia Lake. Dense stands of cedar, spruce and hemlock with an understory of brush line the shoreline. A small gravel beach lies in front of the cabin. Timbered mountain ridges rise up to 2,600 feet. This cabin replaces the older cabin on the east shore.

Water source: stream
Facilities:

- two double bunks
- two single bunks
- table
- bench
- skiff

- oars
- wood stove
- wood supply
- outhouse
- ax

- maul
- broom
- cooking shelf
- cooler box
- cupboard

6 Gateway Juneau
Fishing the TONGASS National Forest

About the Gateway

Juneau is Alaska's capital and the Nation's largest city, covering 3,108 square miles. Most of those miles are wilderness. The city is named after miner Joe Juneau, who discovered gold in the area in 1880.

The city limits sprawl from the edge of the massive Juneau Icefield to the western end of Douglas Island. Strangely enough, the main highway to the north is only about 40 miles long. However, five main harbors provide moorage for most of the town's 2,500 recreational boats and 250 commercial fishing boats.

Juneau is regional headquarters for 22 million acres of National Forests in Alaska. State and federal governments are the main employers.

Population: 23,000
Annual Precipitation: 92 inches
Average Summer High: 62.7 degrees

Fishing the Juneau area

Juneau offers sportfishing variety. About 90 percent of all angling effort in this region occurs in salt water, including Doty Cove, Point Retreat and Benjamin Island. Juneau is a jumping off point for fishing the Admiralty, Baranof and Chichagof Islands and other locations on the mainland and in Glacier Bay. Fishing opportunities in the National Forests in the Juneau area range from good to exceptional.

Near Juneau, marine sport anglers target North Pass, North Shelter Island, Favorite Reef, South Shelter Island, the "Breadline," stretching from Tee Harbor and the Shrine of Saint Terese; Outer Point on Douglas Island. Point Retreat is a popular hotspot for halibut anglers.

When weather is bad, and it often is in this part of Alaska, marine anglers target salmon stocks inside the Auke Bay-Fritz Cove area, and waters near Portland, Coghlan and Spuhn islands. When the spring chinook closure ends, anglers attempt to catch late-arriving chinook moving through near Icy Point, Point Salisbury and Point Bishop. Success at this time is good.

Chinook Salmon

About 50 percent of chinook salmon are taken near communities north of Frederick Sound, with 70 percent of these taken near the Juneau area. The Taku River is the only major chinook salmon producer in northern southeast Alaska (more than ten thousand fish). Juneau anglers typically catch Taku fish in the spring in restricted areas. ADF&G figures indicate that during the peak of the chinook run (May 20 through June 10), it takes about 20 hours or four angler trips to catch one 28-inch-or-larger chinook.

Coho

Over 65 percent of the regional sport harvest of coho salmon occurs in northern southeast Alaska, with nearly 80 percent of that figure taking place in the Juneau area. At least 40 systems in northern southeast Alaska support runs exceeding one thousand coho. The Mitchell Bay-Salt Lake area in Kootznahoo Inlet offers good fishing for coho salmon. These are caught primarily by fly-in anglers, canoeists and lodge guests.

Cutthroat

There are 48 lakes in northern southeast Alaska that contain cutthroat trout populations. The majority of the catch comes from Admiralty, Chichagof and northern Baranof islands. Most of the best waters are lakes or lake-fed streams. Chilkat Lake is also known for its good cutthroat fishing. On Admiralty Island, near Juneau, try Salt Lake and Kanalku Creek for anadromous cutts. Dolly fishing is also very good. One of the best trophy cutthroat lakes is Turner Lake, 20 miles east of Juneau. Two forest service cabins make this a popular recreational fishing hotspot.

Steelhead

While steelhead occur in at least 62 streams in northern southeast Alaska, most streams are not readily accessible to the public. Accessible streams receive heavy angling pressure. Most steelhead in this region are spring fish. Anglers with aircraft fish Bear and Admiralty creeks for steelhead. Berners River, north of the Echo Cove boat launch site, also offers steelhead.

Rainbow Trout

The majority of rainbow trout harvested in northern southeast Alaska are taken from lakes on Baranof Island. A few are taken from Lower Dewey Lake. Less than 10 percent of the rainbows are taken from streams. Northern southeast Alaska hosts three lakes with native rainbow trout, and at least 24 lakes with rainbow trout originating from a stocking program.

Brook Trout

Six of the nine lakes supporting brook trout in northern southeast Alaska support fisheries that yield over ten thousand fish annually. Salmon Creek Reservoir is undoubtedly the most popular brook trout fishery in the Juneau area. The lakes yield approximately 6.5 catchable trout per acre, with Green Lake near Sitka yielding 8.5 fish per acre. It takes seven years to produce a 10-inch fish in Salmon Creek, but only four years in Green Lake.

Grayling

While lakes in the Juneau, Sitka and Haines region contain grayling, most of the harvest comes from Herman Lake near Haines.

For information on recreational cabins in this area, contact:

USDA Forest Service, Juneau Ranger District, 8465 Old Dairy Road, Juneau, Alaska 99803, (907) 586-8800

USDA Forest Service Information Center, 101 Egan Drive, Juneau, Alaska, (907) 586-8751.

Fishing Index

Forest Service cabins in this gateway are listed below. The types of fish available in the vicinity of the cabin are indicated. You can cross-reference the cabin by the F.S. #, a number assigned to each cabin by the Forest Service. A description of the cabin and its facilities can be found on the page listed on the chart, and the page number of the map showing the exact cabin location is listed in the last column.

Gateway 6 — Juneau

Cabin	F.S. #	Page	Cutthroat Trout	Dolly Varden	Grayling	Rainbow Trout	Steelhead	Chinook Salmon	Coho Salmon	Chum Salmon	Pink Salmon	Sockeye Salmon	Halibut	Rockfish	Map pg.
Admiralty Cove Cabin	CH-6	217	•					•		•	•	•			213
Big Shaheen Cabin	CH-10	228	•	•											211
Church Bight Cabin	CH-16	225	•	•					•	•	•	•	•	•	214
Dan Moller Cabin	CH-1	231													213
Distin lake Cabin	CH-14	220	•	•											211
East Florence Cabin	CH-19	222	•	•								•	•		210
East Turner Lake Cabin	CH-5	246	•	•											215
Hasselborg Creek Cabin	CH-13	226	•	•											211
Jim's Lake Cabin	CH-15	230	•	•											211
John Muir Cabin	CH-3	237													213
Katzehin Cabin	CH-23	219		•				•	•	•	•	•	•	•	212
Lake Alexander Cabin	CH-21	232	•	•								•	•		211
Lake Kathleen Cabin	CH-9	234	•	•											210
Laughton Glacier Cabin	CH-22	236													212
Little Shaheen Cabin	CH-11	228	•	•											211
North Young Lake Cabin	CH-7	248	•	•					•		•	•	•		213
Peterson Lake Cabin	CH-24	238						•	•	•	•	•			213
Pybus Bay Cabin	CH-17	241		•					•	•	•	•	•	•	209
Seymour Canal Cabin	CH-20	243		•					•	•	•	•	•	•	213
South Young Lake Cabin	CH-8	248	•	•					•		•	•	•		213
Sportsman Cabin	CH-12	220	•	•											211
Spruce Cabin	CH-2	244	•	•									•		215
West Florence Cabin	CH-18	222	•	•								•	•		210
West Turner Lake Cabin	CH-4	246	•	•									•		215

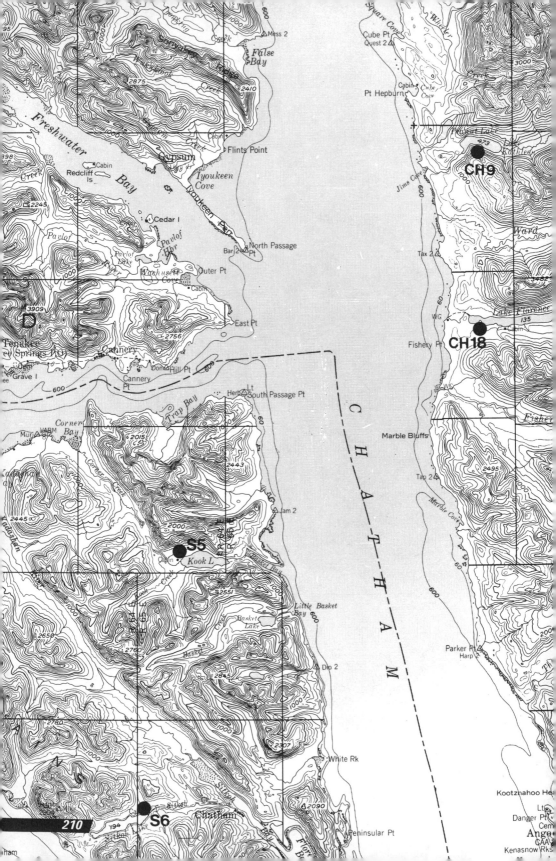

Mess 2

Square Cove

Winder

Cube Pt

Quest 2

Thorofery Creek

False Bay

600

600

1000

3000

2875

False Creek

2410

Pt Hepburn

Cabin

Cube Cove

CH9

Pleasant Lake
273

L Kathleen

Freshwater

Flints Point

Gypsum

Tyoukeen Cove

Cabin

Redcliff Is

Cabin

Jims Cove

600

Ward

Creek

2245

398

1000

Bay

Cedar I

Iyoukeen Inlet

North Passage

Bar 2 Pt

Tax 2

60

Lake Florence
135

3462

Pavlof

Pavlof Lake

Pavlof Hbr

Wachusett Cove

Outer Pt

Cabin

WG

Cabin

CH18

Fishery Pt

3909

D

2756

East Pt

WS

Fisher

Tenakee
(Springs PO)

Cannery

Don Hill Pt

600

Herb Lt

South Passage Pt

Marble Bluffs

600

Grave I

Cannery Pt

60

Trap Bay

Corner Bay

VABM Mur

2015

2443

Jam 2

Tap 2

2495

C
H
A
T
H
A
M

Marble Cove

60

2445

Corner Creek

2000

S5

Kook L

Basket Bay

2551

Little Basket Bay

600

2650

2760

Basket Lake

2845

Dip 2

Parker Pt

Harp 2

2307

210

194

S6

Chatham

White Rk

2090

Kootznahoo He

Lt

Danger Pt

Cem

Ange

CAA

Kenasnow Rks

Peninsular Pt

Dotsons Landing

Death Valley

CH24

Lee Harbor

Auke Mtn

CH3
Auke Bay

Nugget Mtn

Auke Cape

Auke Bay

Coghlan Island

Portland Island

Spuhn Island

Mendenhall Pen

JUNEAU

West Juneau

STEPHENS

Mr Meek

Douglas

Douglas

CH1
Treadwell

Bradley

PASSAGE

Colt Island

Horse Island

Scull Island

Pt Young

Scull

Young Bay

CITY AND BOROUGH OF JUNEAU

False Ardon

Marmion I

CH6

Hawk Inlet

CH7

CH8

CH20

ADMIRALTY

ISLAND

ISLAND

MONUMEN

NATIONAL

CANAL

Pt Windham

510

300

600

S.

PASSAGE

Sunset
Island

K and D Mine

0'

306

Sunset Cove

300

Rocky Pt

Hobart

Gambier Bay

Good

552

Scrub Pt

S.

Raw
Muse

Romp
Gain I

The Twins

Chock I

Church Pt

Chapel I

Gambier
Island

McDonald
Rk

Price I

Pt Gambier

Lawrence I

CH 16

426

540

Pt Hobart

S.

False Pt Pybus

600

Square Pt

60

Sail
Island

360

300

POR

S.

540

Brother (Fox) I

East Brother
Island

Pt Walpole

Crow

Is

West Brother
Island

506

506

Akusha I

San Juan
Islands

198

The Brothers

The
Five Fingers

Fort Pt

Foot I

Southwest

Five Finger
Lighthouse

McNairy Pt

S.

Lt Round Rk

600

Bill Pt

444

Bartlett Pt

2362

330

Whitney
Island

608

5'

600

Storm Is

Cape
Fanshaw

Mt Fa

27200

Bird

Cabin

Duck Pt

1000

330

Fanshaw Bay

Canoe Pt

Cape Fanshaw

1130

S.

600

FREDERICK

Pt Highland

Tar

330

600

Turnabout
Island

396

300

900

S.

216
Pinta
Rocks

Pinta Pt

Schooner

300

600

402

S.

632

Turn Mtn

2867

60

The waters of Southeast Alaska, Blying Sound and Prince William Sound offer good fishing for halibut, ranging from 20 to nearly 500 pounds. Use your own boat, or charter out of the nearest Gateway. Photo courtesy of John Sheedy/Mariah Charters.

Admiralty Cove is on the northern Admiralty Island coastline, accessible by boat or floatplane. One-way flight time from Juneau is approximately 30 minutes. Note: Floatplanes fly into Admiralty Cove only on high tide. (USGS Quad Map Juneau A-2)

Fishing

The nearby creek and tidal flats receive runs of anadromous cutthroat trout and coho, pink and chum salmon. Steelhead fishing is also good in late April and May. The water in the stream is very cold. Best fishing for silvers starts in late August; pinks and chums move in around mid-July and last until mid-August. It's possible to catch and release several limits of salmon a day during the peak of the run.

Other Activities

Deer hunting is popular, as is waterfowl, grouse and bear hunting.

Precautions

The trail to North Young Lake is unmaintained, so use at your own risk. There are 30 windfalls on the trail and 17 bridges. It takes approximately three hours to hike the trail one way.

Cabin

Admiralty Cove Cabin (CH-6)

Admiralty Cove cabin is a cozy, Pan Abode structure that was rebuilt in May 1983. The cabin is on relatively flat ground in a densely wooded, mature forest with a brushy understory. There's an interesting bit of history regarding the woodshed near the cabin. All the wood shakes were split by CCC employee Robert Barren in the 1930s. If you have lots of gear, use a backpack since it's a quarter-mile walk

Pink, chum and coho salmon action await anglers at Admiralty Island. Fish an incoming tide for best success.

from the landing beach to the cabin. The trail is in good shape. It's possible to motor a small boat or skiff from the tidal flats to the cabin on a 17-foot or greater tide. The cabin comfortably sleeps six people.

Water source: creek
Facilities:

- outhouse
- two single bunks
- two double bunks
- table
- bench
- cooking counter
- food cupboard
- shelves
- cooler
- wood stove
- woodshed
- wood supply
- ladder
- ax
- maul
- wedge
- no boat

User Comments:

(no date): "The cabin was clean and there was lots of dry wood. The water was high in the creek from all the rain, so we were able to get our 16-foot skiff to the cabin at high tide. Dollies, cutthroat and a few cohos in the creek. Duck hunting was fairly good. Heard some geese, but they flew on by. Saw bear tracks on the beach down from the trailhead. Later in the week, saw sow and cubs on the tidal flats. Saw no deer except on the last day, when spotted a doe and two fawns on trail. We were lucky to hit the one good week of decent weather in September. Had a great time."

5/2: "Hooters nearby, but evasive. Enjoyed full sunlight (no rain) the whole time. A little too early for steelhead run. Saw a large bear track, an otter and six deer. Also saw a few humpback whales on our departure. Enjoyed it. Great location!"

Admiralty Island has a large brown bear population, estimated to be one bear per square mile. Anglers should use caution when fishing the salmon streams in this area.

The Chilkoot Inlet is southeast of Haines in a spectacular panorama of mountains and fiords in the Upper Lynn Canal. Access is by wheeled plane, roughly 40 minutes from Juneau or 15 minutes from Haines. (USGS Quad Map Skagway A-1)

Fishing

Chilkoot Inlet offers saltwater fishing for salmon. Shore-bound anglers frequently catch silvers as the fish head up nearby rivers in August to spawn. Also available from shore are sockeye and pink salmon and Dolly Varden. A boat is necessary to find the best fishing.

Other Activities

Moose hunting, but no deer hunting available.

Precautions

Skiff access, but no protection for anchoring small craft. If flying in with your own plane, check with Juneau, Haines or Skagway pilots for the latest information on runway conditions.

Cabin

Katzehin Cabin (CH-23)

Katzehin cabin is on the east side of Chilkoot Inlet in relatively flat terrain surrounded by mature spruce rainforest. Unlike the standard USFS cabin, this one is "fine-tuned." Expect curtains, utensils and other items normally not found in cabins throughout the Tongass. The cabin sleeps six.

Located nearby is a 2,000-foot airstrip, with an unimproved, cross-wind runway with day markers and space for aircraft parking. The cabin is about one-eighth mile from the landing strip. A fire ring is available.

Water source: hand-pumped ground water
Facilities:

- two single bunks
- one double bunk
- loft (sleeps four)
- cooking counter
- food cupboard
- shelves
- wood stove
- woodshed
- wood supply
- shovel
- ax
- wedge
- maul
- outhouse
- no boat

User Comments:

7/16-7/18: "The southeast end of the airstrip is grown up, reducing the useable runway to 1500 feet. The northwest end of the runway has three bumps that could cause a problem. Cabin is stocked and well taken care of. Great weather, good time."

Distin Lake

Distin Lake, located on Admiralty Island, is in the central Admiralty Island National Monument Wilderness, and is part of the Admiralty Lakes Recreation Area Trail System for canoeists. Access is by either canoe or float plane. Chartered flight time from Juneau is 50 minutes, one way. (USGS Quad Map Sitka C-2)

Fishing

Cutthroat fishing is excellent, especially in and around the many bays. Anchor on the edge of the lily pads, and cast either flies or small spinning lures. Effective here is a small spinning bubble and Nos. 12 to 14 flies. Salmon eggs also work well. Distin's cutthroat trout can reach lengths to 17 inches. Try fishing the area creeks. The brush along the creek banks can be tough to break through at times, but the fishing is often worth the effort. Dolly Varden are also available in the deeper areas of the lake and in the streams.

Other Activities

The area is in the heart of some of the best wilderness exploring you'll find anywhere. After a day of fishing, take a few minutes to hike the trails that are kept in good condition by the USFS. Trails fan out in all directions. By taking a small "backpackable" inflatable, you can experience an exquisite, several-day adventure.

Take the Distin Lake Trail to Thayer Lake. Row south to the Freshwater Lake-Thayer Lake Trail. Row to the end of the lake. Spend time exploring the Salt Lake intertidal area before hitting the Mitchell Bay Trail. This will take you to Davidson Lake. Explore the lake to about mid-point, where a quarter-mile portage will have you back at Distin Lake. Sportsman cabin is also a popular base for deer hunters in the fall. Good berry picking in the area.

Cabins
Sportsman Cabin (CH-12)
Distin Lake Cabin (CH-14)

Look for Sportsman cabin on the northwest side of Distin Lake in a relatively flat, wooded area with a beach suitable for docking a boat or plane. This A-frame structure sleeps six people. Bunks are movable. A wood-burning stove is provided for heating and cooking.

Distin Lake cabin is an enclosed, Adirondack-style Civilian Conservation Corps structure in poor condition. It can sleep two people. The three-mile hike via trail to Thayer Lake offers an excellent sampling of southeast rain forest. The trail is well-maintained.

Water source: lake and stream at Sportsman cabin, lake at Distin Lake cabin

Facilities:
(CH-12):
- table
- bench
- outhouse
- cooking counter
- food cupboard
- shelves

- cooler
- wood stove
- woodshed
- wood supply
- oars
- two 14-foot semi-V boats

- bucket
- ladder
- ax
- maul
- wedge

(CH-14):
- food cupboard
- shelves
- four single bunks
- table
- bench
- cooking counter

- 14-foot V-bottom boat
- oars
- cooler
- wood stove
- woodshed
- wood supply

- ladder
- ax
- maul
- wedge

User Comments:
Sportsman Cabin:
7/1-7/3: "Cabin condition excellent. Found two dead mice in cabin. From July 1 through July 10 only one brief shower. Fishing was great in creek between Distin and Guerin. Also great at the falls on Hasselborg River. Saw lots of wildlife, including deer, a few ducks and one loon. Saw much more at Mitchell Bay. Had a wonderful trip."

Distin Lake Cabin:
11/1-11/3: "Cabin was in poor shape. Guests should carry hammer and nails. Rustic is not accurate. This place is a shack. Too late for fishing. Not enough snow for deer.

Distin Lake Sportsman Cabin. Photo courtesy USDA Forest Service.

Florence Lake

Florence Lake is a short distance inland from the coastal, western side of Admiralty Island National Monument Wilderness. Access is by floatplane. Charged flight time is roughly 50 minutes from Juneau or Sitka. (USGS Quad Map Sitka D-3)

Fishing

Florence Lake is known for its good to excellent fishing for large cutthroat trout and fair to good fishing for Dolly Varden. The inlet stream near West Florence cabin is good for cutts. Especially effective is trolling attractor lures and cowbells in front of the inlet stream. Fish a zig-zag pattern 10 to 50 feet from shore.

The outlet stream is another excellent place to fish, especially for Dolly Varden. The south side of the lake attracts and holds good populations of cutthroat. Try longline plugs or tiny black or gold Super Duper spoons. At East Florence Lake cabin, a one-mile trail leads to saltwater. Pink and chum salmon are plentiful in the lower outlet creek.

Other Activities

The area is profuse with blueberries, salmonberries and currants. Deer hunting is fair to good.

Precautions

The land surrounding Lake Florence is privately owned and cabin visitors must fill out self-issue permits to use Shee Atika Corporation lands. These can be obtained from the Forest Service.

Cabins
West Florence Cabin (CH-18)
East Florence Cabin (CH-19)

West Florence Lake cabin is a frame structure that sleeps four people. Situated on a small peninsula, the cabin can be reached via trail from either side. The terrain is relatively flat, with dense stands of spruce and hemlock forest with heavy moss undergrowth. Also on the peninsula are beaches for boat docking.

A large A-frame near a small stream, East Florence cabin is nestled in a flat, wooded area with a heavy understory of brush. It can handle six people comfortably. Boat pull-up and float plane docking areas are located directly in front of the cabin.

Water source: lake at West Florence cabin, lake and stream at East Florence
Facilities (CH-18) :

- outhouse
- four single bunks
- loft (sleeps three)
- table
- bench
- cooking counter
- food cupboard
- shelves
- cooler
- wood stove
- woodshed
- wood supply
- 16-foot Jon boat
- 14-foot semi-V boat
- oars
- ax and maul
- wedge
- ladder

(CH-19): Same as West Florence, except it has two double bunks

User Comments:

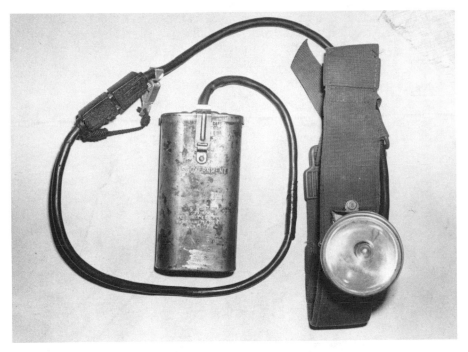

When fishing or hunting the dense rain forests of Admiralty Island, which has approximately one brown bear per square mile, a headlamp with battery pack is a must-have item, especially when traveling at dusk or dawn. The headlamp allows you to see where you are going while keeping both hands free for carrying fishing gear or rifle.

Gambier Bay is in southeast Admiralty Island National Monument Wilderness, to the left of Gambier and Romp islands. Access is via boat or float plane. Charged flight time from Juneau is 70 minutes. (USGS Quad Map Sumdum B-6)

Fishing

Directly in front of the cabin there's fair to good Dolly Varden fishing. From mid-August through September, coho salmon fishing is excellent. With a boat, you can reach the streams in and around Snug Cove that have good runs of pink and coho salmon. On an incoming tide, and for an hour or two after high tide, use flies with plenty of tinsel and/or small coho spoons.

Concentrate on areas with structures that compress migrating fish. These areas include Church Point and other points and peninsulas in and around the cabin. For anglers with a large boat, troll the outside bay for king and coho salmon, and deep-water jig for halibut off any of the islands. Also expect to catch chum and pink salmon, in addition to rockfish, near the rocky and submerged islands to the north and east of the cabin. You'll find cutthroat trout in the upper headwaters of the bay. Use caution when crossing the tidal flats.

Hunting

A good area for deer, waterfowl and bear hunting. Use cabin as a base camp. Use a deer call when heavy snowfall has pushed bucks into the timber. An inflatable boat and motor is a recommended means of hunting this area.

Church Bight cabin at Gambier Bay. Take an inflatable with outboard to reach the best fishing. Photo courtesy USDA Forest Service.

Other Activities

Blueberries are abundant near the cabin and along the fringes of the tidal flats. An excellent opportunity to explore intertidal areas.

Cabin

Church Bight Cabin (CH-16)

Church Bight is a saltwater cabin due to its close proximity to Gambier Bay (southeastern end). An A-frame capable of sleeping six to eight people, this cabin is popular among boaters. Although near saltwater, the cabin sits in old-growth forest and is surrounded by brushy understory and relatively flat terrain. The ground is covered with thick moss. Two freshwater streams are nearby.

Water source: streams
Facilities:

- one single bunk
- two double bunks
- loft
- no boat
- outhouse
- table
- bench
- cooking counter
- cooler (in back)
- wood stove
- woodshed
- wood supply
- bucket
- ax
- wedge

User Comments:

(no date) "Weather fantastic and zillions of horseflies on beach. Cabin in good condition. Lots of firewood and nice foam sleeping pads. Few mice, but not a problem if you keep food cleaned up and put away. No sign of bears or deer. Caught lots of halibut."

Hasselborg Creek, whose headwaters begin at Hasselborg Lake, is located in the central Admiralty Island Monument Wilderness. The river is part of the Admiralty Lakes Recreation Area Trail System. Access is by canoe or float plane. Charged flight time from Juneau is approximately 50 minutes, one way. (USGS Quad Map Sitka C-1)

Fishing

Lake fishing for cutthroat and Dolly Varden fishing is excellent right after ice-out, and as summer progresses, in Hasselborg Creek. This area receives some fishing pressure so please practice catch and release. In front of the cabin, and especially in and around the vicinity of any creeks (one right across the lake from the cabin) are excellent locations for catching cutthroats.

The weedy shoreline to the right of the cabin is a sure bet for a few fish during the evening hours. However, the largest cutthroats come from Hasselborg Lake, so concentrate your efforts near the lake narrows during mid-day. You'll also find fish, although small, hiding amid the lily pads on bright sunny days. Also, silver salmon fishing is good at the mouth of Hasselborg Creek. Steelhead fishing is fair to good in the lower section of stream. Try early May for best success. Pink and chum salmon fishing is good in the intertidal area.

Other Activities

The area is superb for hiking and exploration. Berry picking is excellent, as is wildlife viewing.

Cabin
Hasselborg Creek Cabin (CH-13)

Despite its simple construction, this rustic Adirondack cabin is small and cozy. It has a concrete floor, wood-burning stove and sleeps two. A small fireplace creates a homey atmosphere at day's end. The trail from the cabin to a free-use Adirondack shelter is three-tenths of a mile. From the shelter it is two miles to Guerin Lake. Since this cabin is at the "crossroads" of the Admiralty Lakes Trail System, you might receive unexpected visitors. On the average, don't expect any, especially late in the season. To reach the cabin from the lakeshore, you'll have to hop up a two-foot bank. Good central location for exploratory fishing.

Water source: lake
Facilities:

- outhouse
- two single bunks
- 16-foot Jon boat
- oars
- table
- bench
- cooking counter
- food cupboard
- shelves
- cooler
- wood stove
- fireplace
- woodshed
- wood supply
- ax
- maul
- wedge

User Comments:

(no date) "Wood stove works great, considering the stove is cracked half thru! We killed 11 mice, they weren't too bad a problem. Cabin has lots of holes; would probably be miserable in winter. Don't get me wrong: we loved it! Two slept on the two single bunks, and two slept on the floor. Weather was "partly cloudy with a chance..." and it was! Fishing: we turned too many loose and didn't keep count (true!). We brought home the three big ones and about 25 more. Saw one Canadian goose, mergansers, sea gulls and very fresh deer tracks in the morning in our boot tracks as we came back to the cabin after morning bite (that's when I got the 4-pound cutthroat). Also caught a 3.5-pound cutt in front of Shaheen, trolling 200 feet from the beach. Caught another by the snag at the top of the falls. Flying in we saw deer swimming across the lake—saw the same thing flying out."

(no date) "When it's over 80 degrees, sunny, and the fish still bite, it is very hard to complain. Everything in good shape in and around cabin. Excellent cutthroat fishing (mostly pan-size) in the river and in front of the cabin."

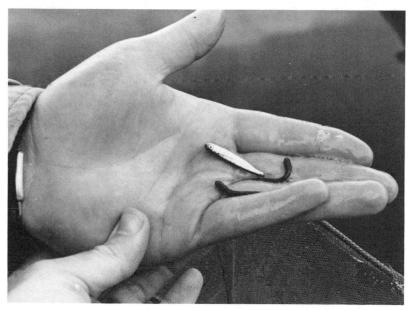

In many areas of southeast Alaska, cutthroats grow to large sizes, due to a diet of salmon smolt. Use Blue Smolt, Coronation and Jansen Minnow fly patterns.

Located in the central Admiralty Island National Monument Wilderness, Hasselborg Lake is part of the Admiralty Lakes Recreation Area Trail System for canoeists. Access is by canoe or float plane. Charged flight time from Juneau is approximately 50 minutes, one way. (USGS Quad Map Sitka C-1)

Fishing

Hasselborg is known for its good to excellent cutthroat trout fishing, both in the lake and in nearby streams. The southern end of the lake, along the shoreline grass and lily pads, is one of the best areas to fish. Those bordering drop-offs are prime locations for catching a trophy. The lake has a profusion of aquatic life. Leech and sculpin patterns are extremely effective on the larger cutts hiding in this vegetation. On dark days, spin anglers should troll a flutter spoon along the steep shoreline north of the cabin. Also try this technique during late evening and early morning hours.

Other Activities

The area receives a smattering of hikers during the summer months. In autumn, the area is a deer hunter's paradise. There is excellent berry picking near the cabin.

Cabins
Big Shaheen Cabin (CH-10)
Little Shaheen Cabin (CH-11)

The two-bedroom, Big Shaheen log chalet cabin was built by the Civilian Conservation Corps in the 1930s. The cabin lies in a relatively flat, wooded area, and offers a good view of the lake. It comfortably handles 8 to 10 people. This lake is one of the author's personal favorites due to the scenery, fishing and overall quality of experience.

Little Shaheen cabin, known as the mother-in-law cabin because it is within 100 yards of Big Shaheen cabin, can handle six people. It is a Pan Abode structure on a peninsula on the east side of Hasselborg Lake. An attractive cabin with beach, it offers an excellent view. A trail connects the two cabins.

Water source: lake
Facilities (CH-10) :

- four double bunks
- bench
- cooking counter
- shelves
- food cupboard
- cooler
- wood stove

- fireplace
- woodshed
- wood supply
- ladder
- saw
- bucket
- ax

- maul
- wedge
- broom
- 16' Jon boat
- 14' Lund boat with oars

Facilities (CH-11):

- two single bunks
- two double bunks
- cooking counter
- food cupboard
- shelves

- cooler
- wood stove
- woodshed
- wood supply
- 16' Jon boat

- outhouse
- oars
- ax
- maul
- wedge

User Comments:

(no date) "Fishing was great in rivers and okay on the lake in spots. Saw loons, marten, ducks and lots of mice. Saw bears on flight in, but not near the cabin. Wonderful vacation!"

(no date) "Could not have been any better. Saw signs of wildlife but nothing more. The cabin was absolutely delightful. The weather was perfect. Caught 20 fish in two days, so cannot complain. Will definitely do it again."

(no date) "The cabin was in excellent condition. Weather was excellent, first day was cloudy with misty rain, second day was mostly sunny, third day was clear skies. Caught 1, 17-inch and 2, 16-inch cutthroat trout in front of cabin. Caught 7 cutthroat and Dolly Varden above outlet falls; caught 30 cutthroat and Dolly Varden below outlet falls; caught six others at various lake locations. Saw a good variety of wildlife, no bears."

During midday, Hasselborg Lake cutthroats hole up near emergent aquatic vegetation. Use ultralight lures or flies for best success.

Jim's Lake

Jim's Lake is in the central Admiralty Island National Monument Wilderness and offers an excellent view of the nearby Yellow Bear Mountains. The area is remote and receives little pressure from hikers. Access is by float plane. Charged, one-way flight time from Juneau is about one hour. (USGS Quad Map Sitka C-1)

Fishing

The lake offers cutthroat trout and some Dolly Varden. A good area to fish is directly in front of the cabin near Jim's Creek. During mid-day, fish the far shoreline with deep-trolling gear or long-line flutter spoons along drop-offs. Also try dry flies or wet flies at the freshwater inlet at the end of the lake.

Hunting

There is good deer hunting at higher elevations in August and September. After the first few snowfalls, hunt the lower hillsides or from a spike camp for a better chance at bagging a large buck. Be prepared to spend at least three days on the mountainside in search of a trophy.

Cabin
Jim's Lake Cabin (CH-15)

This Lincoln-log type structure is roomy and can comfortably sleep six. The cabin is in a partial clearing surrounded by mature forest. There's a spacious beach for boat and airplane docking. Outdoor benches are positioned to overlook the lake and surrounding wilderness. A fire pit is nearby. Expect a moderately steep trail running from the beach area to the cabin.

Water source: lake, stream
Facilities:

- two single bunks
- two double bunks
- outhouse
- 16-foot Jon boat
- oars
- table

- bench
- cooking counter
- food cupboard
- shelves
- cooler
- wood stove

- woodshed
- wood supply
- ax
- maul
- wedge

User Comments:

9/24-9/28: "This was our first time into Jim's Lake, and we were very impressed. The cabin was in excellent condition and adequately housed five of us. Plenty of good wood and the ax and maul were in top condition. Weather was typically southeast. Fishing very good for small trout and even caught one at three-plus pounds. Deer hunting was also good, although the leaves this time of year are a bit of a problem. Deer seemed to be all over, with most of the concentration on top of Yellow Bear Mountain. Nice climb up around the creek half-way down the lake. Steep but quick."

10/12-10/15: "Plenty of wood, lots of fish in the lake. Deer were still up high, but got 11 between four of us. Freshwater clams on beach just on other side of the river next to cabin. Sunny and clear entire three days, I swear!"

The Dan Moller cabin is located in the upper Kowee drainage and designed primarily for winter use. To reach the cabin, take the three-mile Dan Moller Trail from the trailhead in west Juneau. Access by helicopter takes 10 minutes. Snowmobile and ATV access allowed only when there is adequate snow cover. (USGS Quad Map Juneau B-2)

Activities

Excellent cross country skiing and snowshoeing in the bowl area.

Cabin

Dan Moller Cabin (CH-1)

This cabin was originally built in the 1930s by the Civilian Conservation Corps as part of a combined effort by the Juneau Ski Club and the U.S. Forest Service to develop winter recreation in the area. The ski club operated a rope tow and erected a warming hut, and the cabin was used to accommodate overnight guests for many years.

The area was used for downhill skiing from 1939 through 1975, before Eaglecrest Ski Area was developed a ridge away. With the assistance and cooperation of the U.S. Forest Service, the cabin was restored in the winter of 1983-84 by the Vietnam Vets, the Taku Conservation Society, and the residents and merchants of Juneau. The winter snow entrance is at loft level on the south side of the cabin. From 10 a.m. to 5 p.m. daily during the winter, the cabin serves as a warming hut. Maximum two days rental.

Water source: Kowee Creek, one-quarter to three-eighths mile from cabin.
Facilities:
- loft (capable of sleeping 10)
- two single bunks
- two double bunks
- table
- bench
- cooking counter
- food cupboard
- shelves
- wood stove
- woodshed
- wood supply
- rake
- maul
- wedge
- bring own cooking stove & toilet paper.

Lake Alexander

Located on the east-central side of the Admiralty Island National Monument Wilderness, Lake Alexander is part of the Admiralty Lakes Recreation Area Trail System. Access is either by boat, and hiking the 2.3-mile trail from Mole Harbor, or via floatplane from Juneau. Charged flight time is about 50 minutes. (USGS Quad Map Sitka C-1)

Fishing

Fishing for cutthroats is good around the lake perimeter, especially in the deep-water areas near a point of land 100 yards from the cabin. The narrows offer fair fishing. The east end of Beaver Lake provides the most fishing action. Freshwater clams are in the gravel areas of the lake. A two-mile hike down to Mole Harbor offers excellent chum and pink salmon and Dolly Varden fishing. Reaching the trailhead requires a long row across the lake. Lake Alexander and Beaver Lake are connected by a narrow passage.

Other Activities

Good photo opportunities for bear on the Mole Harbor Flats, along with good beachcombing. Hiking trails are many, but an outboard is recommended to reach the far end of Beaver Lake. Good deer hunting.

Cabin
Lake Alexander Cabin (CH-21)

Lake Alexander cabin is a Pan Abode structure on a 25-foot high bluff overlooking Alexander Lake. The surrounding terrain is semi-open rain forest with numerous huckleberries and blueberries. The cabin sleeps six and has a beautiful view of the lake. Good beach for swimming, with morning sun for bathing. A fire ring is ideal for nightly campfires. From the cabin window, a full moon can sometimes be seen rising over the lake.

Water source: lake
Facilities:

- two single bunks
- two double bunks
- table
- bench
- cooking counter
- food cupboard
- shelves
- cooler
- wood stove
- woodshed
- wood supply
- 14-foot semi-V boat
- oars
- ladder
- ax
- wedge

User Comments:

7/27-8/1: "We were on our honeymoon (married 7/25) and this was definitely the "honeymoon cabin." Spacious, comfortable beds (bring pad) and scenic. Must work for the cutthroat. Orange and bronze-colored, 1/8-ounce Rooster Tails, orange and silver Little Cleos worked well. Best areas were the entrance to Beaver Lake and entrance to Hasselborg Lake. Small landlocked salmon (7 to 8 inches) along shoreline back to cabin from Hasselborg entrance. Saw immature eagles, loons and had marten, mice and frogs around cabin. Watch moon rise at night. Great!"

8/3-8/5: "Lake Alexander is a special place for my husband and I. Our first day there, we swam in the lake, which was a wonderful treat. (My first time skinny-dipping!) The water was quite warm. Near the shoreline tiny black tadpoles nipped at our leg hairs. They must have thought the hairs were little black worms. There were hundreds of tadpoles, all along the shoreline. Fishing was good in and around the lily pads. (Thousands of lily pads, with beautiful golden-yellow flowers!) Had to use small lures and flies. Evening was the best time for catching cutthroats. We had a small outboard, and motored to the end of Beaver Lake, and took the trail to Hasselborg Lake. Along the way, we found freshwater clams and watched a mink scurrying along the creek. He looked up, saw me, paused, and for several moments, we made eye-to-eye contact. A very special experience. Later that evening we built a large campfire outside the cabin in the firepit. The heat and light attracted the frogs in the vicinity. Several attempted to jump into the fire, but we saved them. Didn't want to leave this cabin, there was still so much to see and explore. We'll be back. Oh, yes! How could I forget the bowl of huge, ripe blueberries picked just outside the door of the cabin. I'd love to spend all summer here."

Lake Alexander offers solitude as well as good fishing for cutthroat trout. To best enjoy the area and its attractions, take a small 3-hp outboard and a minimum of three gallons of gasoline.

Lake Kathleen is on the northwestern end of the Admiralty Island National Monument Wilderness, about seven miles north of Lake Florence. The lake is surrounded by mature forests of spruce, cedar and hemlock and an impressive range of mountains and hills. In front of the cabin is a small beach for relaxing. Accessible by float plane from Juneau. Flight time is approximately 45 minutes, one way. (USGS Quad Map Sitka D-3)

Fishing

Expect fair to good fishing for kokanee and Dolly Varden. In early morning and late evening, the east end of the lake offers the best success. During mid-day, fish the dropoff in front of the runoff streams near the cabin. The far west end of the lake produces good catches of Dollies in the 18-inch category. Troll tiny Flatfish, Mirro-Lures or wobbling plugs for best success. Cutthroat fishing: fly fishermen should try green midges, caddis or stonefly nymphs fished with a sink-tip line.

Other Activities

Deer hunting is fair to good in late fall. Prime area for wilderness exploration.

Precautions

Lake Kathleen is surrounded by private lands belonging to Shee Atika Corporation. Permit holders must fill out self-issue permits. These can be obtained through the Forest Service. Recently, much of the surrounding forested lands have been harvested.

Cabin
Lake Kathleen Cabin (CH-9)

This small, A-frame cabin is nestled in a remote section of wilderness rain forest where you're unlikely to receive any human visitors. It's common to see squirrels, grouse and other wildlife during the early morning hours, especially at the east end of the lake. The cabin can comfortably sleep six people.

Water source: lake
Facilities:

- two single bunks
- loft
- table
- bench
- cooking counter
- food cupboard
- shelves
- cooler
- wood stove
- woodshed
- wood supply
- 16-foot Jon boat
- oars
- ladder
- shovel
- bucket
- ax
- wedge
- maul
- outhouse

User Comments

9/12-9/14: "Weather was perfect. Clear skies all three days. The cabin was in good shape. Lots of wood, some food, toilet paper, matches, and a few other things had been left here by others. Caught 10 Dollies, one 22-inch, 3 1/2-pounder; one 19-inch and 1½ pounds. Others were a bit smaller. No bear signs except a few tracks a ways from the cabin. They weren't fresh. Enjoyed the boat, but an outboard would be nice."

11/7-11/11: "Didn't fish but saw lots of small ones jumping. Got one deer and saw about 8 others during our stay. Had one bear incident at dusk along the shore on the opposite side of the lake from the cabin. No harm done; scared him as bad as he scared the hunters. Good weather: two overcast with little rain, two days clear. Cabin in good condition, except handle of stove comes off sometimes. Plenty of dry wood, plus three comfortable sleeping pads. No live mice, just two long-dead ones in the cabin's holey coffee pot. Take a motor for the boat. You'll be glad you did. The resident marten in the vicinity of this cabin is quite fiesty. You can thwart his attempts to get your deer, though. Hang the deer from the east side of the porch so that the head is tied to the front cabin wall. That way, you can hear the marten jumping against the side of the cabin at night, and you can bang on the wall. Don't be surprised when he growls back at you. He will. Also, at dusk, watch the bats feeding along the lake."

Lake Kathleen cabin. Photo courtesy USDA Forest Service.

Laughton Glacier

Laughton Glacier drains into Warm Pass Valley, and is located within three miles of the U.S./Canada border. From Skagway, take the White Pass and Yukon Railroad for 12 miles to Glacier Station. There you take the two-mile Laughton Glacier Trail. The trail is in good condition. Distance from Skagway to the glacier moraine is approximately 14 miles. (USGS Quad Map Skagway B-1)

Activities

The area is a prime location for wilderness exploration. This is a total rest and relaxation cabin. Cutthroat trout are occasionally found throughout the area, along with isolated populations of whitefish.

Cabin
Laughton Glacier Cabin (CH-22)

This Pan Abode cabin, located in a small stand of black spruce in relatively hilly terrain, can sleep six. Because the cabin is seldom used, cut wood is not provided. Laughton Glacier is a premier location for the ultimate get-away from civilization or if you're inclined to explore glacial moraines. The cabin is a short hike from the glacier. Five stars for scenic beauty. The cabin can be reserved at the Klondike National Historical Park office in Skagway, located in the old White Pass and Yukon Route Railroad Depot, in addition to regional Forest Service offices.

Water source: stream
Facilities:

- two single bunks
- two double bunks
- table
- bench

- cooking counter
- shelves
- wood stove
- no wood supply

- bring own fuel
- no boat

User Comments:

6/10-6/12: "Cabin is in fairly good repair. Streams are high and those from glacier very turbid, so no fishing attempted. Fresh sign of moose on trail in from railroad to about 200 yards from cabin. No bear sign."

7/13-7/15: "The cabin was very clean. There are several large trees that have fallen across the trail. Saw some bear sign but no bears. The weather was perfect. Laughton Glacier is a piece of heaven!"

From Juneau, take the highway north to Auke Bay. Park your car at the Spaulding Trailhead for a three-mile hike to the cabin, located in a sub-alpine valley above Mendenhall Valley. The trail winds through muskeg, which makes for oftentimes wet hiking during the summer months. Wear ankle-fit hip boots. Helicopter access from Juneau is 10 minutes. Cabin is used chiefly for winter recreation. (USGS Quad Map Juneau B-2)

Fishing

There is no fishing in the immediate vicinity of this cabin. However, anglers on a bare-bones budget have stayed in the cabin and fished the road system during the day.

Precautions

When starting out, follow the blue diamonds 100 yards past the end of the board walk. There, you'll find a trail marked with orange flagging. Contact USFS for trail information.

Cabin

John Muir Cabin (CH-3)

This log cabin is designed especially for winter sports use. The loft can sleep up to eight people. Additionally, two single bunks and three double bunks are available, for a total capacity of 16 people. The cabin has a wood-burning stove for heating and cooking. Maximum two nights rental. Cabin is open to the public as a warming hut between 10 a.m. and 5 p.m. daily throughout the winter.

Water source: Winter: none, bring your own. Summer: Auk Nu Creek, three-eighths mile down the trail.

Facilities:

- table
- bench
- cooking counter
- shelves
- cooler
- wood stove
- woodshed
- wood supply
- ladder
- outhouse
- saw
- ax
- wedge
- maul
- kerosene lamp (bring oil)

Peterson Lake

Juneau's Peterson Lake is accessible via the trailhead at Mile 24, Old Glacier Highway. The trail is 4.2 miles long, one way. (USGS Quad Map Juneau)

Fishing

Coho salmon are available in the lower stretches of Peterson Creek. The USFS indicates Peterson also has cutthroat trout and Dolly Varden, along with a few steelhead in the spring months.

Cabin

Peterson Lake Cabin (CH-24)

Peterson Lake cabin is one of Juneau's newest, and it's capable of sleeping six. It's in a clearing surrounded by mature hemlock and spruce forest with a dense understory of downfall and moss growth overlooking Peterson Lake. Maximum two nights rental.

Water source: stream
Facilities:

- two single bunks
- two double bunks
- table
- bench
- cooking counter

- food cupboard
- shelves
- cooler
- wood stove
- woodshed

- wood supply
- ax
- maul
- wedge
- no boat

User Comments:

11/7-11/8: ''Hike in was very difficult with packs, due to terrain/weather/ice on boardwalks and heavy mud. Took almost three hours each way. Cabin in good condition, with ample pots, frying pan, some foodstuffs. Stove gives off plenty of heat. Weather 30 degrees with sheet ice on lake.''

Whether you bring your own food, or plan to catch it from the stream, Forest Service cabins provide the means to enjoy the splendors of Alaska, while having the many comforts of ''home'' at your disposal.

Throughout most of Alaska, pink salmon fishing is excellent during July or early August. Intertidal areas offer the best fishing.

Pybus Bay

Pybus Bay is in the southeastern Admiralty Island National Monument Wilderness. From Juneau, access is by boat or float plane. Charged flight time from Juneau is about one hour, one way. Floatplanes can land in the bay at high tide. (USGS Quad Map Sitka B-1)

Fishing

Excellent chum and pink salmon fishing in Donkey Bay, a 45-minute hike via bear trail from the cabin. Trail is marked but not maintained. Follow shoreline at low tide, but return route may be under water at high tide, so plan accordingly. For the best action, fish the channel running through the tidal flats. The stream also receives a fair run of coho salmon. Dolly Varden are found at the mouths of streams and near sandy and pebble beaches. Within the bay itself there's king and coho salmon fishing. Halibut and rockfish fishing is excellent. Fly-in anglers should take an inflatable boat.

Other Activities

Good shelling and beachcombing within a half-mile of the cabin. For the naturalist, the area has yellow wood violets in May. Berry pickers favor the area for its ample supply of blueberries and currants. A delightful cabin, away from the hustle and bustle of civilization. Abundant wildlife.

Precautions

Take tide table for planning activities, especially if you cut across tidal flats at low tide. Also, bears are plentiful in the area. Bear protection a must.

Pybus Bay cabin. Nearby streams offer excellent fishing for pink and chum salmon. Bears are plentiful throughout the area, so use caution.

Cabin

Pybus Bay Cabin (CH-17)

Nice, A-frame cabin tucked away in mature rain forest about 50 yards from the bay. Good supply of firewood and fire ring outside the cabin. The surrounding forest is mature timber with a heavy understory of berries and brush. Surrounding terrain is hilly behind cabin, flat in front. The bank leading up to the cabin is semi-steep, but not difficult. An opening through the timber allows you to view a section of the bay. Cabin comfortably sleeps six to eight people, and receives good sun during the summer months.

Water source: creek
Facilities:

- four double bunks
- loft
- outhouse
- table
- bench
- cooking counter
- shelves
- cooler
- wood stove
- woodshed
- wood supply
- ladder
- sledge
- ax
- maul
- wedge
- no boat

User Comments

8/1-8/5: "Cabin in excellent condition. Weather very good. Cool enough at night for campfire. Fished stream at Donkey Bay. Caught two salmon, could have caught a lot more. They were really biting. Saw lots of eagles at Donkey Bay. Walked about a mile upstream and saw some up close. Lots of bear sign at Donkey Bay: trails, prints, scat, fish parts. Only saw two: one in stream, the other in grassy area. Both left quickly."

Seymour Canal is on the northwest corner of Admiralty Island, about 23 miles south of Juneau. Year-round access to the cabin is by either boat or floatplane. Flight time is roughly 15 minutes from Juneau, one way. The closest and most convenient landing area for aircraft and anchorages for boats is Olivers Inlet. Boaters should follow Gastineau Channel south out of Juneau and traverse Stephens Passage from Marimon Point to Olivers Inlet. (USGS Quad Map Juneau A-1)

Fishing

Salmon spawn in two nearby streams from July through September. Saltwater fishing for halibut, rockfish and salmon is good in nearby bays and channels. A boat is necessary to find the best fishing. Dollies can be caught in intertidal areas. Use silver spoons or spinners for best success.

Other Activities

Bear watching is good while salmon are spawning during late July and through August. There are excellent salmonberry patches near the cabin, and muskeg meadows for the botanist. The tramway crosses several of these meadows before ending in an esturine meadow near Seymour Inlet. Seymour Canal has the greatest known concentration of nesting bald eagles in the world, averaging more than one nest per mile of coast line. Photograph blacktailed deer, harbor seals, whales and sea lions, who all use the canal year-round. Trumpeter swans, whistling swans and other migratory waterfowl stop at the island. Admiralty Island National Monument, adjacent to Olivers Inlet State Marine Park, is noted for having one of the largest brown bear populations in southeast Alaska.

Seymour Canal offers myriad photographic opportunities for the novice as well as professional photographer.

Precautions

Olivers Inlet has a constricted entrance and a rock reef which requires a high tide of 10 to 12 feet to motor across. Boaters should exercise caution when entering the inlet and reduce their speed to handle the conditions. When the tide is changing, the entrance to Olivers Inlet resembles a river, with the current flowing in or out from Stephens Passage. Boats anchoring in Olivers Inlet have protection in six fathoms of water, and from predominant southeasterly winds. A 17- to 18-foot tide is required to launch a boat at the end of the tram on Seymour Canal. A 15-foot tide is needed to launch a boat on the Olivers Inlet Side.

Cabin

Seymour Canal Cabin (CH-20)

This saltwater cabin was built on Alaska state park land. It is on a relatively flat area of forest near a grassy, saltwater beach within the Olivers Inlet State Marine Park. A hand-powered tram car helps you carry personal gear and small water craft as you make the one-mile walk across the tramway to Seymour Canal and the cabin. The cabin is a Pan Abode structure capable of sleeping six people. Area surrounding the cabin is relatively flat, with mountains near the coast that rise up 2,000 feet. Also within view is alpine tundra with rock outcroppings and ice fields. Check-out time is noon. You must have in your possession a recreation cabin permit authorizing you to use the cabin on the dates specified. Contact Alaska State Parks, 400 Willowby, Juneau, 99801 (907) 465-4563.

Water source: stream

Facilities:

- two single bunks
- two double bunks
- table
- bench
- cooking counter
- food cupboard
- shelves
- cooler
- wood stove
- woodshed
- wood supply
- ladder
- no boat
- ax
- sledge
- maul
- wedge

The Taku River is a large watershed that winds through the Alaska Panhandle before finally entering Canada. The upper end is extremely rugged and impassable on foot. Access is by floatplane or shallow-keeled riverboat with jet unit. If you fly in, the USFS recommends that you take a small inflatable boat. High water often prevents fly-in parties from reaching the cabin once they've been dropped off. Chartered flight time from Juneau is 45 minutes. The flight into the area is dazzling, with 4,500-foot mountains and glaciers creating a panoramic view. (USGS Quad Map C-6)

Fishing

Expect good cutthroat and Dolly Varden fishing in the many clearwater streams and in Moose Creek and Yehring Creek nearest the cabin. Dollies smash salmon egg patterns in peach and light pink. Fish the flies unweighted on the bottom and along clearwater/glacial water breaklines. Dead-drifting these patterns through the shallow riffles is another excellent tactic. During early August, pink salmon fishing is good. Be sure to bring your own boat.

Other Activities

This cabin is a popular base camp with moose hunters.

Cabin

Spruce Cabin (CH-2)

Spruce cabin is a lincoln-log structure within five miles of the U.S./Canada border. The cabin is located on a riparian plain surrounded by a mature stand of timber. It comfortably sleeps six people. A deep-water bog surrounds the cabin and is impassable on foot after heavy rains. When traveling by boat, look for the marker on the right shore, that indicates a trail to the cabin. Also, wear hip boots on your initial trip in. There is a small stream to cross near the cabin.

Water source: hand-pumped ground water
Facilities:

- two single bunks
- two double bunks
- table
- bench
- cooking counter
- food cupboard
- shelves
- cooler
- wood stove
- woodshed
- wood supply
- ladder
- bucket
- ax
- maul
- wedge
- no boat

Located about a quarter-mile from Taku Inlet, Turner Lake is part of the Turner Lake watershed. Access from Juneau is by float plane or boat and hiking a good trail for eight-tenths of a mile. Charged flight time is approximately 35 minutes, one way. The topography here resembles Norway's fiords, with steep rock cliffs dropping into the lake. Dense rain forest stretches from lake shore to timberline at about 2,500 feet. (USGS Quad Map Taku B-6)

Fishing

Turner Lake offers excellent fishing for Dolly Varden and trophy cutthroat trout up to four pounds. Fishing for both is good in the outlet stream at the base of the falls. Pink, silver and king salmon can be caught in Taku Inlet along with rockfish and halibut. The outlet stream receives a good run of pink salmon. It's possible to catch and release 25 or more fish per day with no boat. However, you need a boat to catch these species in saltwater.

Fishing from shore in Taku Inlet near the cabin is difficult because of extensive tidal flats. When fish are not in the shallows, try deep-water trolling with plugs off the point of land directly north by northwest of the cabin. Farther east you'll find excellent areas to fly fish for cutts. During periods of hot, sunny weather, look for fish holding in the creek. Also, try fishing near the runoffs that empty into the lake. Dollies are plentiful at the lake outlet, especially from July through October. A flutter technique will often catch cruising cutts when standard techniques fail. Egg clusters work well on trout and Dollies when salmon are spawning.

Turner Lake is a popular destination for residents as well as visitors. Rugged mountains surround the lake, which offers cutthroat trout up to four pounds. Photo by Neil Hagadorn, USDA Forest Service.

Other Activities

Salmonberry and blueberry picking is good in the marshy areas and along the beach fringe. Boat to the west end of the lake and hike eight-tenths of a mile to the inlet where mussels, crabs and other marine life wait to be discovered.

Precautions

Keep a clean camp. In August, bears travel through the area searching for berries and salmon. This lake is generally one of the last to thaw in this region so check with your air charter service before flying out. If you're using a boat to reach Turner Lake, use caution when nearing the stream outlet emptying into Taku Inlet. It is very shallow for one to one-and-a-half miles and can only be navigated at high tide. You must follow the channel. Safe anchorage is approximately 40 yards downstream from the first rapids. The pool directly below the rapids is turbulent at low tide.

Cabins
West Turner Lake Cabin (CH-4)
East Turner Lake Cabin (CH-5)

The Civilian Conservation Corps built the West Turner Lake cabin on a solid rock outcropping near the lake. A log chalet structure that can sleep six, it is unique because of its ample closet space and a rock fireplace. A mature rain forest surrounds the cabin, creating a cozy atmosphere. The steep bluff across the lake offers spectacular photographic opportunities, especially in early morning and late evening when the entire lake is ablaze with an orange glow. Snow banks usually remain on some parts of the lake shore. Use the snow as an ice supply to keep food cool.

East Turner Lake cabin is a Pan Abode structure located in a relatively flat area. It is surrounded by dense rain forest and steep-walled mountains, some rising to over 4,000 feet. A good choice for scenery and remoteness. The cabin sleeps six and comes with a wood-burning stove for heating and cooking.

Water source, both cabins: stream and lake
Facilities (West Turner) :

- two single bunks
- two double bunks
- loft (not for sleeping)
- two boats
- oars
- table
- bench

- cooking counter
- food cupboard
- shelves
- cooler
- wood stove
- fireplace
- woodshed

- wood supply
- shovel
- ax
- maul
- wedge

(East Turner) :

- two single bunks
- two double bunks
- outhouse
- aluminum flat-bottom skiff
- oars
- table
- bench

- cooking counter
- food cupboard
- shelves
- cooler
- wood stove
- fireplace
- woodshed

- wood supply
- ladder
- saw
- ax
- sledge
- wedge

User Comments:

(no date) "Fishing good. Caught mainly cutthroats on Dardevles while trolling along shoreline. Largest went 3¾ pounds, several between 1 and 2 pounds."

(no date) "Cabin in very good condition. Recommend bringing some kind of mattress or pad for bunks. Weather excellent. Must have hit 80 degrees and bright sunshine. Hot enough for swimming. Water is cold. Caught some small salmon and a couple of trout. Fish bit instantly on egg clusters, but I only had a couple from the salmon I caught. Without clusters, the trout followed spinners without striking."

(no date) "The cabin was in excellent condition. The party before us left it super clean. Weather was super. Almost too hot for anything...no shortage of bugs...fishing was excellent...nothing big...14 inches...but no shortage of fish either...no problem catching enough to eat...and bring home our limits. Odd thing this year...did not catch one Dolly. First time this has happened. No bear, or sign of, around camp. No wildlife seen at all except for the loons, and the seagulls with two young ones and a merganser with broods. Lots and lots of kokanee. Must have caught and released 50 or more. All taken on mosquito fly #12. Some fun."

7/1-7/4: "Weather mixed. Some showers, two magnificent days. Came in by boat. Lots of packing! Fly-in is the way to go. "Kleppered" around the lake, a great experience. Fishing very good. Caught a 3 1/2-pound cutthroat while trolling. Lots of pan-sized trout, salmon on flies. An unforgettable experience."

7/9-7/13: "Mostly rain and bugs, but the scenery made up for them for us visitors from the Lower 48. Boats, tools, oars in great shape. Wear raingear on trail to inlet, especially if leaves are wet. Compacted snowslide 3 miles up lake on north side. Carry splitting maul to collect camp ice. Blueberries almost ready, and cutthroats and Dollies very tasty when baked in foil with lemon, butter, salt and pepper."

8/2-8/4: "Cabin was great. Lots of dry wood. The weather was clear and hot. Fishing was fantastic. We caught lots of cutthroat and landlocked salmon. There was a beaver swimming in front of the cabin and a black bear about a mile north of the cabin. It was a fantastic trip."

8/21-8/25: "Couldn't see the scenery because it rained! It rained steady, hard and loud. Lake rose almost four inches in three days. Waterfalls were magnificent. Fishing in the river was great. We hit a run of pinks and lots of Dolly Varden. Also, five seals in the inlet and lots of birds—and rain. Cabin in good shape. Good idea to take a stove along to cook on. Fishing in lake poor due to high water. No bears. Even with the rain, we had a great, soggy time."

8/27-8/30: "Cabin was in clean condition. Area was abundant with blueberries. Saw no wildlife. Cutthroat fishing out the back of the cabin was terrific! The river was full of fresh pinks, not many Dollies yet. The waterfalls were spectacular. Went full perimeter of lake on 4 hp outboard in about 6 hours, taking it easy for sightseeing. Skiff was in good condition, one was not so good. We (2 dads and 2 boys) had a great time."

Young Lake

Young Lake is on the north end of Admiralty Island just east of Admiralty Cove. The lake is accessible by boat and hiking trail from Admiralty Cove, or by floatplane. Flight time from Juneau is 30 minutes, one-way. (USGS Quad Map Juneau A-2).

Fishing

Dolly Varden, cutthroat trout and kokanee fishing is good. Trail leads to steelhead fishing at Admiralty Cove. Most fly fishermen fish the lake and stream for cutts and Dollies. Fishing here ranges from fair to very good. Longlining spoons and plugs is often considered the best tactic for catching cutthroats from this lake. Dolly Varden overwinter in the lake. Pink, silver and chum salmon available in the lower outlet creek. Fish an incoming tide for best success.

Other Activities

Deer and bear hunting is good during their respective seasons. Deer hunting often requires a strenuous 2,000-foot hike to nearby mountaintops. Good berry picking, especially elderberry and blueberries.

Precautions

The trail to Admiralty Cove is unmaintained. Use at your own risk. There are approximately 30 windfalls and 17 bridges. Takes about three hours to hike, one way.

Cabins
North Young Lake (CH-7)
South Young Lake (CH-8)

North Young Lake cabin (sometimes called John Kennedy cabin) is a lincoln-style log structure that can sleep six people. The lake has a long beach bordered by heavy brush. A stream is nearby, along with muskeg that you'll need hip boots to explore.

Built in 1981, South Young Lake is a frame cabin that sits at the base of some of the tallest mountains on Admiralty Island. Many claim that the view from this cabin is the most scenic on all of Admiralty. The cabin has two lower double bunks and two single upper bunks that can sleep six comfortably. There is a beach a short walk away where you can load and unload your floatplane easily, and tie it down.

Dolly Varden fishing is good in Young Lake and at Admiralty Cove. Although Dollies can be caught year-round, the best time is from late July through freeze-up.

Water source: lake
Facilities (North Young Lake):

- two single bunks
- two double bunks
- bench
- cooking counter
- food cupboard
- shelves

- cooler
- wood stove
- woodshed
- wood supply
- ladder
- shovel

- ax
- maul
- wedge
- outhouse
- two boats
- oars

(South Young Lake):

- two double bunks
- two single bunks
- table
- bench
- cooking counter
- wood supply
- woodshed

- wood stove
- cooler
- shelves
- food cupboard
- 14-foot Jon boat
- oars
- ladder

- shovel
- ax
- wedge
- maul
- outhouse

User Comments

9/26: "Cabin in good shape. One set of oars fine. Weather was superb! Sunny during the day: 60 degrees plus! The northern lights were out at night. Couldn't be better. Fishing was sporadic. Caught a big cutthroat, but couldn't put it into the boat. Hadn't planned on serious fishing, and had no net. Broke my line as I pulled it toward boat. So there's a nice fish out there with a hook and line still in its mouth. Saw otter, eagle and sign of deer. Great, relaxing trip."

10/19: "Cabin in good shape. Rain nearly every day. High southeast winds also. No fresh bear sign. Mice have found their way into "refrigerator box" on side of cabin. Deer are all up high (2,000-feet plus). Hunted five days, got four deer."

(no date) "Cabin was in great shape! Need new maul and oar holders fixed on the boat. The weather was a bit rainy off and on, but that kept the bugs to a minimum. The fishing in the lake was unsuccessful, but we hiked down the creek at the north end and the trout fishing was fantastic in the creek. Fresh deer tracks on the trail, and bear sign, but didn't see any in the 'flesh.' Lots of beavers!"

(no date) "The cabin was clean and squared away when we arrived. Of our three days there, it was about half rain and drizzle and half partly sunny and overcast. Not bad, not great. Fishing was decent, but only small cutthroat. Only caught about a dozen, released seven. The largest was about 10 inches. I would have loved to have had the gear to go very deep and see if there are any large cutthroat out there. The beaver was very entertaining and the loons lent a true sense of wilderness to the scene. Also saw a kingfisher on several occasions and one doe with twin fawns. No bear, or sign of any, was around. Our Coleman cooking stove and lantern kept the cabin plenty warm. Left the cabin as we found it. The sense of wilderness was rudely shattered though, when five guys came in as we left with umpteen cases of beer, guns, a TV and a VCR with a generator to run it."

(no date) "Cabin was in great shape. Weather incredible...suntans too! Best fishing seems to be to the south at the beaver dam on other side of the lake. We caught around 50 cutthroat in 4 days, but put some back. One was about 12 inches long and delicious. Plenty of waterfowl and beaver. Oh yes, single salmon eggs or belly strips catch the most fish."

7 Gateway Skagway
Fishing the TONGASS National Forest

About the Gateway

Haines and Skagway are located at the northern end of the Inside Passage. In 1881, Haines was established when thousands of prospectors flocked there to reach the Klondike gold fields. Haines is one of the towns on the southeast Alaska ferry system that is connected to interior Alaska by road. Each year, from October through January, as many as 1,500 bald eagles gather to feed on a late chum salmon run in the Chilkat River.

Skagway began with a population of two in 1897. With the Klondike Gold Rush, that population jumped to 10,000 in less than a year. This is the take-off point to see the famous Chilkoot Trail, one of the most famous hiking trails in Alaska.

Population: Haines: 1,800   Skagway: 900
Annual Precipitation: 53 inches
Average Summer High Temperature: 64.9 degrees

Fishing the Haines/Skagway Area

The marine chinook fishery in the Haines area runs from midApril through early June. Later in the year, a marine fishery also exists for coho salmon and halibut. Most of the marine fishery takes place within 10 miles of Haines. Portage Cove and Lutak Inlet on the Chilkoot side of town are popular fishing areas, while on the Chilkat River side, Seduction Point to Letnikof Point offer good fishing for salmon.

Anglers find good fishing for pink and coho salmon and Dolly Varden off the beaches of the Chilkat Peninsula. Try surf casting for Dollies from June through October, pinks in July and August and coho in late August through early October.

Chilkoot Lake and River supports one of the largest freshwater sportfisheries in Alaska. The road-accessible fishery takes place primarily in the outlet lagoon and stream area. The majority of anglers are non-residents who harvest mostly pink, sockeye and coho salmon and Dolly Varden. The peak of the coho fishery generally takes place around October 12, with campgrounds and road-side pull-offs and area hotels filled with anglers intent on catching salmon.

The Chilkat River, although glacial in nature, is also fished for coho and chum salmon. It is a popular Dolly Varden water in late March and April. Chilkat Lake offers excellent fishing for cutthroat trout and Dolly Varden, and considered by many to be the finest in this region. Mosquito Lake offers relatively unexploited fishing for Dolly Varden and cutthroat trout. Located six miles northwest of Klukwan, this lake is popular with ice fishermen. Round whitefish are also available. Skagway offers limited sportfishing opportunities. At a slough near its mouth, the Taiya River offers fair fishing for Dolly Varden. Numerous lakes in the region have trout populations that receive minimal fishing pressure.

For information on recreational cabins in this area, contact:

Juneau District Ranger, Tongass National Forest, 8465 Old Dairy Road, Juneau, Alaska 99803, (907) 586-8800.

Fishing Index

Forest Service cabins in this gateway are listed below. The types of fish available in the vicinity of the cabin are indicated. You can cross-reference the cabin by the F.S. #, a number assigned to each cabin by the Forest Service. A description of the cabin and its facilities can be found on the page listed on the chart, and the page number of the map showing the exact cabin location is listed in the last column.

Gateway 7 — Skagway

Cabin	F.S. #	Page	Cutthroat Trout	Dolly Varden	Grayling	Rainbow Trout	Steelhead	Chinook Salmon	Coho Salmon	Chum Salmon	Pink Salmon	Sockeye Salmon	Halibut	Rockfish	Map pg.
Green Top Harbor Cabin	H-1	255	•			•				•			•	•	252
Salt Lake Bay Cabin	H-2	256		•				•	•	•	•	•			253

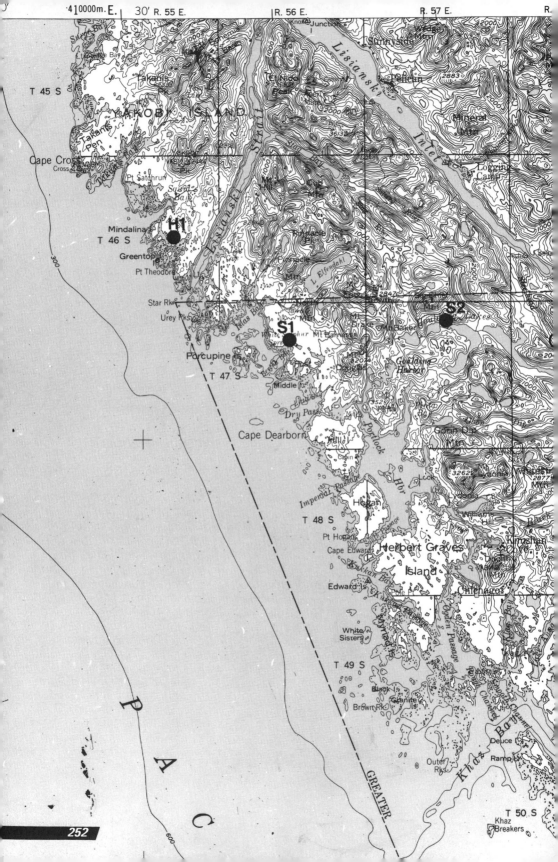

Green Top Harbor is about 70 miles northwest of Sitka. The cabin is on the southwest corner of Yakobi Island, 70 miles northwest of Sitka and roughly the same distance from Juneau. Flight time from either Juneau or Sitka is about 50 minutes, one way. (USGS Quad Map Sitka D-8)

Fishing

Excellent halibut fishing. Good freshwater coho salmon fishing in nearby Takanis Bay. Rainbow and cutthroat trout and sockeye salmon are in the Takanis watershed. A boat is necessary for fishing.

Other Activities

The cabin is a welcome stop for people kayaking along the outer coast of Yakobi Island, which is part of the West Chichagof-Yakobi Wilderness. The most dramatic feature of this area is the rugged Pacific coastline, characterized by exposed, wind-swept, offshore islands and rugged, blocky highlands. The area supports a variety of wildlife, including Sitka blacktailed deer and brown bear. View large sea lion rookeries at White Sister Islands, Cape Cross and Cape Bingham. Seals inhabit most of the coastline.

Precautions

When entering Green Top Harbor by boat, use charts. The harbor has many hidden rocks and is a trick to navigate. Floatplanes can land easily in the bay to the right of the cabin. Safe taxi water lies below the cabin. Also, streams may be low at certain times of the year, so bring your own water.

Beachcombing, as well as salmon and trout fishing, awaits recreationists visiting the West Chichagof-Yakobi Wilderness area. Take a small daypack for collectibles, lunch and gear.

Cabin
Green Top Harbor Cabin (H-1)

Green Top Cabin is an attractive, yet rustic structure built by an old fisherman in the 1940s. A handful of permanent residents live nearby. A flagged trail goes to Lisianski Straight. There is a nice scenic view from the cabin. A wood-burning stove is furnished for heating and cooking.

Water source: stream
Facilities:

- three single bunks
- one double bunk
- two tables
- chairs

- outside cooler
- wood stove
- wood supply
- ax

- broom
- dustpan
- no boat
- counter

User Comments:

6/7: "Wonderful cabin, great change of pace from standard USFS-built structure. I'm shocked at the number of people who refuse to financially support their use of Green Top. I hope the buildings can be properly maintained and preserved. The wood cookstove allowed us to prepare a scrumptious meal. The trail to Lisianski Straight is nice, but rough enough that boaters should know they'll need a backpack to haul their gear, rather than trying to carry an armload of boat bags or loose equipment. Trail is very wet, and needs more flagging in a few places, especially at straight-end trailhead."

Salt Lake Bay

Salt Lake Bay is on the south shore of Port Frederick, 15 miles southwest of the town of Hoonah on northcentral Chichagof Island. It is 65 miles north of Sitka, or 50 miles southeast of Juneau. Access is by boat or float plane. Flying time charged is 45 minutes from Juneau or Sitka, 10 minutes from Hoonah. (USGS Quad Map Sitka D-5 and D-6 or Juneau A-5 and A-6)

Fishing

Fishing is good in nearby Neka Bay for sockeyes from mid-June through July; coho from late August through September; pinks and chum salmon from July through mid-August. Nearby Port Frederick offers fair to good king salmon trolling. Sockeye, pink and coho salmon and Dolly Varden can be caught from shore on their migratory runs, and at the heads of bays fed by small streams. Be sure to check ADF&G regulations for salmon fishing restrictions in this area. Tip: A boat is required for the best fishing.

Cabin
Salt Lake Bay Cabin (H-2)

Salt Lake Bay cabin is a plywood structure that sleeps three people. The terrain is relatively hilly, with moderate stands of brush and timber. Located across from the cabin is a log transfer facility. Expect active logging activity in the area. The nearest water source is about a quarter-mile south of the cabin.

Water source: stream
Facilities:
- two double bunks
- bench
- cooking counter
- wood stove
- wood supply
- broom
- dustpan
- outhouse

8 Gateway Yakutat
Fishing the TONGASS National Forest

About the Gateway

The village of Yakutat sits at sea level on Yakutat Bay, one of the few refuges for sea-going vessels along this long stretch of coast in the Gulf of Alaska. Yakutat started as the principal winter village of the Yakutats, a subtribe of the Tlinget Indians. The economic structure was based first on the fur trade, then gold, followed by commercial salmon fishing. The first cannery was built in 1904. Fishing and processing of salmon, halibut, crab and black cod is now the mainstay of the economy, although timber harvesting and oil and gas exploration has been introduced.

Another major draw to the area is the spectacular beauty of the Malaspina Glacier, largest on the North American continent. In June 1986, the Hubbard Glacier surged, sealing off the mouth of Russell Fiord and threatening the safety of Yakutat. Cannon Beach, close to town, has good beachcombing and a picnic area.

Population: 456
Annual Precipitation: 130 inches
Average Summer High Temperature: 60 degrees F., 16 degrees C.

Fishing the Yakutat Area

The Yakutat region offers some of the richest fisheries in the Tongass National Forest. All five species of Pacific salmon are found here, with coho and sockeye salmon stocks the most abundant and chinook, pink and chum salmon available in lesser numbers. Also available are steelhead/rainbow trout, cutthroat trout, Dolly Varden char, halibut and rockfish.

Saltwater fishing is popular in the area, with halibut the most sought-after species. Chinook and coho salmon trolling is popular in Yakutat Bay, from the Yakutat side to Humpback Creek.

In recent years, anglers have discovered the Situk River, the most productive of Alaska's steelhead rivers (excluding major transboundary rivers such as the Taku and Stikine). The river offers both numbers and size of steelhead. On a positive note, in a survey conducted by ADF&G, most anglers said they were primarily interested in catching and releasing Situk steelies.

There are two distinct runs of Situk steelhead: fall-run fish enter the river in late August through December and overwinter in the river's deep pools or in Situk Lake. Starting in March, spring-run fish enter the river, with some unconfirmed accounts of fish entering as early as January or February. Spawning takes place from early April through mid-June. Research shows that in 1982, at least 5,000 steelhead spawned in the Situk. Adults outmigrate through mid-July.

Angling pressure is highest during April and early May. Anglers stay at nearby lodges, in U.S. Forest Service cabins and hotels. Lodges and hotels are usually booked a year in advance for the peak steelhead and coho seasons. The Forest Service has implemented a lottery system for cabin use during peak periods.

The region also offers excellent lake fishing, with Situk and Mountain lakes two of the most productive in southeast Alaska (Schmidt, 1981). Fourteen additional streams and five lakes were ranked as excellent or offering exceptional sportfishing values (wilderness, scenery, fish-catching opportunities). The Yakutat area is the only place in southeast Alaska where you can freshwater sportfish for chinooks. The largest in-river sportfishery for chinooks takes place in the Situk River, although the East River offers fair fishing. The best season is from mid-June through mid-July.

The coho salmon fishery in the Yakutat area is world famous. Historically, the Situk has been the most popular. Recently, however, anglers have found excellent fishing at the East and Italio rivers. The Lost River area and the Ankau Lagoon-Kardy Lake area is also popular. One reason for the widespread effort in the Yakutat area is the countless sloughs, streams, and side tributaries that host runs of coho salmon. A little known and infrequently fished hotspot, the Tsiu-Kaliakh drainage, offers excellent fishing for coho. Most anglers surveyed indicated they want to take home as many cohos as possible.

Most of the pinks in the Yakutat area are taken from the Situk River, which hosts returns of over 500,000 fish in odd years, with even years seeing less fish. Humpback Creek is also a good choice for pinks.

Anglers on the Situk claim the most sockeye taken in the Yakutat region. Fish are currently not harvested in large numbers by anglers. However, recent advances in techniques have increased the harvest and reputation of this once-termed "non-biter."

Very few chum salmon occur in Yakutat streams and rivers. The East River supports the largest run, yet is seldom fished for this species. Cutthroats are widely dispersed throughout the region, yet no single watershed provides any large numbers of this species. On the average, the annual take is several hundred fish. The best fisheries occur in a stretch of sloughs, bays and backwater intertidal areas stretching from the Italio River to Dry Bay. Look for both resident and anadromous cutts in the Italio, Akwe, Ustay, Tanis, Situk, and East Doame rivers, Tawah Creek and Ankau Lagoon. The Italio and Akwe are reported to have the best cutt fishing, taking place in the spring and fall. Various lakes and ponds also support fair numbers of resident fish. Rainbow trout fishing is best in the Situk drainage, which includes Situk and Mountain lakes. Good to excellent rainbow trout fishing is also available in the tributaries of Williams Creek, Doame River, lower Doame Lake, Humpback Creek, Italio River, Redfield Lake, and the Akwe River. In these systems, the smaller rainbows caught by anglers may be rearing steelhead.

Distributed widely throughout the Yakutat region, in both fresh and salt water, Dolly Varden char are most frequently caught from the Situk and Italio rivers, probably as an incidental species to anglers fishing for steelhead and salmon. At times, during the salmon runs, Dollies are thick in pools, and anglers find it difficult to keep the fish off their hooks. Resident Dollies are caught from Mountain, Square, Situk, Aka and Summit lakes. In the headwater region of the Ahrnklin River, four small lakes are known to contain populations of northern pike. According to biological reports, these populations are unique to southeast Alaska, and are thought to be remnant stocks pre-dating recent glaciation. These fish receive virtually little fishing pressure. Arctic grayling are only present in Clear Creek, at Dry Bay. According to reports, (Mattson, 1971), this stock likely originated in interior British Columbia, and migrated down the Alsek River.

For information on recreational cabins in this area, contact:

Yakutat Ranger District, P.O. Box 327, Yakutat, Alaska 99689, (907) 784-3359.

Fishing Index

Forest Service cabins in this gateway are listed below. The types of fish available in the vicinity of the cabin are indicated. You can cross-reference the cabin by the F.S. #, a number assigned to each cabin by the Forest Service. A description of the cabin and its facilities can be found on the page listed on the chart, and the page number of the map showing the exact cabin location is listed in the last column.

Gateway 8 Yakutat

Cabin	F.S. #	Page	Cutthroat Trout	Dolly Varden	Grayling	Rainbow Trout	Steelhead	Chinook Salmon	Coho Salmon	Chum Salmon	Pink Salmon	Sockeye Salmon	Halibut	Rockfish	Map pg.
Dry Bay Cabin	DB	263		•							•	•			262
Harlequin Lake Cabin	Y-4N	264													262
Harlequin Lake Cabin	Y-4S	264													262
Italio River Cabin	Y-11	265	•	•		•			•	•	•	•	•	•	261
Lower Dangerous River Cabin	Y-3	266													261
Middle Dangerous River Cabin	Y-9	267							•				•		261
Middle Situk River Cabin	Y-2N	270		•					•	•	•	•	•	•	261
Middle Situk River Cabin	Y-2S	270		•					•	•	•	•	•	•	261
Situk Lake Cabin	Y-1	268		•				•	•	•	•	•	•	•	261
Situk Wier Cabin	Y-10	272		•				•	•	•	•	•	•	•	261
Square Lake Cabin	Y-5	274	•						•						262
Tanis Mesa Cabin North	Y-6N	275													262
Tanis Mesa Cabin South	Y-6S	275													262
Upper Alsek River Cabin	Y-7	276		•											262

MILLER

GLACIER

YAKUTAT

NOVATAK

GLACIER

ONA

Harlequin
Lake

YN

Y4S

River

BRABA

Mt Redburn

Chamberlain Glacier

FOREST

Ibis
Lake

Bodman Gl.

Fassett Gl.

Martin Gl.

River

Dewe
Lake

Canyon Glacier

Triangle
Lake

Ustay
Lake

River

Tanis Lake

Landing Strip

Y6N
Cabin

Akwe

River

Square
Lake

Y6S

Y5

TRACTOR

Williams Creek

Clear Creek

Cabin

Slough

Cabin

ALSEK

Landing

Y7

817

TRAIL

Cemetery Creek

Muddy Creek

Creek

Cabin

Landing
Strip

Bear
Island

Landing Strip

818

861

862

Dry Bay

Landing
Strip

DB

863

Cabins

Tidal flat

905

906

907

Cabin

262

908

949

950

951

952

The East Alsek River is located about 60 miles southeast of Yakutat on the boundary of Glacier Bay National Park. Wheeled plane access from Juneau or Yakutat. An airfield is within easy walking distance of the cabin. (USGS Quad Map Yakutat A-2)

Fishing

This river system supports king, silver, chum and sockeye salmon, and Dolly Varden. The clear-water tributaries (especially two streams to the north of the cabin) offer the best salmon fishing. Take the overgrown tractor trail to these streams.

Hunting

Brown and black bear hunting is fair to good, especially in spring and fall. Fall moose hunting is fair. Drawings are held for cabin usage during the October-November moose hunting season. Good waterfowl hunting on the flats from September through November.

Other Activities

Wildflowers and berries during the summer months. Excellent opportunities to observe waterfowl during the spring and fall months.

Precautions

The cabin is on land designated as Glacier Bay Preserve. Hunting is allowed over to the Dome River, approximately six miles to the east. The east side of the Dome River and beyond is Glacier Bay National Park, where hunting is prohibited. Also, expect extremely high winds in this area during the fall and winter months.

Cabin
Dry Bay Cabin (DB)

This one-room, 12' x 14' Pan Abode cabin is located in a flat and easily traversed section of spruce and willow forest on the west bank of the East Alsek River. The Alsek River-East Alsek River/Dry Bay tidal flats are two-and-a-half miles south of the cabin. Although this cabin belongs to the National Park Service, reserve it through the U.S. Forest Service.

Water source: river
Facilities:

- four single bunks
- table
- benches

- aircraft tie downs
- shelves
- oil stove

- open shed
- outhouse

User Comments:

9/7-9/10: "Cabin was clean and comfortable. Rained 9 out of 12 days there. Salmon spawned out (reds) but great deal of waterfowl including swans (40 on river while there). No moose or wolf sighted. Enjoyable stay."

Harlequin Lake

Harlequin lake is southeast of Yakutat on the east bank of the Dangerous River. Access is by wheeled plane from Yakutat or automobile (32 miles along Forest Highway 10). Note: At the time of this writing, Dangerous River Bridge is closed to vehicular traffic. (USGS Quad Map Yakutat B-3)

Hunting

The cabin is used primarily as a base camp during moose and mountain goat hunting seasons. Black and brown bear hunting is fair to good during the spring and fall seasons. Special drawings held for cabin reservations for the moose hunting season. There are no fish in the lake.

Other Activities

Two main trails lead away from the cabin: the northbound trail follows the lake shore and offers scenic views, berry picking and patches of wildflowers. The other trail runs south to the Middle Dangerous River cabin with its cottonwood and willow meadows and examples of post-glacial plant succession. Good berry picking in late summer.

Precautions

Trails leading from the cabin can be flooded during periods of heavy rain. Extremely high winds are common in this area during fall and winter. Bring your own water or catch rainwater. Lake is glacially silted.

Cabins
Harlequin Lake Cabin (Y-4N)
Harlequin Lake Cabin (Y-4S)

This is a duplex-style, double-ended A-frame that measures 14' x 40' and has north and south entrances. Each section, or cabin, is a single, 14'x 20' room. Mixed spruce, willow and cottonwood forests are near the cabins. The terrain is relatively flat and easily traversed. The outlying area offers outstanding scenic views of Harlequin Lake and its massive icebergs, Yakutat Glacier and the Brabazon Range, which rises to 4,000 feet and surrounds the lake area.

Water source: bring your own
Facilities:
- four single bunks and one double bunk (Y 4S)
- two single bunks and two double bunks (Y 4N)
- loft
- table
- benches
- shelves
- oil stoves
- open shed
- outhouse
- no boat

The Italio River is 25 miles southeast of Yakutat. Access is via boat or wheeled plane. The airfield is located on the tidal flats between the cabin and ocean. Tiedowns are available. The region is notoriously famous for its high winds and frequent storms, so always plan on spending an extra day or two when booking this cabin. (USGS Quad Map Yakutat B-3 and B-4)

Fishing

The Italio River is one of the finest freshwater fishing streams in the area. You'll find Dolly Varden, rainbow and cutthroat trout throughout the river, as well as excellent silver fishing. Also available are pink and chum salmon. At one time, several years ago, the river flowed in front of the cabin. It now flows several miles to the southeast, requiring an extensive hike to reach. Carry a backpack for hauling gear and fish.

The Italio is an excellent choice for the fly fisher. A 10-weight rod is often necessary to cast large salmon flies into the ever-present wind. The region is an excellent choice for a hunting/fishing adventure trip. You can spend 10 days indulging in excellent fishing for silvers at different streams and creeks within a 15-mile radius of the Italio.

Other Activities

Bear and wolves can often be seen passing through the area. Fall moose hunting is considered fair to good, while pass shooting for waterfowl is excellent.

Cabin

Italio River Cabin (Y-11)

Italio River offers a 14'x 20' A-frame Pan Abode cabin in a flat, easily traveled intertidal area. The cabin sleeps four downstairs plus two in the loft. The geography in this region consists of sandy beaches, tidal sloughs and flats.

Water source: stream
Facilities:

- two double bunks
- loft
- oil stove
- shed
- outhouse
- table
- bench

User Comments

8/23-8/30: "Fishing was good at the mouth of the new Italio River. Commercial fishermen will take you to the mouth aboard three wheelers for a nominal price (well worth it). Fishing not good in the old Italio. Fishing impossible last two days due to high river water, wind and rain. New cabin stove works good. Roof leaks in places on left side."

9/6-9/13: "Rained four days, plus lots of wind. Cabin in reasonable shape. NO fish in what is left of Italio River that used to be near the cabin. Must hike 3½ miles to the southeast to reach river and fish."

The Lower Dangerous River is located about 18 miles southeast of Yakutat. Access is by wheeled plane. During wet-weather months, (May, June and September) the airfield near the cabin can be soft and slick. (Refer to USGS Quad Map Yakutat B-4)

Fishing

This camp is generally used as a base camp by people who fly their own planes to other streams (Situk, Italio) to fish for the day.

Hunting

The area offers fair moose hunting, excellent black and brown bear hunting, and fair to good waterfowl hunting in season. Special drawings are held for cabin use during the moose hunting season.

Other Activities

A limited amount of beachcombing is available. Use the trail leading from the cabin to the mouth of the Dangerous River, a hike of about four miles, one way, to reach the beach.

Precautions

Weather can be extremely severe in this area, especially during the fall months. Plan a few extra days into your schedule for the return flight.

Cabin

Lower Dangerous River Cabin (Y-3)

The one-room, 12' x 15' plywood-frame cabin is located on the west bank of the Dangerous River. Surrounding terrain is relatively flat and easily traversed with mixed willow and cottonwood forests. During heavy rains, the area surrounding the cabin becomes flooded, making foot traffic difficult. The cabin's water supply is from a well. Bring water for priming the hand-operated pump.

Water source: well
Facilities:

- four single bunks
- table
- benches
- oil stove
- open shed
- outhouse
- shelves
- aircraft tiedowns

User Comments

10/14-10/21: ''Cabin clean, stove worked well. Bagged one small bull moose.''

(no date): ''Hunting was not good. One young bull shot by a party who flew in with their own plane. We sighted eight cows, no bulls were taken.

Middle Dangerous River

The Dangerous River is located southeast of Yakutat. Take Highway 10 for 32 miles to Harlequin Lake. Take the four-mile trail to the river and cabin. Trail can be flooded during heavy rains, so use caution. (USGS Quad Map Yakutat B-3 and B-4)

Fishing

The Dangerous River supports a good run of silver salmon. Sockeye spawn in the upper stretches of the main channel. However, other streams in the area offer better fishing. Some anglers (mostly hunters in late fall) concentrate their efforts where clearwater breaklines meet with glacial water breaklines.

Hunting

Brown bear and moose hunting is considered fair to good in season. Wolves are sometimes hunted in this area. Waterfowl hunting is excellent in the fall, as is grouse and ptarmigan hunting in the uplands.

Other Activities

Waterfowl observation and photography is excellent during both spring and fall migrations. Late May and early October are best for photos. The trail to the cabin is a naturalist's delight, with numerous wildflowers, berries and examples of post-glacial plant succession.

Precautions

At this time, Dangerous River Bridge is closed to vehicle traffic.

Cabin

Middle Dangerous River Cabin (Y-9)

This one-room, 12' x 16' Pan Abode cabin is located in a mature stand of timber on the east bank of the Dangerous River. The trail to the cabin courses through young spruce forests and open willow/cottonwood meadows. Bring fuel for the oil stove, and pack in a lightweight cookstove.

Water source: catchment: bring your own water supply, as river water is silty.
Facilities:

- four single bunks
- table
- benches
- shelves
- oil stove
- open shed
- outhouse

User Comments

10/21-10/28: ''Rained each day, water standing everywhere (90 inches) during September and October in Yakutat. Lots of bear, mostly sows with cubs, saw 13 in this period. No wolves, some hares, a marten, owl, ducks and geese. Lots of salmon in rivers and streams. Cabin generally in good repair. Leaks in corner. Plenty of water in streams nearby for cabin use.''

(no date): ''I didn't get a chance to use the cabin. Fishing was too good at the Lost and Situk rivers, and Situk Lake. Maybe some other time.''

Situk Lake is a short distance northeast of Yakutat. Access is by floatplane (15 miles) or a 6-mile trail that leaves Forest Highway 10 at a point about 11 miles from Yakutat. The hike is over relatively flat, forested terrain. Trail can be flooded during heavy rains. (USGS Quad Map Yakutat C-4)

Fishing

Fishing is excellent in the lake for rainbow trout, kokanee and Dolly Varden. In the river expect good to excellent fishing for steelhead, sockeye, king and silver salmon, with chum and pink salmon predominant in the lower stretches.

Fish the outlet, especially during the sockeye run. Use Glo-bug imitations to catch Dollies near sockeye spawning redds.

Also, consider fishing Mountain Creek, which empties into Situk Lake. Fishing at the inlet or in the creek itself is good. Mountain Lake also offers good fishing for rainbows, kokanee and Dolly Varden. There is a two-mile trail that connects Mountain Lake to Situk Lake.

Other Activities

The area is good for viewing black and brown bears. The marshy area surrounding the lake is a primary nesting, feeding and resting area for waterfowl during their fall and spring migrations. Numerous trails for the hiker.

Cabin
Situk Lake Cabin (Y-1)

This one-room, 12'x 16' Pan Abode cabin is on the southeast shore. A mountain range rising to 4,000 feet begins across the lake from the cabin. A boat is provided for your enjoyment.

Water source: lake

Facilities:
- four single bunks
- table
- shelves
- skiff
- oars
- wood stove
- wood supply
- outhouse

User Comments

9/18-9/20: "Cabin was clean and in very good condition. A real pleasure to stay in. What can I say about the weather? Most rain ever recorded in Yakutat. No fish in the outlet of Mountain Lake. Fished lake for only one hour—no luck. Saw small bear, loon, ducks, eagle. Saw sign of moose. Nice cabin and location."

(no date): "Weather excellent, only two days of rain. Fishing for cutthroat and Dollies very good in lake outlet and stream. Caught a few rainbows in outlet stream, some coho in lake, most at lower end. Didn't see any bear, but lots of fresh sign. One walked across sandbar between cabin and lake one night. Thanks for an outstanding vacation."

(no date): "Slight problem finding trail. About half a mile in, must stay to the right. Trail very wet. Overcast whole time. Can't go up to Mountain Lake without hip boots. Saw lots of footprints: bear, wolf and moose. Actually saw two moose and a swan. We didn't try fishing."

World-class rainbow trout and steelhead await anglers at the Situk watershed.

The Situk River is in the Yakutat Forelands area of southeast Alaska. From Yakutat, the river is accessible by trail, vehicle or boat. Taxi and fishing guide service available in town. (USGS Quad Map B-5)

Fishing

Favored by veteran steelheaders and salmon anglers, this section of the river is not affected by tide and the water generally runs clearer. The fishing for steelhead, Dolly Varden, king, coho, sockeye and pink salmon is outstanding. The cabin is usually reserved by anglers, but occasionally by hikers or people floating the river. See the Situk Weir Cabin entry (page 272) for additional information. All Situk River cabins are subject to drawing lotteries for use during April through mid-May, August to mid-September, and October to mid-November.

Other Activities

The outlying areas offer good black and brown bear hunting in season.

Precautions

The Situk is not a whitewater river. It flows at approximately two to three miles per hour and is ideal for float fishing trips for steelhead and salmon. However, caution is advised, as there are logjams and sweepers to avoid.

Cabins
Middle Situk River Cabin (Y- 2N)
Middle Situk River Cabin (Y- 2S)

Combining two cabins into one, this duplex-style cabin is northeast of Yakutat on the east bank of the Situk River. It is an A-frame that measures 14x40: the north side has one room, 14x20, and the south side has one room of the same dimensions. Each cabin is equipped with two bunks, a loft and oil stove.

Access to the cabin is by trail, wheeled plane (six miles from Yakutat) or float craft. To reach the float craft landing, take Forest Highway 10 to a point about nine miles from Yakutat and take a three-mile trail to the landing. The trail weaves through mixed spruce and willow forest, is relatively flat and easily traversed. Caution: the trail can be flooded during periods of heavy rain.

Water source: river
Facilities (Y 2N cabin):

- two double bunks
- loft
- table
- benches
- shelves
- oil stove
- open shed
- outhouse

(Y 2S cabin):

- four single bunks
- loft
- table
- benches
- shelves
- oil stove

User Comments

(no date): "Cabin OK, lots of mice, bats in loft. Water low and very wadeable. Fishing best upstream from cabin. Caught and released four king salmon, then concentrated on pinks, silvers and red salmon. Four species of salmon in river. Saw no bears, perhaps because we were all wearing bells on our sleeves. Saw otter, two moose, eagles, bear tracks and evidence of them eating fish. Saw wolf tracks around landing strip. Noticed one bullet hole in roof of cabin. I was with my wife and another couple. Enjoyed our stay and would like to return. People in town very accommodating."

(no date): "We caught Dolly Varden and pinks. River too low for coho. Don't expect them to come up until Saturday or Sunday. Outdoor fire pit OK except it holds six inches of water because there is no opening for it to get out. Would be great in a desert where it does not rain. Rains too much here. Had a good time. Enjoyed your state."

(no date): "Bats and mice have taken over the cabin. The situation is bad enough that it is hard to get a good night's sleep with all the noise the critters make. Suggest leaving some traps or bait on site. The new outhouse is excellent. Caught and released some nice kings. Floated the river to the mouth and caught many pinks."

4/26-5/10: "Fishing excellent—plenty of steelhead. Saw moose, but no bear sign. Heavy use of river by fishermen."

5/3-5/10: "Snowed Thursday night. Fuel can was missing, cabin very cold. Rest of cabin was very good. Water temperature 34 degrees. Fishing slow. Saw lots of fish Saturday, caught and released some."

9/14-9/20: "Cabin was comfortable. Fair amount of trash left around the cabin by previous occupants. Weather was too nice, river too low. Coho weren't running. River filled with stinking dead pinks. Went upstream approximately 1.4 mile to small stream entering Situk to get drinking water since river was so bad. Caught nice Dolly Varden (2-3 pounds) at junction of Situk and Old Situk. Caught some coho (8-16 pounds) but they were pretty soft. Lots of bear and wolf sign but did not see any. Saw two bulls, one cow and one calf moose. We enjoyed the stay and the opportunity to use the cabin. Note: We floated in and out with John (sic) Boats."

Jim Oatfield with a Situk River steelhead. When you're through fishing the river, don't pass up the fishing opportunities at Situk Lake, which offers rainbow trout and Dollies.

Situk River

The Situk River is in the Yakutat Forelands area of southeast Alaska. The river is accessible by trail, vehicle or boat from Yakutat. Taxi and fishing guide service available in town. (USGS Quad Map B-5)

Fishing

The Situk River offers what is perhaps some of the best steelhead fishing in Alaska. The river regularly produces the annual state record for the largest steelhead. Most recently, it was a 23-pound, 9-ounce fish. A skilled angler with the right timing and a bit of luck can expect to catch a couple steelies in the 15- to 20-pound range, along with a dozen or more fish in the 8- to 14-pound category.

Fishing in the Situk starts picking up in November, and stays good as long as the river stays open. Best fishing is from late March through early May. Expect crowds during this timeframe. Hotspots on the river include the DMZ area, potmarked with numerous snags; and where the little Situk merges with the Situk.

Sight casting to fish is what makes fishing the Situk so enjoyable. Use flies, spinning or casting gear. Veteran Situk steelheader Jim Oatfield prefers Hot Pink Sparklers and Babine Specials fished with a sink-tip line and 36- to 48-inch leader. Spin anglers should use drift lures in fluorescent pink, red, peach, orange and chartreuse. Spinners and spoons also work well in the deeper runs. The river also offers good to excellent fishing for king, red, coho, pink and chum salmon, Dolly Varden, cutthroat and rainbow trout. See other Situk entries for additional information.

Other Activities

Wildlife viewing opportunities are abundant in the area. Brown bear are numerous, and moose are common. Waterfowl hunting is good on the tidal flats south of the cabin.

Cabin

Situk Wier Cabin (Y-10)

Rebuilt in 1987, the Situk River Wier cabin is a 12'x 14' structure in a spruce-hemlock forest southeast of Yakutat, near the mouth of the Situk River. The half-mile trail leaves the Situk Landing (10 miles from Yakutat on the Lost River/Situk River Road) and courses along the river bank. Caution: the trail can be very muddy and slippery. The cabin is frequently used as a final stopover point for visitors, fishing parties floating the river, and hikers.

Water source: river
Facilities:
- wood stove
- six single bunks
- table
- benches
- outhouse
- counter
- table

User Comments

6/15: "The weather was rainy, but cleared up. River dropped 2 1/2 feet and fishing picked up for kings. Caught 25 kings. Caught lots of returning steelhead. Saw two cow moose. Caught about 50 other fish in big pool."

8/17-8/24: "Cabin was being painted and new heater was there to be installed. Understand cabin burned to ground in October or November. Hope it gets rebuilt to same size. Fishing for pinks is great late July to mid-August. Some silvers were caught week we were there, but silver fishing is best in early September. Saw bear daily at river; moose once and lynx once, eagle nest in area. Floating river from Nine-Mile Bridge is nice and takes 8 to 10 hours if you fish a little. Be sure to drive 30 miles out to Dangerous River and Yakutat Glacier. There is a trail down to the lake: take it."

9/7: "Cabin in good shape. Fishing was poor, but those are the breaks. Better luck next time. Information on licenses could have been more accurate. We were lucky we had time to buy them in Juneau. They were not available anywhere in Yakutat on Sunday. Stove oil and Coleman fuel were also unavailable on Sunday."

9/17-9/21: "Fishing very slow. We did not catch our limit of silvers any of the seven days. A few Dolly Varden. Thanks, it was great."

9/20-9/27: "Cabin was nice. Stove worked well, although wood had to be dried first before it would burn well. Weather was rainy. Fishing was fair compared to other year. A large otter would come and retrieve fish parts out of the river while the fish were being cleaned. It would rest on the river bank 20 feet away and watch and eat. Thanks for furnishing such a nice place."

George Sturgill is pleased with this Situk River steelhead he caught on a Glo-Bug fly in late April.

Square Lake

Square Lake is located 38 miles southeast of Yakutat. Accessible by floatplane, the immediate area is surrounded by marsh and muskeg, and interlaced with rivers. (USGS Quad Map Yakutat A-2)

Fishing

Cutthroat and rainbow trout fishing is fair in neighboring streams and outlets. Fish range from 6 to 12 inches, occasionally larger. Use weighted black marabou streamers to catch the bigger fish holding in deep channels and pools. Successful spin fishermen use ultralight spoons and bait.

Hunting

Brown bear and moose hunting is considered fair in season. Waterfowl hunting is good.

Other Activities

Swans nest at the head of the lake and should be admired but not disturbed. Otter and beaver are present.

Precautions

Pull skiff well up on beach and turn it upside down before leaving camp.

Cabin
Square Lake Cabin (Y-5)

Square Lake offers a 12'x 14' Pan Abode cabin on the southeast shore of the lake. The area around the cabin is marsh, intermixed with stands of spruce and willow forest. There are numerous streams and rivers draining the area. Special drawings are held for cabin bookings during the moose hunting season.

Water source: lake
Facilities:
- four single bunks
- table
- benches
- shelves
- skiff
- oars
- oil stove
- outhouse

Tanis Mesa is 45 miles southeast of Yakutat. Access is by wheeled plane. (USGS Quad Map Yakutat A2 and B2)

Hunting

Mountain goat hunting is fair, especially in late fall when snow storms drive the animals down from the higher peaks. Spring black and brown bear hunting can be excellent. Fall moose hunting is rated as fair. Wolves frequently pass through the area.

Other Activities

Wildlife includes a family of beavers south of the cabin area. Summer brings numerous wildflowers and wild berries. Excellent hiking and exploring opportunities.

Precautions

Extremely high winds, fog and storms are common in this area during the fall and winter months. Bring drinking water during the summer months as creeks in the area often go dry or become silty. Tie down aircraft securely.

Cabins

Tanis Mesa Cabin North (Y-6N)
Tanis Mesa Cabin South (Y-6S)

The cabin is a 14' x 40' A-frame structure broken into north and south wings. It is located in a broad, scenic valley between the Brabazon Range (4000-foot elevation) and the Tanis Mesa (600-foot elevation). Trails lead into a mixed spruce/cottonwood/willow forest.

Water source: water supply is by catchment; however, bring your own supply.
Facilities (for both cabins):

- two single bunks
- loft
- outhouse
- open shed
- airfield
- oil stove
- table
- benches
- shelves

User Comments

9/20-9/27: "We had extremely high winds for about 60 hours. It forced us to attempt to seal air leakage along the bottom of the roof as the wind inside the cabin was blowing things off the table. I recommend the cabin be sealed tighter against the wind. Seat belts in the outhouse would be handy! Hunted bear and goat. Saw no bear, Goats too high. Saw 1 large moose. No bear or wolf sign."

(no date): "Weather terrible, rain every day and high winds. Scenery is great when you can see it. Very little wildlife here. Four days of hard hunting by four people. Saw a few cow moose, one ermine and few birds and nothing else."

Upper Alsek River

The Alsek River is located about 50 miles southeast of Yakutat. Access is by wheeled aircraft. Chartered flying time is about 30 minutes, one way. The Brabazon Range (elevation 4,000 feet) begins about two miles to the north. (USGS Quad Map Yakutat A-2)

Fishing

The Alsek River watershed contains numerous streams and lakes that hold over-wintering populations of Dolly Varden. The closest of these to the cabin is Tanis Lake. The main river supports populations of king salmon, silver salmon, steelhead and Dolly Varden. Fish the clearwater streams north of the cabin during the salmon runs. Other streams and rivers to the south offer better fishing opportunities. A riverboat is a must for fishing this area. Because resident and anadromous species move frequently, scout various sloughs until you find fish.

Hunting

This cabin is primarily used as a base camp for hunters. Spring brown and black bear hunting is often good to excellent. Goat hunting in the Brabazon Range, two miles to the north of the cabin, is considered fair. Moose hunting is considered fair to good.

Other Activities

Excellent area to observe waterfowl and songbirds. Numerous wildflowers and berries during the summer months. Wonderful scenery.

Precautions

Extremely high winds prevail during the fall and winter months.

Cabin

Upper Alsek River Cabin (Y-7)

This one-room, 14' x 16' Pan Abode cabin sits in a willow/alder/cottonwood forest about one mile west of the Alsek River. Surrounding terrain is flat. There's a special drawing for this cabin for the late fall moose hunting season.

Water source: creek
Facilities:

- four single bunks
- table
- benches
- shelves
- oil stove
- open shed
- outhouse
- airfield

User Comments

11/4-11/10: "Saw four moose and two brown bear, one at 20 yards or less. Rain hail, sleet and wind. Cabin in good condition, with the exception of stove leak. One can (5 gallons) of fuel lasts almost 3 nights if stove is not used during the day. Good trip."

9 Gateway Anchorage
Fishing the CHUGACH National Forest

About the Gateway

You can enjoy the riches of the Chugach National Forest from the cities of Cordova, Whittier and Seward, and of course, Alaska's most populated city, Anchorage. Known as the "Land of Many Uses," the Chugach is the second largest forest in the United States. It offers a variety of recreational uses from boating, off-roading, camping, hiking, horseback riding, wildlife photography, whitewater kayaking, and of course, fishing and hunting. During the months of May through September, daytime temperatures usually range from 40 to 50 degrees F. Temperatures range from 18 to 38 degrees from October through April, and from 0 degrees and below during cold snaps. Backcountry travelers may encounter heavy rains near sea level, and snow at higher elevations year-round.

Fishing the Anchorage Area

With over 3,500 miles of saltwater shoreline, the Chugach offers plenty of "elbow room" for saltwater and intertidal fishing. Unlike the Tongass, which has a multitude of freshwater rivers and streams with healthy populations of resident sportfish, many of the freshwater systems within the Chugach are glacially silted and do not support populations of resident sportfish. However, rivers such as the Kenai and Russian rivers (parts of which run through the Chugach) account for a lion's share of the state's total sportfishing efforts. In recent years, anglers have discovered that the Copper River tributaries offer some of the hottest sportfishing available in southcentral Alaska. Many streams within the Chugach are dying. The 1964 earthquake affected critical salmon spawning habitat throughout areas of Prince William Sound. Land was uplifted, draining significant spawning and rearing habitat. Consequently, sport and commercial fishing suffered.

In recent years, natural salmon stocks in Prince William Sound have been enhanced by over 120 fisheries rehabilitation projects in the Chugach Forest. Private hatcheries have created unbelievable returns of salmon, and equally impressive sportfishing opportunities. While most of the returning fish are pink salmon, hatcheries are gearing up their production of silver, sockeye and king salmon. The waters near Solomon Gulch Hatchery near Valdez, for instance, provide some of the best pink salmon fishing you'll find anywhere in the state. The hatchery has also been responsible for revitalizing an enemic coho and king salmon saltwater fishery. Keep in mind that some recreational cabins located on the shores of Prince William Sound are not located near prime fisheries, nor can anglers experience salmon action as found at other cabins located in the sound. Check the listings for each cabin before making your reservation.

For information on recreational cabins in this area, contact:
Chugach National Forest, 201 East Ninth Ave. Suite 206, Anchorage, Alaska 99501-3698, (907) 271-2500
Glacier Ranger District, Monarch Mine Road, P.O. Box 129, Girdwood, Alaska 99587-0129, (907) 783-3242
Cordova Ranger District, 612 Second St. Cordova, Alaska 99574-0280, (907) 424-7661
Seward Ranger District, P.O. Box 390, Seward, Alaska 99664-0390, (907) 224-3374

Fishing Index

Forest Service cabins in this gateway are listed below. The types of fish available in the vicinity of the cabin are indicated. You can cross-reference the cabin by the F.S. #, a number assigned to each cabin by the Forest Service. A description of the cabin and its facilities can be found on the page listed on the chart, and the page number of the map showing the exact cabin location is listed in the last column.

Gateway 9 Anchorage

Cabin	F.S. #	Page	Cutthroat Trout	Dolly Varden	Grayling	Rainbow Trout	Lake Trout	Chinook Salmon	Coho Salmon	Chum Salmon	Pink Salmon	Sockeye Salmon	Halibut	Rockfish	Map pg.
Aspen Flats Cabin	S-5	323		•		•							•		286
Barber Cabin	S-12	323		•		•							•		286
Beach River Cabin	C-6	292		•					•		•				289
Caribou Creek Cabin	A-2	293													286
Coghill Lake Cabin	A-6	294							•	•	•	•			281
Crescent Lake Cabin	S-2	295		•	•	•									286
Crow Pass Cabin	A-3	296													280
Devil's Pass Cabin	S-11	298		•											286
Double Bay Cabin	C-1	301								•		•	•		283
East Creek Cabin	A-1	302													286
Fox Creek Cabin	A-10	302													286
Green Island Cabin	S-14	303		•					•		•		•	•	289
Harrison Lagoon Cabin	A-7	304							•	•					288
Hook Point Cabin	C-5	305							•	•					283
Jack Bay Cabin	C-12	306							•	•		•			290
Juneau Lake Cabin	S-8	308				•	•	•							286
Log Jam Bay Cabin	C-9	331	•	•						•	•				282
Lower Paradise Lake Cabin	S-3	314				•									287
Martin Lake Cabin	C-4	309		•				•		•			•		285
McKinley Lake Cabin	C-15	311	•	•						•			•		284
McKinley Trail Cabin	C-7	311	•	•						•			•		284
Nellie Martin River Cabin	C-14	313		•						•		•	•		282
Paulson Bay Cabin	A-8	315								•	•	•	•	•	288
Pete Dahl Cabin	C-2	317								•			•		284
Pigot Bay Cabin	A-4	318									•	•	•	•	288
Port Chalmers Cabin	C-17	320	•	•						•		•			289
Resurrection River Cabin	S-13	321													287
Romig Cabin	S-7	308				•	•								286
San Juan Bay Cabin	C-10	324								•					282
Shrode Lake Cabin	A-5	326		•						•		•	•		288
Softuk Bar Cabin	C-16	327													285
South Culross Passage Cabin	A-9	329		•							•	•	•	•	288
Stump Lake Cabin	C-8	331	•	•						•		•			282
Swan Lake Cabin	S-9	332		•			•						•		286
Tiedeman Slough Cabin	C-3	317								•			•		284
Trout Lake Cabin	S-6	334		•	•	•	•								286
Upper Paradise Lake Cabin	S-1	314				•									287
Upper Russian Lake Cabin	S-4	323					•								286
West Swan Lake Cabin	S-10	332		•			•						•		286

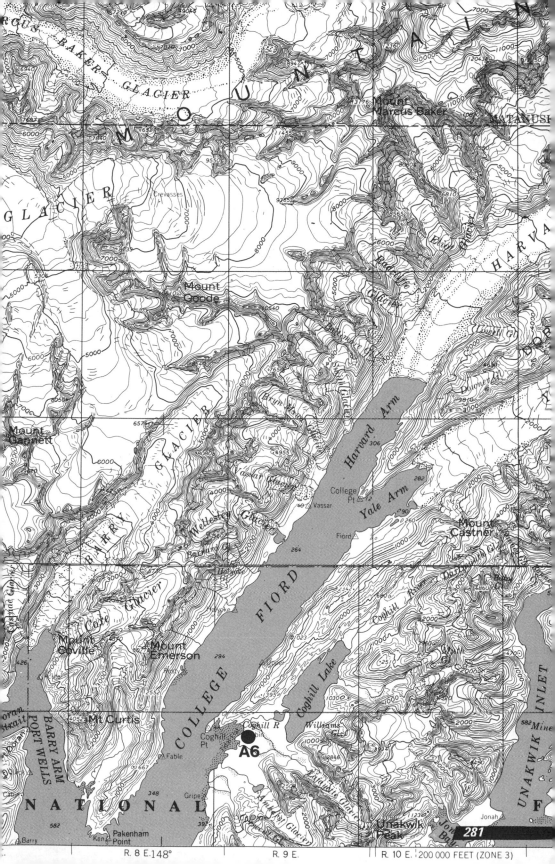

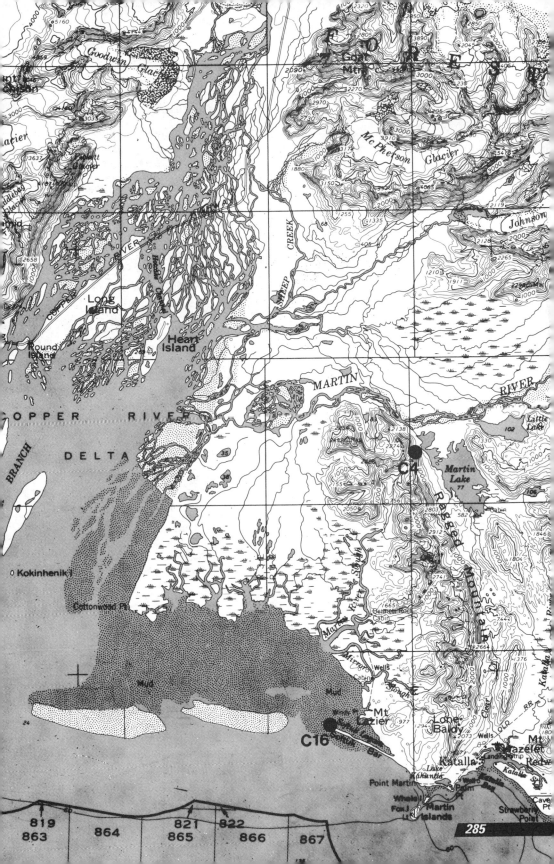

Located 70 miles southwest of Cordova, Beach River is north of Patton Bay on the Gulf of Alaska side of Montague Island. Access is only by wheelplane at low tide. Minimum, one-way flight time charged from Cordova is 45 minutes; from Seward, 50 minutes. A short, gravel/sand beach landing strip is located within a quarter-mile of the cabin. (USGS Quad Map Blying Sound D-2)

Fishing

Beach River is located about 300 yards south of the cabin, and contains fair fishing for Dolly Varden after ice out and from late July through September. Pinks are caught from mid-July through August, and a good run of silvers enters the river in mid-August. Attractor flies are good, as are spoons, spinners in silver and gold, and other hardware. A boat is helpful in fishing and exploring the area.

Farther up the drainage in late August, look for silvers holding in sidewater sloughs or deep runs. Tiny lures and No. 6 purple/black-colored streamers are effective, especially if water levels are low.

Hunting

Hunting is fair for deer and brown bear. In years of heavy snowfall, deer can be successfully hunted near the beach fringe. Early in August and September, climb to the higher elevations and glass alpine meadows and fringes of timber.

Many of the beaches throughout the Sound offer access at low tide to small planes. Use established landing areas, and exercise caution and good judgement always.

Other Activities

The Beach River Valley offers a good day hike. From the cabin, hike up the valley to the higher elevations. There, traveling is easier and photographic opportunities are many. Expect to do some brush busting along the way. The Gulf of Alaska side of Montague offers beachcombing for Japanese fishing floats, starfish, old bottles and the like. Also expect to see Steller sea lions and sea otters, especially during late summer. Enjoy, but do not disturb the historic and archaeological sites in the area.

Precautions

The gravel landing strip in front of the cabin is not maintained and should be attempted by experienced pilots only. Boat access to Beach River cabin is not possible due to unprotected anchorages and high surf. Storms can be severe in this region, so take three to five days worth of extra fuel and food. Also, the cabin is near private property. Contact the Chugach National Forest office or Chugach Alaska Corporation in Anchorage for information regarding the location and use of these private lands.

Cabins

Beach River Cabin (C-6)

Beach River Cabin is a 12' x 20' cabin located in a flat, thickly wooded area with a beach view. It is capable of sleeping six, and is equipped with both wood and oil stoves. The beach has an excellent supply of driftwood for burning. The immediate area offers seclusion and scenic vistas of the Gulf of Alaska.

Water source: rainwater catchment; bring your own
Facilities:

* wooden bunks
* oil stove
* table

* bench
* wood stove
* outhouse

* cooking counter
* saw
* ax

In many areas throughout Prince William Sound, beachcombers have the opportunity to search for glass-ball commercial fishing floats. They are coveted collector's items.

Caribou Creek is located on the Resurrection Pass Trail System on the Kenai Peninsula, seven miles south of the north trailhead near Hope. Access is by foot. (USGS Quad Map Seward D-8)

Fishing

Minimal fishing opportunities in this area.

Hunting

Ptarmigan and spruce grouse hunting is fair to good. Moose, black and brown bear, Dall sheep and wolf hunting is fair to good in season. Some hunting is on a permit basis. Before heading afield, check out regulations, boundaries, and permit-only areas with ADF&G.

Other Activities

Recreational gold panning is allowed in designated areas along the trail. Avoid active mining operations north of the cabin. Equipment belongs to miners and is private property. Snowmobile access from December 1 through February 15. Popular hiking and cross-country skiing trail.

Cabin
Caribou Creek Cabin (A-2)

Caribou Creek Cabin is 12' x 14' and sleeps six. It has a wood-burning stove for heating and cooking. The cabin is on the edge of an alpine meadow with a panoramic view of mature spruce forests, Caribou Creek and the surrounding Kenai Mountains. Elevation is 1,000 feet.

Water source: creek
Facilities:
- wooden bunks
- table
- benches
- outhouse
- wood stove
- maul
- saw counter

Coghill Lake

Coghill Lake is on the east side of College Fiord in Prince William Sound. One-way access by floatplane is 50 minutes from Anchorage or 60 minutes from Cordova. (USGS Quad Map Anchorage A-3)

Fishing

Coghill Lake offers a variety of fishing opportunities, and is ideal for the angler looking for a get-away salmon fishing adventure. Sockeye enter the river in mid-June, pink and chum salmon enter in early to mid-July, lasting through mid-August, and silver salmon in mid-August through September. For best success, try the stream or lagoon at the lake outlet. Because the river is deep and wide, try hardware or bottom-bouncing tackle. Start with 7/8-ounce lures before going to smaller sizes. Many anglers prefer eggs for silvers, although plugs do work well when backtrolled at the lake outlet and river. Coghill Lake supports a commercially important sockeye salmon fishery. For best success, look for areas where sockeye are concentrated near shoreline or holding in current. Because no boat is provided, you'll find access to productive fishing spots easier if you bring a small inflatable and outboard kicker.

Hunting

Coghill Lake is a good base of operations for a black bear hunt. A large inflatable or boat is necessary for best success. Spring hunts, May and early June, are good. Waterfowl hunting is fair to good for puddler and sea ducks, with some divers.

Other Activities

This area offers scenery that is mesmerizing, and, aside from the fishing, is the main attraction of this cabin. Wild berries abound.

Precautions

A boat is necessary to cross the Coghill River. Also, the U.S. Forest Service indicates the lagoon near the cabin is generally deep enough to taxi a plane to the cabin's boardwalk.

Cabin
Coghill Lake Cabin (A-6)

Coghill Lake Cabin is a 16-foot A-frame with loft, nestled on the edge of a spruce forest. A very impressive panorama of mountains and alpine glaciers surround the cabin. When flying in, look for the cabin on the southern shore of the lake near a lagoon a short distance from the outlet. The cabin has a wood-burning stove for heating and cooking. Firewood is available, but requires a bit of searching to find. Cabin can sleep up to 10.

Water source: lake
Facilities:

• wooden bunks	• splitting maul	• counter
• loft	• saw	• shelves
• table	• outhouse	• no boat
• wood stove	• benches	

Crescent Lake is three miles north of Kenai Lake on the Kenai Peninsula. Access is by trail (6.5 miles from Crescent Creek Trailhead). Also accessible by float plane, 15 minutes from Moose Pass or 20 minutes from Cooper Landing. (USGS Quad Map Seward B-7, C-7, C-8)

Fishing

Crescent Lake is noted for its good to excellent arctic grayling fishing. Fish have been known to reach lengths of 16 to 18 inches, although most average 9 to 14 inches. Fly fishermen do best at either end of the lake over flat, sandy bottom in 10 to 20 feet of water. Muddy bays are also good, especially when a mayfly or caddis hatch is taking place. Grayling can be seen dimpling the entire surface of the bay at these times, a common occurrence in late June. Also try along the southern shoreline near mid-lake. Spin fishermen should longline a spinning bubble and fly, or troll small spinners or spoons in black or red/yellow. Nearby Juneau Creek offers grayling, Dolly Varden and rainbow fishing. Practice catch and release.

Hunting

Hunting is available, but not considered exceptional. In the forest surrounding the lake, hunters will find grouse, ptarmigan and snowshoe hare, along with black bear and moose. Moose are plentiful in the area, and hunting is good. Waterfowl hunting can be good in late autumn. During high-use periods in late August and early September, cabin must be reserved through special drawings.

Precautions

Extreme snow avalanche danger on Crescent Creek Trail in winter and early spring. Use the Carter Lake Trail to reach the lake during winter months, and cross frozen Crescent Lake to the cabin.

Cabin
Crescent Lake Cabin (S-2)

Located at the northwest tip of Crescent Lake, this cabin is a 12' x 14' structure capable of sleeping four. It has a wood stove for heating and cooking, and a good firewood supply. The cabin sits in a flat area filled with trees, shrubs, grasses and wildflowers. View of the lake from the cabin door. Elevation is 1,450 feet. Note: Cabin is located two feet from the trail, and offers little privacy.

Water source: lake
Facilities:

• wooden bunks	• saw	• counter
• table	• 14-foot boat	• shelves
• wood stove	• oars	• outhouse
• maul	• benches	

Crow Pass is accessible via the Crow Pass trailhead, located at Mile 90 Seward Highway (35 miles south of Anchorage). Turn at a T-intersection leading to Mount Alyeska Resort. At Mile Two, turn left onto Crow Creek Road. The trailhead is at road's end. The trail is part of the Iditarod National Historic Trail that was used to transport mail and supplies between Turnagain and Knik arms. (USGS Quad Map Anchorage A-6)

Fishing
No fishing in immediate area.

Hunting
Ptarmigan and grouse hunting is good starting in September. Limited big game hunting. Check with the Alaska Department of Fish and Game for regulations and species availability.

Other Activities
The cabin is primarily for the non-consumptive outdoor user. Cross-country travel, hiking and wildlife viewing opportunities abound. The three-mile hike gains 2,080 feet in elevation. A popular overnight trip for a family. Along the trail you'll find Girdwood Mine Ruins at Mile 1.7. A waterfall, a quarter-mile farther up the trail, makes an ideal picnic spot. After your arrival at the cabin, keep hiking to Mile 4, where you'll come to Raven Glacier. Glaciers and peaks offer advanced challenges to the experienced climber. Dall sheep, mountain goats, bear and ptarmigan are occasionally seen while hiking the trail.

Precautions
The Crow Pass Trail is a hazardous avalanche zone, and is not traveled during the winter months. Snowstorms, whiteouts and gale-force winds are commonplace throughout the winter. Trail is usually snow-free by mid-June.

Cabin
Crow Pass Cabin (A-3)
The cabin is at 3,500 feet, above timberline in open, alpine tundra. A panorama of mountains surrounds the cabin, and Crystal Lake is a short hike away. The cabin is a 16-foot A-frame with loft, capable of sleeping 10. It is not furnished with a wood stove.

Water source: glacial stream. Boil, and allow silt to settle before drinking.
Facilities:
* wooden bunks
* table
* outhouse
* counter
* no boat

U.S. Forest Service cabins located on lakes and several major rivers come furnished with a boat or skiff. You need to provide your own life vests, outboard motor and fishing equipment.

Devil's Pass

Devil's Pass is in the Kenai Mountains on the Kenai Peninsula, 10 miles from the Devil's Pass Trailhead and 18 miles from the south trailhead of the Resurrection Pass Trail. (USGS Quad Map Seward C-8)

Fishing

A small population of golden fins, or landlocked Dolly Varden, exists in Devil's Pass Lake. These fish are generally less than eight inches. No other fishing in the immediate area.

Hunting

The area is extremely popular with ptarmigan hunters in early fall and throughout the winter months. Bear and moose are also available, and hunting is considered fair to good in the alpine areas. Bear hunting is best in September, when berry stocks are ripe.

Precautions

Devil's Pass is a hazardous avalanche zone, and this route is not recommended for winter use. Winter recreationists use the Resurrection Pass Trail to reach the cabin. After a heavy snowfall, the trail from East Creek to Resurrection Pass may be difficult to travel.

Cabin
Devil's Pass Cabin (S-11)

This 16-foot A-frame cabin with loft can sleep 10, and has an oil-burning stove for heating. The cabin is situated in alpine tundra at 2,400 feet elevation. It is one of a series of cabins on the 72-mile, Hope-to-Seward trail system. The Devil's Pass Trail provides access to seldom traveled alpine valleys branching from the main route. The area is patchworked with wildflowers, shrubs and grasses. Geological formations include steep and narrow canyons. Awaiting your visit is wonderful scenery that includes forests, meadows filled with alpine wildflowers, streams, lakes and rugged mountain peaks.

Water source: creeks
Facilities:
- wooden bunks
- loft
- outhouse
- table
- bench
- counter
- oil stove

When hunting moose in the alpine areas, keep high and watch the timberline for bulls, especially in the morning or late afternoon.

Double Bay

Double Bay is southwest of Cordova on the north shore of Hinchinbrook Island. Access is via float plane at high tide only. One-way flight time is 20 minutes from Cordova. Boat access is possible, but not advised. From Cordova, the distance by boat is 35 miles. (USGS Quad Map Cordova B-7)

Fishing

Pink salmon fishing is excellent in July and early August. Walk the shoreline and cast into the surf, or fish the mouths of streams where salmon congregate. At times, expect fish-a-cast action. Chartreuse spinners work well, especially the elongated variety of Rooster Tail. Use larger lures in the deeper holes. Silvers mill around the area but are not abundant. Troll herring or plugs at the mouth of the bay on an incoming tide for best success. Surf casting from a boat near freshwater streams is also productive. Use lightweight flutter spoons and light tackle. Halibut fishing is good outside of Double Bay.

Hunting

In October and November, waterfowl hunting is good for divers, puddlers and sea ducks. Deer and brown bear hunting is available. Use the cabin as a base of operations and set up camps at various locations. A small, easily handled inflatable and outboard is a must for successfully hunting this area.

Other Activities

The islands in this region were originally settled by the Chugach Eskimos. The Russians established the first permanent European outpost here at Port Etches. More recently, the 1964 earthquake uplifted Hinchinbrook by 15 feet, creating large beachfronts around the island. The numerous bights and channels of Double Bay and nearby Anderson Bay are exciting places to explore by dinghy. Without a boat, it's still possible to explore the gravel spits and beaches. Because of dense brush, stream banks are tough to navigate, but are the best way to reach the island's interior. Wear ankle-fit hip boots when hiking in this country. On a clear day, a hike north of the cabin will offer a panoramic view of Port Fidalgo and Columbia Glacier. The immediate area offers excellent opportunities to photograph deer, waterfowl, harbor seals and sea otters.

Precautions

At low tide, the shallow-water lagoon is a potential danger to boats and float-planes attempting access. At high tide, the USFS recommends that you anchor in 40 feet of water at the mouth of the bay. To the west will be a point of land, and large islands will be to the east. However, caution is advised, as this anchorage williwaws badly in strong southeasterlies.

Cabin

Double Bay Cabin (C-1)

The Double Bay cabin is a 12' x 14' structure located inside Double Bay, and surrounded by mature spruce interspersed with muskeg. Terrain is very wet, and often makes for difficult walking. The cabin sleeps six, and comes equipped with an oil stove for heating. Elevation is about 25 feet.

Water source: streams
Facilities:

- wooden bunks
- table
- oil stove (with oven)
- benches
- outhouse
- covered meat rack
- counter
- no boat

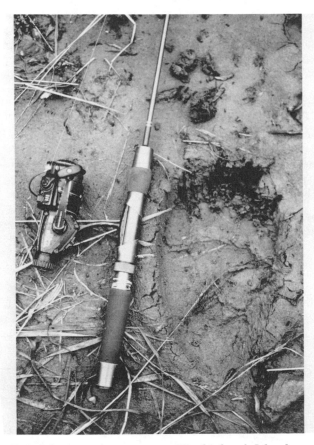

Brown bears are common on Hinchinbrook Island. Familiarize yourself with bear avoidance procedures prior to your trip.

East Creek is on the Resurrection Pass Trail, 14.5 miles from the trailhead at Hope. Fox Creek is located at Mile 11.5 (USGS Quad Map Seward C-8)

Fishing

The immediate area does not support a sport fishery.

Hunting

Ptarmigan, grouse and snowshoe hare hunting along the ridges and in the alder patches from August through season closure. Big game hunting also available, however, most hunters use the cabin as a base camp. Moose and bear hunting is considered fair.

Other Activities

Recreational gold panning is allowed in designated areas along the trail. Active mining operations are visible along the trail north of the cabin. Mining equipment is private property. Area is popular with hikers and cross-country skiers. Snowmobile access from December 1 through February 15. Closed to motorized vehicles from Feb. 16 through November 30, and pack animals from April 1 through June 30.

Cabins
East Creek Cabin (A-1)
Fox Creek Cabin (A-10)

Located a short distance from the main trail, the 12' x 14' rustic East Creek cabin is near alpine meadows filled with shrubs, flowers and grasses, with occasional stands of spruce. Elevation, 2,200 feet. Wood stove is furnished for heating.

Fox Creek cabin is nearly identical to East Creek cabin. Elevation, 1,500 feet.

Water source: creek
Facilities:
- wood bunks
- wood stove
- table
- bench
- counter
- maul
- saw
- outhouse

Moose hunters use pack horses to carry moose meat and antlers many miles from field to highway. Photo courtesy USDA Forest Service.

Green Island is in Prince William Sound, 45 minutes by air from Cordova or 80 minutes from Anchorage. By boat, distances are 100 miles from Seward, 70 miles from Whittier and 65 miles from Cordova. (USGS Quad Map Seward B-2)

Fishing

This area is best fished from a boat or inflatable. There is no "good" fishing within walking distance of the cabin, although there is limited fishing for pinks in or near the intertidal area. Look to Gibbon Anchorage for the best fishing opportunities. There, pink salmon arrive in mid-July and last through mid-August. In mid-to-late August, catch silvers while trolling along shoreline structure. One mile north of the cabin is a stream that is reported to have good Dolly Varden fishing. Halibut fishing is good at the mouth of bays and along flat, sandy bottoms. Look for rockfish and lingcod near underwater islands and protruding points, and along rocky shorelines with sudden dropoffs.

Hunting

Fair to good deer hunting, and good waterfowl hunting. A boat is necessary, as are decoys for the best waterfowling. Dark, drab decoys are good if hunters don't have eider, old squaw or harlequin dekes. Later in the season, outside points and protected bays offer good pass shooting.

Other Activities

Fair to good photographic opportunities for brown bear and deer. Otters, sea lions and seals are plentiful. Many hiking opportunities.

Precautions

Brown bears available in good numbers. Boaters should use caution when passing through the area. Uncharted rocks, rapidly changing weather and sea changes are common. Due to the island's higher elevation caused by the 1964 earthquake, many lakes are running dry. The Forest Service cautions that some features, such as lakes and streams, which are shown on topo maps, may no longer exist.

Cabin

Green Island Cabin (S-14)

Green Island cabin is a 12' x 14' wood structure with loft. Located in a protected bay in Gibbon Anchorage, the cabin sleeps six, and has an oil stove for heating. Surrounding the cabin is mature Sitka spruce and hemlock rainforest with open patches of muskeg. The area was originally settled by the Chugach Eskimos.

Water source: catchment
Facilities:
- wooden bunks
- oil stove (with oven)
- outhouse
- table
- bench
- counter
- no boat: bring own

Harrison Lagoon

Harrison Lagoon is located on the west side of Port Wells about two miles north of Hobo Bay, in West Prince William Sound. One-way access by floatplane is 40 minutes from Anchorage and 60 minutes from Cordova, or 34 miles by boat from Whittier. (USGS Quad Map Seward D-4)

Fishing

Pink and chum salmon migrate into Harrison Lagoon and mill around in Lagoon Creek. Fishing is fair. For best success, cast for fresh pinks on an incoming tide. Bring pots for shrimping. Finding concentrations of shrimp can be difficult, but rewarding.

Hunting

Waterfowl hunting is fair. Deer and black bear hunters use this cabin as a base camp. Best hunting is along the beaches and at the head of bays at low tide, or in early morning. Swampy areas with feeder creeks offer excellent black bear hunting during the spring months. Deer hunting is best after a heavy snowfall.

Other Activities

Wildlife in the area includes harbor seals, sea otter, Dall porpoises and sea lions. Whales are occasionally seen in the open ocean. A boat opens up a vast and lengthy shoreline for exploration. The area has good crops of edible berries in July and August. On the mountainside between Hobo Bay and Harrison Lagoon is Granite Mine, the last hard rock gold mine in Prince William Sound.

Precautions

Harrison Lagoon drains at low tide. The Forest Service recommends that the shoal to the north of the lagoon only be used for short-term anchoring. There is a dangerous shoal stretching over a mile offshore from the northern point of Harrison Lagoon and Point Packenham at the mouth of Barry Arm. Drinking water is accessible by boat from Lagoon Creek, or at times via runoff found by walking south of the cabin along the shore at low tide. Because wood is scarce, and often wet when you do find it, take a small gas stove for cooking.

Cabin

Harrison Lagoon Cabin (A-7)

This 16' x 20' cabin sleeps six, and has a wood-burning stove for heating. The cabin is on a gravel spit that separates the ocean from Harrison Lagoon. The rugged and brush-covered terrain makes for difficult hiking. The cabin offers seclusion and privacy. The scenery is magnificent, with steeply rising mountains and alpine and tidewater glaciers.

Water source: streams accessible only by boat; bring your own.

Facilities:
- wooden bunks
- outhouse
- table
- wood stove
- splitting maul
- saw
- bench
- counter
- shelves
- no boat

Hook Point

Hook Point is on Prince William Sound's Hinchinbrook Island, about 25 air miles southwest of Cordova. One-way flight time from Cordova is 15 minutes by wheeled aircraft. (USGS Quad Map Cordova B-7)

Fishing

Starting in mid-July, the stream near the cabin offers fair to good fishing for pink salmon, and for silver salmon in mid-August through September. Salmon are also available in a stream one mile east of the cabin. Streams are affected by intertidal fluctuations, and are difficult to cross at high tide. Plan your fishing time accordingly. Salmon are in select holes at low tide, and well into the stream at high tide. In some years, silvers are difficult to catch because of the overabundance of pink salmon. The same lures and flies that are effective in streams on Montague are effective here.

Hunting

Bear and deer hunting is available. Use calls to attract deer during late October and November. During years of heavy snowfall, hunt deer in and along beach fringe areas. Also look for them eating kelp on the beach during an early morning or late evening low tide.

Other Activities

Hook Point is an excellent choice for hiking, exploring, and especially beachcombing immediately after a storm. Concentrate your efforts at the sea cliffs to the west of the cabin. High breakers deposit a variety of items along the beach. The marine environment and geological structures make for excellent photographic opportunities. In late July and August, photograph seals feeding on salmon. Look for them at high tide, in or near the creeks. During a minus tide, flat, sandy areas offer good clamming.

Precautions

The landing strip is a quarter-mile from the cabin, so take a backpack for hauling gear. The bay in front of the cabin goes dry at low tide, prohibiting access.

Cabin
Hook Point Cabin (C-5)

Located 1.5 miles west of Hook Point, the cabin is a 16' x 16' A-frame with loft and capable of sleeping eight. It has an overview of beach and muskeg, and is surrounded in back by mature timber. A stream is nearby. This area offers seclusion and is a perfect choice for a weekend getaway. The cabin comes equipped with an oil and wood-burning stove.

Water source: stream
Facilities:
- wooden bunks
- loft
- table
- benches
- saw
- ax
- maul
- woodshed
- meat rack
- outhouse
- no boat: bring your own

Jack Bay is immediately off Valdez Narrows, 10 air miles southwest of Valdez. Access is either by floatplane (15 minutes from Valdez, 30 minutes from Cordova) or 20 miles by boat from Valdez. (USGS Quad Map Valdez A-7 and Cordova D-7)

Fishing

This is a marine fishery that requires a Zodiac inflatable or larger boat. Silver salmon fishing is fair to good, as is pink salmon in and around the points outside the bay and at the mouths of the streams within Jack Bay. Halibut fishing is fair in Valdez Arm, although you'll enjoy better fishing farther out in the Sound. Salmon sharks inhabit Jack Bay. The area is frequently visited by tour boats and other fishermen.

Hunting

Use this cabin as a base camp to hunt for mountain goat, black bear and deer, although some hunting can be done from the cabin. Expect tough going. Waterfowl hunting is good from October through December.

Precautions

Jack Bay is a popular anchorage, however, strong northeasterly winds can create large swells that may cause anchoring problems. The Forest Service recommends the bay as a fair weather anchorage only. Jack Bay is a good base for exploring other bays and Columbia Glacier.

Cabin
Jack Bay Cabin (C-12)

The 12' x 14' log cabin is at the head of Jack Bay. It sleeps six and has an oil-burning stove. Steep mountains and cliffs surround the cabin in back, with ocean and beach in front.

Water source: runoff; bring your own initial supply.
Facilities:

- wooden bunks
- oil stove (with oven)
- table
- outhouse
- benches
- counter
- no boat: bring your own

Sea lions, seals and sea otters are common throughout Prince William Sound, and in many areas can be observed while anglers fish for salmon, halibut or rockfish.

Located in the Kenai Mountains on the Kenai Peninsula, Juneau Lake is on the Resurrection Pass Trail System. A nine-mile hike from Mile 52, Sterling Highway, will get you to the lake, as will a chartered flight from Cooper Landing (10 minutes) or Moose Pass (20 minutes). (USGS Quad Map Seward C-8)

Fishing

Juneau Lake offers a variety of species, including lake trout, rainbow trout, whitefish, burbot and arctic grayling. The best fishing for rainbows and lakers is in spring, right after break-up. The north inlet stream is perhaps the best. Anchor or drift parallel to shoreline structure, using brown or black muddler patterns for rainbow and lakers, and gold Flashflies for lakers feeding in shallow water. Scud patterns also work extremely well, especially in and around the weed beds during the summer months. Many anglers are successful with deep-water trolling gear, one to six ounces of weight and a gold or silver flutter spoon. Bronze or copper plugs such as Wiggle Warts and Killer Baits also are effective in catching both species. For burbot, concentrate efforts in 20 to 40 feet of water, using fresh whitefish or herring scraps. Check ADF&G set line and hook size information. Best fishing is done at night, however, burbot do hit lures fished near the bottom, especially jigs tipped with bait. Whitefish require gossamer, 7X tippets and size 18 nymphs, dries, or caddis patterns. Concentrate your efforts during feeding cycles: watch for dimples on the lake. Whitefish migrate around Juneau Lake in schools, so where you'll catch one, you'll catch several. If you're not catching fish, experiment with various patterns and sizes.

Grayling fishing is best in Juneau Creek. Walk upstream, casting to holding structures such as riffles, pools, undercut banks and around logs and boulders. Almost any small, non-descript nymph or wet fly pattern works here. Although Juneau Creek grayling are not large, they are fiesty. Depending on time of year and water levels, fishing can range from poor to good.

Romig cabin. Photo courtesy USDA Forest Service.

Hunting

Moose, black and brown bear hunting in their respective seasons. Ptarmigan hunting is good on the higher ridges, while grouse and snowshoe hare hunting is fair to good at lower elevations. During high-use periods in August and early September, cabins must be reserved through special drawings.

Other Activities

This area is a popular destination with hikers and snowmobilers. Check with the USFS for restrictions on snowmobile, ATVs and pack animals.

Cabins
Romig Cabin (S-7)
Juneau Lake Cabin (S-8)

Romig and Juneau cabins are 12' x 14' structures surrounded by rolling hills covered with willow, spruce and birch. Find Juneau cabin on the eastern shore, and Romig on the southern shore. Elevation, 1,300 feet. Wood-burning stoves are furnished for heating. The cabins offer an ideal setting for a weekend fishing trip. Each cabin sleeps up to six people.

Water source: lake
Facilities:

- wooden bunks
- table
- bench
- wood stove

- wood supply
- maul
- saw
- outhouse

- counter
- boat
- oars

Silver and/or gold plugs longlined behind a boat is an effective technique for catching Kenai Peninsula lake trout.

Martin Lake is located 42 miles southeast of Cordova in the Copper River Delta. It's a 20-minute, one-way flight from Cordova. (USGS Quad Map Cordova B-2)

Fishing

Martin offers good fishing for lake trout year-round, however the best fishing for lunkers is immediately after ice out and in early October. Cut bait fished with a slip-sinker rig on the bottom in 20 or more feet of water has produced good catches of lakers. Starting in mid-June, sockeye salmon enter the Martin River. Dolly Varden and silver salmon are available for catching in mid-to-late August. Bright, fluorescent colored lures or flies are necessary for successful salmon fishing in this watershed. Occasionally, an anadromous cutthroat is caught. The lake is usually frozen from late November until late April or early May. Cabin must be reserved through special lottery drawings from late August through late September.

Hunting

Opportunity to hunt black and brown bear, moose and mountain goats from the cabin, or use it as a base camp for hunting further afield. Hunting is fair to good, but expect plenty of brush busting. Waterfowl pass through the area on their southward migration in late October and offer good pass shooting. This is a popular cabin with hunters, so apply early for best selection.

Cabin
Martin Lake Cabin (C-4)

The 12' x 14' cabin is located on the western shore of Martin Lake. It sleeps six, and is equipped with an oil-burning stove and oven. Situated in a very scenic area, the cabin has steep mountains behind it, the lake 50 yards from the front door, and a window view of the Martin River valley. Watch for loons or ducks on the lake, as well as fish rising for a hatch. The Eyak Indians originally settled the area, and it was popular with trappers in the late 19th century.

Water source: lake
Facilities:
- wooden bunks
- oil stove
- outhouse
- table
- bench
- counter
- covered meat rack
- boat/oars

McKinley Lake is in the Copper River Delta area, accessible via the McKinley Lake Trail. Find the trailhead at Mile 21 of the Copper River Highway; 10 minutes by floatplane from Cordova; or via boat or canoe up the Alaganik Slough (Mile 22 Copper River Highway) two miles to McKinley Lake. (USGS Quad Map Cordova B-4)

Fishing

Excellent fishing for cutthroat trout in the lake and stream. Longlining chrome/red or chrome and orange spoons is extremely effective. Fly fishermen use nymph patterns in late evening or early morning. There are Dolly Varden, but the largest fish are caught after late July, when sockeye salmon enter the stream. Silver salmon fishing is best from mid-August through mid-September. Sockeyes and silvers can be caught on 7/8-ounce Pixees, attractor patterns and brightly colored spinners. A popular hotspot for silvers is Alaganik Slough. After some pressure, fish often refuse to strike. Fish elsewhere and return an hour or two later.

For a more unusual type of fishing, go after the burbot in McKinley Lake.

Hiker/anglers enjoy the Pipeline Lakes Trail for additional good fishing for trout, grayling and char.

In August and September, the Copper River Delta is a berry-pickers delight, with huckleberries, blueberries and salmonberries found in abundance.

Hunting

There is good black and brown bear hunting in season. McKinley Lake cabin is insulated and suitable as a base for ice fishing and grouse hunting expeditions.

Other Activities

These cabins offer good wildlife viewing. Seals often follow salmon into the slough. Beaver, loons and Canada geese are common and photograph easily. The trail from the road to the cabin is in good condition. This is a popular family weekend outing destination. Day hikes include walking to the abandoned Lucky Strike Gold Mine, a half-mile north of the cabin, or exploring McKinley Peak. The area was once a mining capital. During the ''Copper Boom'' in the late 19th century, there were over 4,000 mineral claims in and around the Copper River. Blueberries and salmonberries are abundant throughout the area.

Precautions

Limited boat access mid-June through September during periods of high water.

Cabins

McKinley Trail Cabin (C-7)
McKinley Lake Cabin (C-15)

Capable of sleeping eight people, the 16' x 16', insulated McKinley Lake Cabin nestles in a mature rain forest about 40 feet from the lake's edge. The surrounding area is intermittent muskeg with steeply rising mountains.

McKinley Trail cabin, 16' x 20', with room to sleep six, is located 80 yards northeast of the Copper River Highway on the McKinley Lake Trail.

Water source: lake
Facilities:

- wooden bunks
- table
- wood stove
- deck

- outhouse
- table
- benches
- ax

- maul
- boat/oars

Nellie Martin River is 80 miles southwest of Cordova on the southwest end of Montague Island where it drains into Patton Bay. Access is by wheeled-plane via beach landing. Charged flight time from Cordova is 50 minutes; 45 minutes from Seward. (USGS Quad Map Blying Sound D-2)

Fishing

The Nellie Martin River silver salmon run offers some of the best salmon fishing in Prince William Sound. During the third week of August, the area receives moderate to heavy use from fly-in anglers. Fish the incoming tide for best fishing, and move upstream with the tide and salmon. At low tide, concentrate on fish holding in pools in the intertidal area or further upstream. The intertidal area also hosts a population of pink salmon from late July through mid-August. Dolly Varden are caught during the same time on spoons, Glo-bugs, needlefish or smolt patterns. Patton Bay offers fair to good fishing for halibut, most averaging 30 pounds or less, with an occasional fish over 100. Drift parallel to structure in 20 to 30 fathoms, jigging herring, metal Vi-ke or Diamond jigs or use salmon heads on a 10/0 hook for larger fish.

Nellie Martin River offers excellent silver salmon fishing. Due to the popularity of this fishing area, cabins must be reserved through special lottery drawings.

Hunting

The cabin is popular with deer and bear hunters in late fall. Good waterfowl hunting in October.

Other Activities

The Nellie Martin River basin offers myriad opportunities for day hikes and exploration. When water level is high, pack an inflatable to assist in crossing the river. Beachcombing is good in Patton Bay, a short hike from the cabin. Salmonberries and blueberries are abundant.

Precautions

The lower beach is the recommended landing site for this cabin. The upper landing strip consists of soft sand. It is bumpy, and not recommended for use. The tide affects the depth of the river and intertidal area, so calculate the time required to travel to and from fishing or hiking areas. Don't become stranded. Private lands border the cabin. Request information regarding use of these lands from Chugach National Forest or Chugach Alaska Corporation in Anchorage.

Cabin

Nellie Martin River Cabin (C-14)

Located in a clearing on the north bank of the Nellie Martin River, this 12' x 14' log cabin sleeps six and has both an oil stove and a wood stove with oven. The beach offers an excellent supply of driftwood for burning. This cabin receives high use from early August through mid-September. Cabin must be reserved through special lottery drawings.

Water source: river
Facilities:

- wooden bunks
- outhouse
- table
- bench

- cooking counter
- shelves
- ax
- saw

- wood stove
- oil stove
- no boat

Paradise Lakes

Paradise Lakes are behind Sheep Mountain, about eight miles east of the Seward Highway. Access is by floatplane, 15 minutes from Moose Pass or 20 minutes from Seward. (USGS Quad Map Seward B-6)

Fishing

Upper and Lower Paradise lakes offer fair to good fishing for 9- to 16-inch arctic grayling. Although it's possible to catch grayling anywhere in the lake, look for fish near the feeder inlets and outlets. Black Furies work well, as do small spoons. Grayling here are not finicky. However, a boat is necessary to reach the best fishing. Find concentrations of fish by watching for rises in early morning, late evening or throughout the day. Don't forget to fish deep along the bottom, as grayling here also feed on snails and aquatic nymphs.

Hunting

Hunting for grouse, ptarmigan and hares is fair to good. The cabin can be used as a base camp for hunting moose, bear and goats when in season and if the appropriate permits have been issued. Check ADF&G for more information.

Other Activities

Backcountry hikers will delight in knowing the lake is accessible from Ptarmigan Creek Trail via the Snow River Pass. Good orienteering skills are necessary, as no trail exists. Climb up and over the saddle at the head of Upper Paradise Lake to view numerous glaciers and the Sargent Icefield.

Cabins
Upper Paradise Lake Cabin (S-1)
Lower Paradise Lake Cabin (S-3)

Located at 1,200 and 1,340 feet of elevation, the 12' x 14' cabins are surrounded by 4,000-foot, glacier-crowned mountains, dense spruce forests and flower-filled alpine meadows. The area is one of the most scenic on the Kenai Peninsula. Both cabins are located near the lake and each can sleep six. Each has a wood-burning stove for heating.

Water source: lake
Facilities:
- wooden bunks
- outhouse
- table bench
- counter
- shelves
- wood stove
- maul
- saw
- 14-foot boat
- oars

Upper Paradise Lake. Scott Harrison, USDA Forest Service.

Located southeast of Whittier at the west end of Cochrane Bay in Prince William Sound, Paulson Bay is 40 minutes by floatplane from Anchorage or 60 minutes from Cordova. From Whittier, the distance by boat is 18 miles. (USGS Quad Map Seward C-4)

Fishing

Starting in early July and lasting until August, pink salmon fishing in and around the bay is good. Try the creek near the cabin for the best pink and chum fishing. Excellent fishing for rockfish and lingcod can be had at any of the islands or rocky points in Cochrane Bay. Halibut fishing can be good, but not exceptional in this area. Keep fishing new areas every 20 minutes until you locate fish. Shrimping is reported as good. Sockeye salmon are available in a stream about two miles south of the cabin.

Hunting

Bear and waterfowl hunting is good throughout the region. During a high tide, look for ducks at the heads of coves. Good black bear hunting to the west and north of the cabin.

Other Activities

This area is especially attractive to hikers because of little or no brush-busting. A good trail leads from the cabin to the creek, a hike of about three-quarters of a mile. Take a boat to help expand your range of exploration.

Precautions

Beware of submerged rock ledges between islands and off coastal points. Sight in on the Forest Service buoy, as the cabin is hidden in thick timber and difficult to locate.

Cabin

Paulson Bay Cabin (A-8)

Located in a thickly forested area surrounded by patches of open muskeg, this 12' x 14' cabin sleeps six and has a wood-burning stove for heating. If you're boating in, finding the bay may be difficult. The mouth is obscured by five small islands. Enter from the north, well to the right of center (along the northwestern side of Cochrane Bay). Look for the cabin at the head of the bay. From the cabin you'll have a spectacular view of Port Wells and into College Fiord, with Harvard Glacier dropping down majestically in the background.

Water source: creek
Facilities:

• wooden bunks	• saw	• counter
• table	• woodshed	• no boat
• wood stove	• outhouse	
• splitting maul	• bench	

Pete Dahl Cutoff Slough

Peter Dahl Slough is southeast of Cordova. It is accessible by boat by driving the Copper River Highway to Mile 17. Turn south on Alaganik Road. You'll find a boat ramp at the end of the road (Mile 3). The area is floatplane accessible, requiring a 10-minute, one-way flight from Cordova. Access should be attempted only at high tide. Tiedeman Slough is located seven miles down Alaganik Slough, and is on the right before reaching open water. (USGS Quad Map Cordova B-4)

Fishing

There is no fishing in the immediate area due to water turbidity caused by glacial run-off. However, fishing for sockeyes (late June-July) and silvers (August-Sept.) can be had in Alaganik Slough. See McKinley Lake (page 310) for more details.

Hunting

The Copper River Delta is a major resting and feeding area for as many as 20 million waterfowl and shorebirds of the Pacific Flyway. Waterfowl hunting is exceptional. Hunters can expect mallards, pintails, green-winged teal, shoveler, widgeon and gadwall. Hunting is best at the start of the season, and again in mid-October, when the northern birds move through on their southward migration. Decoys are a must here for best success. Silhouettes as well as full-bodied floaters are popular. Type depends on boat size and area hunted. Many hunters carry both, allowing them to hunt low as well as high tides. Geese concentrate on the flats at low tide. You'll enjoy good action by watching for concentrations of birds, and setting up silhouettes early the next day as the tide is going out. Brown bear hunting is also a favorite activity in this area.

Flash flies and flutter spoons are effective in catching sockeyes holding in or near backwater sloughs.

Other Activities

This is an ideal location if you're a bird watcher. May is the best time to reserve the cabin. You'll find bears, foxes, coyotes and land otters hunting for eggs and molting, flightless birds. Photographic opportunities are abundant and one-of-a-kind. However, expect several days of inclement weather.

Precautions

This area is an epicenter for major storms. If you're canoeing or rowing to the cabin, keep in mind that high winds may keep you at or near the boat ramp. A small outboard is preferred. Also, travel to the cabins is at high tide only. Foot travel on the mud flats can be dangerous. Always travel in pairs.

Cabins
Pete Dahl Cabin (C-2)
Tiedeman Slough Cabin (C-3)

Both cabins are 12' x 14' wooden frame structures that can sleep six. They are in the flat, sprawling Copper River Delta, an area of immense grasslands and ponds. Each cabin is equipped with an oil stove, so bring your own fuel.

Water source: none; bring enough for the length of your stay.
Facilities:
- wooden bunks
- table
- oil stove
- outhouse
- bench
- counter
- no boat

Pigot Bay

Pigot Bay is in West Prince William Sound, northeast of Whittier on the west side entrance to Port Wells. By float plane, it's 40 minutes from Anchorage or 60 minutes from Cordova. By boat from Whittier, the distance is 18 miles. (USGS Quad Map Seward D-4)

Fishing

Pink and chum salmon fishing is good in the freshwater braid of streams at the head of the bay. These salmon can also be caught on an incoming tide by fishing the intertidal areas and outer saltwater sections with spoons and flies. Halibut fishing can range from poor to good, depending on weather and time of year. Fishing is excellent for a variety of rockfish and ling cod along the western shore of Esther Island, and at the mouth and rocky points of Pigot Bay. Try 180 feet and deeper for yelloweye rockfish. Use large metal jigs for best success.

Hunting

Deer hunting in the outwash valley is fair, and bear hunting is fair to good in the spring.

Other Activities

Take along your crab pots and clam shovels, as good populations of Dungeness crab and butter clams inhabit Pigot Bay. Best clamming is at the head of the bay on easily identifiable gravel beaches.

Precautions

Anchor at the head of the bay near its north shore, using the Forest Service mooring buoy. Keep your eye out for sudden storms.

Cabin
Pigot Bay Cabin (A-4)

Located in a thickly forested area surrounded by patches of open muskeg, this 12' x 14' cabin sleeps six and has a wood-burning stove for heating. If you're boating in, finding the bay may be difficult. The mouth is obscured by five small islands. Enter from the north, well to the right of center (along the northwestern side of Cochrane Bay). Look for the cabin at the head of the bay. From the cabin you'll have a spectacular view of Port Wells and into College Fiord, with Harvard Glacier dropping down majestically in the background.

Water source: creek
Facilities:

- wooden bunks
- table
- wood stove
- splitting maul

- saw
- woodshed
- outhouse
- bench

- counter
- no boat

Port Chalmers is on the northwest side of Montague Island, and accessible by boat or floatplane. Flight time is 50 minutes from Cordova, 75 minutes from Seward. By boat, it's 65 miles from Cordova, 70 miles from Whittier and 100 miles from Seward. (USGS Quad Map Seward A-1)

Fishing

Chalmers River offers fair fishing for cutthroat trout and Dolly Varden char. The mid-to-upper headwaters offer the best angling opportunities. Walk up river and fish pools and currents where they join side streams. In early August, the intertidal area of the bay has a good run of pink salmon. You can also catch these fish in the Chalmers River. For silver salmon, first try surf casting on an incoming tide, then fish the river. The silver run starts in late August. Catch them through mid-September by fishing holes or backwater sloughs. Late-season silvers readily strike plugs. I prefer silver Wee Warts.

Hunting

Waterfowl hunting in the area is good for both puddlers, divers and sea ducks. Season opens early September. Deer hunting is good, especially if you have water transportation such as a cruiser or inflatable. Brown bear present year-round. Deer season runs from August through December. Many hunters choose this area for a combo fishing/deer hunting trip.

Montague Island has a healthy population of Sitka blacktail deer. Look for them along beach fringe areas and in high alpine meadows.

Other Activities

The rainforest of Montague and the intertidal areas offer many hiking opportunities. At low tide, take a hike across the tidal flats to the other side of the bay. At high tide, you'll need to follow the shoreline. Discover an abundance of marine life. Pack a magnifying glass, collector's sack and tide book. An inflatable and outboard can save much travel time, and opens up for exploration other bays in the area. Take field glasses for observing whales, porpoises, sea otters and sea lions in the waters of Montague Strait. Observe breeding colonies of black-legged kittiwakes and sea lions on The Needle, 15 miles southwest of Port Chalmers. Caution: Only undertake this journey in a boat 18 feet or longer.

Precautions

If traveling by floatplane, arrive at high tide. It's then possible to land in front of the cabin. At low tide, the bay goes dry. If arriving via boat, the best anchorage is behind the cabin to the west.

Cabin

Port Chalmers Cabin (C-17)

Located at the southern end of Port Chalmers, this 12' x 14' cabin is surrounded by hemlock/spruce forest and offers a good view of Port Chalmers and the mountains of Montague Island. It sleeps six, and has both wood and oil stoves.

Water source: difficult, bring your own. Nearest stream quarter-mile south of cabin.

Facilities:

- wooden bunks
- oil stove
- wood stove
- outhouse

- bow saw
- ax
- table
- bench

- counter
- shelves
- no boat

Resurrection River empties into the head of Resurrection Bay near the city of Seward on the Kenai Peninsula. It is fed by the snow and glacial melt of the Kenai Mountains and Harding Icefield. (USGS Quad Map Seward B-8)

Fishing

Resurrection River is glacially silted, and does not support populations of resident fish.

Hunting

The trail offers access to some excellent black bear hunting in the Kenai Mountains and surrounding drainages. However, the going is difficult. Best hunting is done on foot above timberline, or with the use of pack animals. Moose, brown bear and wolves are also available. Check season openings and permit availability with ADF&G. Hare, grouse and ptarmigan are hunted during the fall and winter months.

Other Activities

This trail receives relatively little use, and thus offers a secluded experience for the hiker or cross-country skier. The trail is closed during parts of the year to motorized vehicles and pack animals. Check with the USFS for specific information. This trail is a good choice for the family desiring a weekend hike. The terrain is relatively flat and easily walked.

Precautions

Bears have scratched the cabin in various places, and destroyed the screening. Keep a clean camp.

Cabin
Resurrection River Cabin (S-13)

The 12' x 14' cabin is 6.5 miles from the Resurrection River Trailhead. Take a short spur up and off the main trail to the cabin, which overlooks a small pond with a picturesque view of the surrounding Kenai Mountains. Spruce trees are predominant throughout the area, with some alder and willow. The trail to the cabin has been used for thousands of years by Indian tribes on the Kenai Peninsula. The cabin sleeps six, and has a wood-burning stove for heating and cooking. Elevation, 500 feet.

Water source: river, creeks
Facilities:
- wooden bunks
- outhouse
- table
- wood stove
- shelves
- benches
- saw
- ax
- no boat

The Russian River and Lakes can be reached by taking the Anchorage Highway south to the Kenai Peninsula and turning into the Russian River Campground. The lakes can be reached by floatplane, 25 minutes from Seward. (USGS Quad Map Seward B-8 and Kenai B-1)

Fishing

The Russian River is the largest and most heavily hit sockeye salmon fishery in Alaska. Fishing for sockeyes is not permitted above the Russian River Falls. Fish the lower stretches of river before hiking to the cabin. However, there is good fishing for Dolly Varden and rainbow trout in the Russian River. Best fishing is in Upper Russian Lake for rainbow trout 21 inches and larger. Smolt and sculpin patterns take the most fish, along with egg and Odonata nymph imitations.

Hunting

During winter, snowmobilers and cross-country skiers use this cabin as a base for ptarmigan and grouse hunting. The cabin can be used as a base camp to hunt wolves, moose, and black and brown bear in their respective seasons. Hunters take note: The trail is closed to saddle/pack stock from April 1 through June 30. It is closed to motorized vehicles from May 1 through November 30.

Other Activities

Photographers often take photos of bears fishing for Russian River sockeyes. The area is also popular among winter recreationists. The cabin is part of the Russian Lakes Trail System, which connects to the Resurrection River and Resurrection Pass trails. When combined, these form a 72-mile trek from Seward to Hope. The trail is relatively flat, and offers easy hiking for those wishing to enjoy the beauty of Alaska's backcountry.

Precautions

Severe avalanche danger exists for winter travelers between Russian River Campground trailhead and the south end of Lower Russian Lake. Recommended winter access is through Cooper Lake trailhead. Trail may be difficult to follow after heavy snowfall.

Cabins
Aspen Flats Cabin (S-5)
Barber Cabin (S-12)
Upper Russian Lake Cabin (S-4)

The Aspen Flats cabin is nine miles from the Russian River trailhead and 12 miles from the Cooper River trailhead. A 12' x 14' rustic cabin that sleeps six, it is near the river in a mixed forest of spruce and black cottonwood. Elevation, 600 feet. A wood-burning stove is provided for heating and cooking.

The 16' x 20' Barber cabin, named in memory of Forest Service District Ranger Dave Barber, is on the eastern shore of Lower Russian Lake, three miles south of the Russian River Campground. Elevation, 400 feet. Boat and oars included. This cabin has been specially built to accommodate wheel-chair visitors. Features include: ramps to front and rear doors, outhouse and boat dock.

Upper Russian Lakes cabin is located on the north shore of Upper Russian Lake. Access is 12 miles by trail, starting at the Russian River Campground trailhead or nine miles from the Cooper Lake trailhead. Also accessible via a 20-minute flight by floatplane from Seward. Elevation, 700 feet. Dimensions, 12' x 14'.

Water source: river/lake
Facilities:
- wooden bunks
- table
- wood stove
- maul
- saw
- shelves
- counter
- benches
- outhouse
- boat/oars

(at Barber and
Upper Russian cabins)

The Russian River is the most popular sockeye salmon fishery on the Kenai Peninsula. Rainbow trout fishing is good in the Russian Lakes.

San Juan Bay

San Juan Bay is 100 miles southwest of Cordova on the southwest end of Montague Island in Prince William Sound. Access is by wheeled plane only. Charged flight time is 60 minutes from Cordova, 40 minutes from Seward. (USGS Quad Map Blying Sound D-3)

Fishing

The San Juan River north of the cabin offers good to excellent silver salmon fishing in August and September. Access is via beachfront. Salmon are caught on both flies and hardware.

Hunting

Opportunities to hunt deer and bear.

Other Activities

The area has an abundance of scenery, vegetation and wildlife. Photograph or observe deer, whales, porpoise, sea otters, sea lions and harbor seals in the waters of Montague Strait. Birdwatchers will find the nearby meadows a haven to birds of all types. A scenic waterfall is an easy quarter-mile hike from the cabin. Cross a rock berm to the west and follow the stream south. If it's a clear day, take the ridgeline to the east for a spectacular view of Montague Island and surrounding ocean. Hiking is strenuous, but worth the effort.

Precautions

Due to frequently rough seas, pilots should not attempt to land in the bay. Take a backpack with frame to haul gear, as the cabin is a quarter-mile from the landing site. Hip boots are a must item. You'll need to cross a stream before reaching the cabin. During periods of heavy rain, the stream becomes swollen, and is difficult to cross.

Cabin

San Juan Bay Cabin (C-10)

The 14' x 16' rustic log cabin sleeps six and is equipped with both wood and oil stoves. Located on the edge of a meadow bordered with stands of alder and spruce, the cabin provides a scenic view of mountains and forest to the east. This area was uplifted 38 feet during the 1964 earthquake. Before the earthquake, the large meadow near the cabin was a saltwater lagoon. The area is remote, and offers seclusion and unlimited recreational opportunities.

Water source: catchment
Facilities:

- wooden bunks
- wood stove
- oil stove
- ax
- bow saw
- covered meat rack
- outhouse
- bench
- table
- counter
- wood supply nearby
- no boat

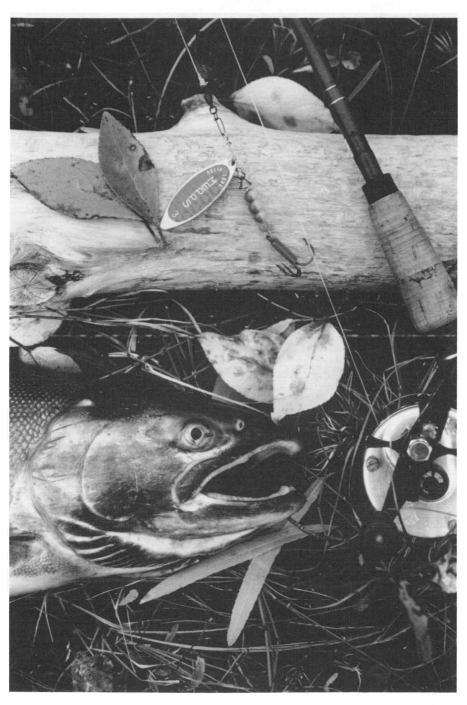

Mepps spinners with prism blade patterns in sizes three to five are popular among anglers fishing the San Juan River.

Shrode Lake

Shrode Lake is in West Prince William Sound, southeast of Whittier, near Long Bay off Culross Passage. By floatplane, access is 45 minutes from Anchorage or 55 minutes from Cordova. By boat, the distance from Whittier is 25 miles to Long Bay, and a one-mile hike to the lake. (USGS Quad Map Seward C-4)

Fishing

The area offers fair to good fishing for several species of salmon. In mid-July, sockeyes enter Shrode Creek, but quickly move into the lake, making themselves virtually inaccessible to anglers. During the same time, pink salmon enter the stream by the thousands, offering excellent fishing, both in freshwater and salt. In mid-August, silver salmon arrive, with the peak of the run taking place toward the end of the month. There are four areas to fish: the saltwater, which is Long Bay, a one-mile hike from the cabin; the lagoon between saltwater and the creek mouth; the creek itself (which offers the best fishing); and Shrode Lake. In August and September, expect good fishing for Dolly Varden char. Use salmon egg patterns or salmonberry spinners for best success. Fish are often spooky in the creek when you fish downstream on them, so walk to the lagoon and fish upstream for best success. Time this to coincide after peak high tide. Going is often rough. Use the trail to skirt around the tougher areas.

Hunting

The area offers fair to good hunting for blacktails and black bear in the spring. Waterfowl hunting is fair in September and improves in October and November.

Other Activities

Hikers enjoy the half-mile trail to Jack Lake or Three-Finger Cove, west of Shrode Lake, for bird watching and photographic opportunities. Discover a variety of plant life in the rain forest. Berries are abundant in August and September.

Precautions

During summer only, boaters can use the anchor buoy in Long Bay. At high tide, only shallow-draft vessels can proceed as far as the lagoon at the head of Long Bay. Use caution, as rock hazards are numerous in both the channel and lagoon.

Cabin
Shrode Lake Cabin (A-5)

This 16-foot A-frame sleeps 10, and has an oil stove for heating. The cabin is near timberline in a grassy/muskeg area surrounded by snow-capped mountains. Excellent scenery and isolation. Due to its high elevation, ice-out does not occur until mid-June.

Water source: lake
Facilities:

- wooden bunks
- loft
- table
- benches
- oil stove
- outhouse
- counter
- shelves
- boat
- oars

Softuk Bar is on the mainland near Mount Lazier, 55 miles southwest of Cordova. Access is by wheeled plane only at low tide. Flight time from Cordova is 30 minutes, one way. (USGS Quad Map Cordova A-2)

Fishing

No fishing in this area. However, razor clamming is good at low tide.

Hunting

Softuk Bar offers good to excellent waterfowl hunting in the fall, featuring puddlers, divers and sea ducks. It is also a good base for bear hunters who hunt the Martin River Slough and Ragged Mountain area. A riverboat or small inflatable with outboard is a must for hunting the area. Decoys are not necessary, but add to the enjoyment of the hunt. Time your arrival and departure times with the tides, as low tide can leave you stranded in the dark.

Other Activities

The U.S. Forest Service says this cabin offers variety for all users. The sand beaches allow easy walking to various shorelines and distant points of interest. There is excellent beachcombing, especially for Japanese fishing floats (glass balls) and commercial floats of all types. After heavy storms, look for crab pots that have washed ashore. The area is an excellent wildlife viewing area. Expect to see gray whales hug the shoreline in the spring on their northward migration. Closer to shore, sea otters, shorebirds, harbor seals and sea lions are common. If you're an explorer, take a hike to the abandoned townsite of Katalla. A metal detector will provide some interesting finds. At the east end of Softuk Bar, you'll find an overgrown roadbed that leads into town. Take a bucket, as strawberries are abundant and delicious.

Cabin

Softuk Bar Cabin (C-16)

This cabin is located on the outside beach of this mud/sand bar that is surrounded by alder and spruce thickets. The 12' x 14' log cabin can sleep six, and has wood and oil stoves for heating. Water source is limited, so bring an initial supply. Nearest source of freshwater is half a mile from the cabin. About 40 yards from the cabin is a good view of the Gulf of Alaska. On a sunny day, sunbathe and soak in the scenery on the sandy beach.

Water source: half a mile from cabin
Facilities:

• wooden bunks	• ax	• counter
• table	• bow saw	• no boat
• wood stove	• outhouse	
• oil stove	• bench	

South Culross Passage

Culross Passage is on the southwestern side of Culross Island, about 25 miles southeast of Whittier, in West Prince William Sound. Access is by boat or floatplane; charged air time, one-way, is 45 minutes from Anchorage; 55 minutes from Cordova. (USGS Quad Map Seward C-4)

Fishing

Pink salmon fishing is fair in July, and increases in intensity as the month progresses. Best fishing is in the cove. Chum salmon are also available. Use small 1/8-ounce spoons in silver/chartreuse or No. 4 or 5 Rooster Tail spinners. On an incoming tide, wade into the cove and cast to individual fish. If you have a boat, try rockfish and cod fishing in and around the various islands of the passage. Six-ounce lead-headed jigs work very well, especially when tipped with a white twister tail. In the immediate area, steamer clamming and shrimping is good.

Hunting

Waterfowl, black bear and blacktail deer hunting is fair to good near the cabin. Access to a small inflatable or dingy will increase your chances of success. Such a craft should be large enough to handle the open ocean. A boat is a must for serious waterfowl hunting. Without a dog or a boat, ducks may be impossible to retrieve on a gusty day.

Other Activities

This cabin offers marine photographers the chance to photograph harbor seals, orca whales in the main channel, porpoises and sea otters. Behind the islands are numerous intertidal plant and animal communities awaiting to be discovered. Secluded beaches are ideal for secluded and private picnics. The area is excellent for salmonberries and blueberries.

Chum salmon, also known as dog salmon, are aptly named due to the large teeth males grow prior to spawning. This species is a spunky fighter on light tackle.

Precautions

Because the inner lagoon is dry at low tide, anchor large boats in the outer bay and use the skiff to reach shore. A trail from the inner spit leads to the cabin on the north shore of the lagoon.

Cabin

South Culross Passage Cabin (A-9)

This cabin is a 12' x 14' log structure that sleeps six. It is nestled at the head of a lagoon and surrounded by rock bluffs. A wood-burning stove is furnished for heating. In late July and August, the number of dead and dying pink salmon impart a fishy smell to the area. Near the cabin, a waterfall offers exceptional photographic opportunities. A deep pool below the falls makes for a cold, yet invigorating dip. Access to the falls is at low tide only.

Water source: creek

Facilities:

- wooden bunks
- table
- benches
- maul
- saw
- woodshed
- outhouse
- counter
- shelves
- no boat

Stump Lake

Stump Lake is 85 miles southwest of Cordova on the southeast end (Gulf of Alaska side) of Montague Island. Access is by air only, 45 minutes from Seward, 50 minutes from Cordova, 80 minutes from Anchorage, one way. The lake is accessible via floatplane, but be cautious of logs or stumps near the surface, when landing. Two miles from the cabin, a beach allows wheeled plane access at low tide only. (USGS Quad Map Blying Sound D-2)

Fishing

Stump Lake offers year-round fishing for cutthroat trout and Dolly Varden. Fish are often holding in or near the bank, under floating logs, in weedbeds and in and around stumps. The log jam areas are especially productive in late afternoon and during twilight hours when there is no direct sunlight entering the water.

Before the salmon runs begin, expect fair cutthroat fishing in the creek emptying the lake. Pink salmon fishing starts in July; catch the freshest pinks at the creek mouth. The creek also receives a small run of silver salmon. Don't fish for them at the lake. Find migration routes in the stream, or fish the mouth for best success. Dollies are available, but not abundant. Try late August and September for large fish. Attractor flies, woolly buggers, leeches and dries are effective in taking cutthroats and Dollies; hardware, flies and eggs are good choices for taking silvers. Small tippets are required for the cutts, especially on sunny days. Lake is frozen from mid-November through mid-April. The boat at the cabin can handle up to a 10-hp outboard.

Western Prince William Sound is a favorite among saltwater anglers pursuing salmon and bottomfish. Alpine and tidewater glaciers provide spectacular photo opportunities.

Hunting

Waterfowl hunting is fair to good in mid-to-late October and November, as is blacktail deer hunting. Brown bear hunting is difficult due to the dense brush and forest. Because the muskeg has thigh-deep "holes," wear ankle-fit hip boots if hunting this area. Pass shooting for sea ducks is good in October and November.

Other Activities

Steller sea lions, harbor seals and sea otters are common in and around salt water. The beach offers miles of easy hiking and beachcombing opportunities. Stump Lake cabin provides a unique opportunity to witness the death of a lake. Since the 1964 earthquake, the water level has dropped steadily. Through plant succession, the lake will eventually drain and become a meadow.

Precautions

Access into this area with large boats is not possible due to high surf and unprotected anchorages. An inflatable and outboard is a good transportation choice. Carry bear protection.

Cabins

Stump Lake Cabin (C-8)
Log Jam Bay Cabin (C-9)

The 16' x 20' Stump Lake cabin is surrounded by a dense stand of spruce and hemlock forest and brush with patches of muskeg. Both wood and oil stoves are provided. Room to sleep six. A good trail leads from the lake to salt water. If you plan on landing on the beach, take a pack with frame to haul goods to and from the cabin.

The 12' x 18' Log Jam Bay cabin is located on the northeast end of Stump Lake. It doesn't have a covered meat rack, otherwise it is equipped identically to Stump Lake cabin.

Water Source: lake
Facilities:

- wooden bunks
- table
- wood stove
- oil stove

- ax
- bow saw
- covered meat rack
- 14-foot skiff/oars

- outhouse
- cooking counter
- bench

Swan Lake

Swan Lake is on the Resurrection Pass Trail, 13 miles from the south trailhead at Mile 52 Sterling Highway. Access is also by floatplane: 15 minutes from Cooper Landing or 30 minutes from Moose Pass. (USGS Quad Map Seward C-8)

Fishing

Swan Lake offers lakers, rainbow trout and Dolly Varden in the lake and nearby streams, and sockeye salmon starting in mid-July and lasting through August. The lake is narrow, and fish are generally suspended at or below the thermocline. For best success, deepwater trolling is necessary. The southeastern end of the lake offers the most opportunities for fly and spin fishermen. Use salmon egg patterns and attractor spoons for best success. Check Crescent and Juneau Lake entries for additional how-to fishing information.

Hunting

Caribou hunting is allowed by permit only. Moose, brown and black bear and wolf hunting is best done via horseback on an extended hunt, using a spike camp. Terrain is rugged and steep. Most hunters concentrate their efforts in the alpine areas north of the lake. Grouse and ptarmigan hunting on the slopes surrounding the cabin is good to excellent. The cabin is popular during late August and early September seasons, and may be reserved only through special drawings.

Other Activities

Good hiking during summer and fall, especially a possible cross-country trek to American Pass. Cross-country skiing and snowmobiling opportunities in winter. Snowmobile access from December 1 through February 15 only. Restrictions on pack animals.

Cabins
Swan Lake Cabin (S-9)
West Swan Lake Cabin (S-10)

The 12' x 14' Swan Lake cabin is located on the lakeshore in a grassy field surrounded by birch, spruce and moderately rolling terrain.

West Swan Lake cabin is located near the northwest corner of the lake. Each cabin sleeps six and has a wood-burning stove for heating. Elevation, 1,400 feet.

Water source: lake
Facilities:

- wooden bunks
- table
- bench
- counter

- outhouse
- maul
- saw
- boat

- oars
- wood stove
- wood supply

In spring and fall, expect to catch large lake trout in relatively shallow water and at depths to 40 feet. Silver and gold jigging lures and spoons catch the most fish.

Trout Lake can be reached by taking the Resurrection Pass Trail, which starts at the south trailhead, Mile 52 Sterling Highway. It's a seven-mile hike to reach the half-mile access trail to the lake. If you're in a hurry, the lake is accessible via a 10-minute flight from Cooper Landing or 20-minute flight from Moose Pass. (USGS Quad Map Seward C-8)

Fishing

Trout Lake offers whitefish, rainbow and lake trout. Fishing is fair to good, depending on weather conditions. Nearby Juneau Creek offers fair to good fishing for grayling, rainbow and Dolly Varden. Fishing is fair where Thurman Creek empties into the lake. During summer, fish for lakers at the northwest end in 20 to 30 feet of water, going deeper if necessary. Use ultralight tackle or fly gear for rainbows and lakers in the southeast end of the lake when the fish come into the shallows to feed, usually during the hours of dusk and dawn. Small flatfish from one to two inches in blue, gold and red work well when trolled very slowly around the lake structure. Add weight for fishing deeper water. Whitefish require small dry flies, translucent-wing nymphs or egg patterns.

Hunting

The area offers a good base for moose hunting. Expect to see examples of controlled burning to enhance moose habitat. Black bear hunting is fair in the low-lying creekbeds. Hunting here is difficult, and requires a tree stand in the heavily forested areas.

Other Activities

The scenery and easy trail make this cabin and area a popular choice with skiers, hikers, cross-country travelers and dog mushers. The trail may be difficult to follow after a heavy snowfall. Resurrection Pass Trail is closed to saddle/pack stock from April 1 to June 30, and motorized vehicles from February 16 to November 30.

Cabin
Trout Lake Cabin (S-6)

The cabin at Trout Lake is a 12' x 14' A-frame with loft capable of sleeping 10. It is furnished with a wood-burning stove, and fair to poor wood supply. Bring your own cook stove. Rolling hills covered with birch, spruce and willow surround the cabin, which is located on a slight rise overlooking the lake at 1,200 feet elevation.

Water source: lake
Facilities:

- wooden bunks
- loft
- table
- benches

- wood stove
- maul
- saw
- outhouse

- boat
- oars

Epilogue

The friendship that we've established from sharing the adventures in this book doesn't have to end here. Write us about your Alaska fishing experiences, the things you've discovered, the sights you have seen and the fish you have caught in Alaska's National Forests.

Because no one person knows all there is to know about Alaska sportfishing, we're always eager to learn about new techniques, theories and successes that you've discovered, either on your own or with the help of our fishing books and periodicals.

Nothing would please us more than to hear about them directly from you, the reader of this book and our friend in Alaska sportfishing.

Let us share this common bond in an uncommon land. Write to us at P. O. Box 83550, Fairbanks, Alaska 99708.

Until then, Good Fishing.
Chris and Adela Batin

Cabin Index

Airline Reservations to Alaska

You've chosen your destination, the fishing tackle has been purchased and packed, and you're ready to travel. We recommend you choose Alaska Airlines for airline transportation to any of the Gateways listed in this book.

There are several reasons why Alaska Airlines is our Number 1 choice. The first is service. The airline's commitment to quality is reflected, in part, by how your baggage is handled. Over the last 10 years, we've checked fishing rod cases, kayaks, rifles, backpacks and even a fishing rod without a case. We have yet to experience a mishap or the broken equipment often experienced with other airlines. And if you want to ship your catch back home, Alaska Airlines will, space permitting, refrigerate or freeze your catch in storage lockers until your flight is ready to depart.

Another reason to fly Alaska Airlines is the amount of baggage you can ship. Smaller airlines often implement a weight restriction on bags (50 pounds total for all bags, per person), and charge you per pound for any excess. Alaska Airlines allows two bags of 70 pounds each and a carry-on.

Small courtesies also keep customers coming back year after year. The in-flight crew often conveys the wonder and excitement of Alaska from the moment you board to the time you deplane. Examples include co-pilot narrations of the geographical and geological sights along the Alaska coast. At times, the crew bantering becomes hilarious, and draws a hearty laugh from all on board.

Meals are excellent, with first-class service the best we've experienced on any U.S. airline. Alaska Airlines also spends more to prepare your coach-class meal: $7.50, compared to $3.75 for the other airlines. They place value in customer feedback. The executive chef spends a day each month flying unannounced on various Alaska Airline routes, sampling the meals and requesting comments from passengers. Comment cards are analyzed for positive and negative trends. The airline's officers meet twice a week in the executive dining room. Coach and first-class meals prepared in Alaska Airline kitchens in Seattle, Los Angeles and other destinations are flown in that day for the executive lunch.

The accolades don't stop here. For the past three years, Conde Nast readers voted Alaska as the best domestic airline. In July, 1991, Consumer Reports chose Alaska as the best domestic airline carrier. And from a financial management and safety standpoint, Air Transport World recognized Alaska as the world's best airline.

Because weather in Seattle, San Francisco and southeast Alaska can oftentimes be treacherous, Alaska Airline pilots are specially trained on 727 simulators that can be programmed with any city Alaska flies to. The technicians can program a variety of hazards into the system, from wind shears and fog to engine failure.

Alaska Airlines is the only passenger carrier airline that has the HGS 1000 on its 727 jets, a holographic heads-up guidance system often referred to as ''The Fog Buster.'' As a result, the landing minimums for Alaska are much lower than other air carriers. In a nutshell, chances are good you'll reach your destination on time when you fly Alaska Airlines.

Alaska Airlines flies from most western U.S. cities, with connecting flights to the major Gateways listed in this book, as well as Cordova, Yakutat, Nome, and of course, Anchorage and Fairbanks.

The in-flight magazine also offers a variety of travel tips and information on Alaska to prep you for your fishing adventure.

For more information on making reservations on Alaska Airlines, contact your travel agent or call Alaska Airlines direct at **1-800-426-0333** from anywhere in U.S.

About the Authors

Chris and Adela Batin are one of Alaska's most widely published husband/wife outdoor photojournalist teams. They have authored and produced the popular, award-winning books *"How to catch Alaska's Trophy Sportfish"*, *"Hunting in Alaska: a Comprehensive Guide"* and *"Chris Batin's 20 Great Alaska Fishing Adventures."*

Chris is editor-in-chief of *The Alaska Angler®*, a publication that provides a comprehensive look at current research in Alaska sportfishing techniques, lodge and guide reviews, do-it-yourself fishing opportunities and "inside information" on Alaska sportfishing.

The couple enjoys nationwide exposure for their work in promoting Alaska sportfishing. In the last 10 years, they have appeared on the covers of over 20 national and regional publications and have received recognition in numerous articles, radio talk shows and tv appearances.

Chris and Adela's dedication to producing quality work have won them over 50 national and regional writing and photography awards. These include several first-place awards for their book, *"How to catch Alaska's Trophy Sportfish,"* considered by many to be the bible on how to fish Alaska. *Field and Stream* magazine reviewed it as "Alaska Fishing Book Unparalleled." Chris is also the recipient of 32 trophy fish certificates sponsored by various state and national organizations.

Far from being an "arm-chair outdoor writer," Chris spends from 150 to 180 days per year traveling throughout Alaska. Much of that time is spent personally researching various tips and techniques that help anglers catch more fish. He has hiked into volcanoes, rafted glacial rivers, climbed wilderness mountains and survived Alaska's worst weather to search out and experience the state's unique and undiscovered as well as most popular sportfishing opportunities. Chris and Adela's photo file, which contains over 35,000 Alaska sportfishing transparencies, is a testimonial to this continuous quest.

The International Gamefish Association appointed Chris to be their Alaska representative. He helps promote the conservation goals of the organization and assists in verifying world-record fish.

When Chris isn't fishing some remote area of Alaska, he is in great demand for seminars and instructional classes. He is now entering his 12th year of teaching the extremely popular "Advanced Alaska Fishing TechniquesTM," an intense, eight-week seminar designed to help anglers increase their skills in Alaska sportfishing. Since 1984, he has been a featured speaker at the Great Alaska Sportsman Show, where hundreds of people fill the bleachers to hear his dynamic presentations.

His fishing experience extends beyond Alaska. Chris has fished throughout Canada and the Lower 48, Mexico, Sweden, Germany, Hawaii, Japan and Russia. He says he has yet to find a place that offers the variety and quality of sportfishing that Alaska offers.

While he fly fishes for personal enjoyment and research, Chris frequently uses other types of gear to "learn whatever is necessary to increase my knowledge about fish and fishing, and pass this information on to my readers." He is equally adept at catching lunker halibut on deep-sea rigs as he is bottom-bouncing drift lures for salmon or dancing mini-jigs on a five-foot ultralight for lake trout.

Adela grew up fishing and hunting in Alaska and developed a love for Alaska's beauty and adventure. She has been able to share this love through her photographs, which have appeared in many national publications including *Sports Afield, Western Outdoors, Pacific Northwest Outdoors, L.A. Times, Alaska Airlines magazine and Western's World.* Adela is a professional graphic designer, photographer and publisher. She is the owner of AWARD DESIGN, which specializes in travel brochures, publications and book design.

Adela was chosen as one of the Top Ten Businesswomen in the nation by the American Business Women's Association. She is an active member of the Outdoor Writer's Association of America and is listed in Who's Who of American Women.

Chris and Adela are strong advocates of catch and release, which they practice on all freshwater and anadromous fish unless the fish are mortally wounded. They always try to keep a few sockeye salmon for their annual 40-below barbeque in mid-December, weather and grill permitting.

Chris and Adela live on a five-acre homesite outside Fairbanks, Alaska with their dog, Tiger Lily and yellow-naped Amazon parrot, Juliet. The couple is always interested in hearing about their readers' fishing adventures in Alaska.

Field Notes

Periodicals

Each Issue of The Alaska Angler® Provides You With 10 Benefits:

Lodge Reviews

You don't need to spend $4,000 to discover if a lodge has a four-star rating or whether it's a fly-by-night operation. We visit the lodges and provide you objective reports on the number of fish you can expect to catch, accommodations and compare it with other lodges. We take the risks, you benefit from our experience.

Do-it-Yourself Alaska Angler

Tired of fishing with the crowds? Receive inside information on affordable trips you can enjoy, both from the road system and fly-out trips. You receive everything necessary to duplicate our successes: names of air taxi services, contacts, detailed maps, what to use and how to fish it: First-hand information because we've been there, and want to share these great fisheries with you!

Advanced Alaska Angling Techniques

With each issue, you become an instant expert with a crash course on a specific angling situation you're likely to encounter while fishing Alaska. You'll be on the cutting edge of the most popular and effective fish-catching techniques as well as field-proven flies, lures and equipment. The result? You'll be catching fish when others are not.

Guide Review

In a recent field survey, over 60 percent of the fishing guides we fished with were judged to be incompetent. Why fish with a guide who will catch you five fish, when you can fish with a guide who can help you catch 20 fish, and larger ones at that? I review the best guides, investigate their success ratios and score them against the industry's best.

Alaska Angler Field Notes

Bringing a loved one to Alaska, or looking for a trip that caters to women? Perhaps a secluded cabin you can rent for dollars a day, away from the crowds but in the thick of the salmon? Or specific technical data on water flow, speed, substrate, forage fish and hatches on streams? I tell you the specifics, and the best patterns you need to catch the big ones. I know because I've been there, having earned more than 30 trophy fish certificates and awards, so that you can benefit from this experience, NOW.

Alaska Angler Field Reports

Read about the successes or failures of other anglers who fish Alaska as they rate the best and worst of Alaska fishing...valuable information that will help in taking home personal experiences of catching and releasing trophy fish...not just stories of the catch someone else made last week.

Short Strikes

Brief news notes on items that will enhance your fishing knowledge, making you a better angler. Some recent topics include "Techniques for finding and catching trophy gray-ling"; "Forage fish preferences of Alaska rainbow trout"; "Three steps to catching 10-pound-plus fish when all else fails"; and "When do fish feed during Alaska's 24 hours of daylight".

Alaska Angler Notebook.

Trip discounts, last-minute fishing closures, and field notes regarding Bush travel, suppliers of inexpensive, quality flies for Alaska fishing, uncharted steelhead fishing and more information on how you can fish Alaska on a shoestring budget.

Custom Trip Consulting

Planning on making a trip soon? Subscribers can take advantage of our low-cost information service on lodges, guides, resorts or areas you plan on visiting in 1991. We'll tell you what to expect, and if you'll be better off going elsewhere! We provide harvest statistics, success ratios, lures, tackle equipment for specific areas and contacts over the telephone if you need them in a hurry or by mail if you want to share them with friends.

Special Reports

Discover the behind-the-scenes story major magazines won't publish, stories that will change how you view so called "blue ribbon" fisheries. In the past, we've covered the problem of Alaska's widespread incompetent guide problem, the demise of the Iliamna watershed fishery, the advertising hype surrounding the Brooks River fishery, and more.

Not Available in Stores!

The Alaska Angler® is available only by subscription...it is not sold on newsstands or to libraries. Thus, our information stays among our close-knit network of subscribers.

If our bi-monthly reports were made available through newspapers, magazines and tv, the good fishing I reveal would cease to exist. But I'm willing to share this information with you, a fellow sportsman who cares about Alaska's fishery resources.

Why You Need to Act Now!

The Alaska Angler® has become the information source for anglers who want the very best in Alaska sport-fishing. Here's what our subscribers have to say:

"Informative, concise, well worth the investment." Dr. R.T., New York, N.Y.

"Excellent information on Alaska sport-fishing. We have planned trips because of articles in The Alaska Angler."
I.H., Anchorage, Alaska

Receive over 60 pages of special reports and information a year...the cost of a couple flies or a fishing lure per issue. And the price includes first-class postage to your home or office.

The Alaska Angler......$49 per year.

Chris Batin's 20 Great
Alaska Fishing Adventures

by Christopher Batin

The greatest adventures in Alaska sportfishing that you can experience today!

Frustrated by shoulder-to-shoulder crowds... mediocre Alaska fishing opportunities...and fish that are small and too few in number?

If so, get ready to fly into a glacial-rimmed volcanic crater and fish nearby streams where you will land 50 salmon a day... a wilderness mountain retreat where you catch 11 different species of sportfish in one week... or discover a remote river where anglers catch several, 10 to 17-pound rainbow trout each day!

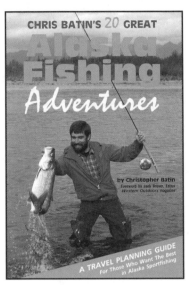

CHRIS BATIN'S 20 GREAT

Alaska Fishing Adventures

by Christopher Batin
Foreword by Jack Brown, Editor
Western Outdoors magazine

A TRAVEL PLANNING GUIDE
For Those Who Want The Best
in Alaska Sportfishing

ISBN 0-916771-09-1

Free information on contacts, charter pilots, lodges, road-access routes, telephone numbers...everything you need to plan your Great Alaska Fishing Adventure THIS YEAR!

It's an adventure book you won't want to put down!

This book is also chock-full of Alaska wilderness fishing adventure stories and anecdotes that not only entertain, but inform. Only a handful of anglers experienced in the world's best fishing have known about many of these areas.

At your fingertips is everything you need to duplicate the author's successes...as well as specific travel details necessary for you to plan one of Alaska's 20 finest fishing adventures NOW.

Many fisheries are so remote, only a handful of anglers visit them each year!

This book has over 150 photos and maps...showing you what you can expect first-hand. See the rivers...country... fish...and the adventure you can expect on each trip!

This book offers you detailed information on where to find fish at each location...forage fish and hatch information...and personal observations on the habits of these sportfish so you can make outstanding catches...and releases... of trophy fish Alaska is famous for.

A comprehensive listing of the most productive flies for each area, based on actual field tests.

"In 20 Great Alaska Fishing Adventures, Chris Batin captures the spirit and excitement of Alaska sportfishing adventure!"

Jack Brown, Western Outdoors magazine

"In recent years, Chris and Adela Batin have become synonymous with and trusted sources for Alaska fishing information.

Twenty Great Alaska Fishing Adventures stresses the best in Alaska sportfishing and details trips that qualify in that 'adventure of a lifetime' category. The book also offers a commendable emphasis on catch-and-release fishing."

The International Angler

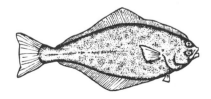

Chris Batin's 20 Great Alaska Fishing Adventures.................$19.95

How to catch Alaska's Trophy Sportfish

By Christopher Batin

"Alaska Fishing Book Unparalleled" *Rich Landers*
Field and Stream magazine

Over 30,000 anglers around the world have benefited from this advanced guide.

Anyone can catch four-pound rainbows or 12-pound salmon. But if you want to catch 60 to 80-pound Alaska king salmon, 300-pound halibut, 20-pound silvers, 30-inch rainbow trout, trophy grayling and steelhead, **"How to catch Alaska's Trophy Sportfish"** is your must-have, on-stream guide.

ISBN 0-916771-03-2

This Book Gives You A PH.D. Crash Course In Alaska Fish Habits and Biology Necessary for Success

"How to catch Alaska's Trophy Sportfish" translates volumes of biological data into terms every angler can understand and use to catch trophy sportfish.

You'll learn about:
■ aggravation responses that catch 70-pound salmon,
■ social hierarchies that tell you where to find fish before you reach the water,
■ stream equations necessary for catching the largest trout and char.

We show you how each species of Alaska trophy sportfish respond to stimuli, and how you can duplicate those responses through our proven field tips and techniques. If you order NOW, you can have this knowledge today...at your fingertips.

Use this book when you go shopping for flies and tackle.

You receive sixteen full-color pages showing the different sportfish and the best flies and lures you need for success, all of which have earned the highest marks for catching trophy sportfish in 10 years of testing.

With this advice, you'll spend your time catching fish, rather than wondering what to catch them on.

This book is also a must-have volume to fully understand the author's fishing recommendations in "Fishing Alaska on $15 a Day."

"Batin's long time on Alaskan waters (over 30,000 hours) gives his new book singular value. What fisherman wouldn't pay for a decade of experience condensed into plain English? The author's experience shows. No matter what the species being sought, Batin's book is a great place to start." Joe Bridgman
The Anchorage Times.

This book can make your Alaska fishing trip a success with its:

■ 368 pages and 120 action-filled photos showing you the fish-catching secrets that has enabled the author to catch and release thousands of sportfish.

■ Fly fishing techniques for Alaska's lakes and streams.

■ Detailed information, life histories, and feeding habits for all of Alaska's 17 major sportfish species.

■ Over 500 specific areas in Alaska where you can catch your trophy sportfish.

■ 16 full-color pages identifying Alaska's trophy sportfish plus color charts of the most effective lure and fly patterns.

■ Detailed charts and illustrations showing you where to find trophy sportfish.

■ Fish-catching secrets of over a dozen guides and biologists.

"If you plan to go to Alaska, or already live there, read this book thoroughly and you fish it better. Chris Batin IS Alaska fishing."
Homer Circle
Angling Editor, Sports Afield magazine

How to catch Alaska's Trophy Sportfish
Softcover $24.95
Hardcover-Limited Edition............$45.

The Alaska Hunter®

Dear Alaska Hunter:

Before you make another Alaska big game hunt, heed this warning: **The hunting crowds are getting worse.**

...In many areas, game animals are not as large as they used to be.

The market is flooded with incompetent guides out to make a quick buck.

Statistics show that guides typically harvest 8-foot bears because they lack the skill and knowledge to find larger bears for their clients.

And do-it-yourself hunters who don't have an insider providing them with Alaska hunting information seldom enjoy the areas they are in, or the fruits of a successful hunt...

However, now YOU can regularly receive the inside scoop on:

■ Where the largest big game animals are taken,

■ The undiscovered, do-it-yourself trips that offer near 100 percent success rates;

■ The guides with high success rates for big bears, trophy moose and caribou.

These successful hunters all have one thing in common. They subscribe to **The Alaska Hunter®**.

With **The Alaska Hunter®** as your guide, you become one of the state's most knowledgeable hunters. Why? Because with each issue, you receive the most current reports and analyses necessary for success.

You can look elsewhere for this information, but don't expect to find it. Conventional sources of information offer you fluffy stories with no substance. Rarely do these stories satisfy the informational needs of knowledgeable hunters who demand specifics such as harvest figures, game densities, access corridors, and information on guides and outfitters offering outstanding trips, or do-it-yourself hunts with high success ratios.

The Alaska Hunter provides you with all this information...and more.

We cater to you, the experienced hunter who wants the very best. And with **The Alaska Hunter®**, you receive specific answers to your Alaska big game hunting questions.

In each issue, you can expect...

At least a dozen new contacts necessary for a successful Alaska hunting trip...outfitters, guides, air charter operators, biologists, hunting experts. Save valuable time and money by allowing us to do the legwork for you. Just the contacts and references you receive each month are worth the yearly subscription price in money saved from expensive long-distance phone calls!

With **The Alaska Hunter®**, you receive the facts without bias from booking agents, bribed writers or advertisements.

Our only allegiance is to you.

We receive no commissions for the trips or contacts we report. No gun reporting or adventure stories. Only unbiased objective reports on Alaska hunting. You won't find this information anywhere else. Pure and simple.

In each bi-monthly issue, you receive specific answers to your Alaska big game hunting questions. You'll receive:

Do-It-Yourself Alaska Hunter
A special page with complete where-to, how-to information on planning your Alaska big game hunt, by yourself or with a group. Prices, logistics, transportation, chances of success, special equipment, game populations, best ways to ship home trophies and meat, companies that rent float hunting gear.

Hunt Reviews
The best and worst do-it-yourself and guided hunts for every species of Alaska big game. In future issues, discover Alaska's best trophy moose area, where record-book bulls are dying of old age...read where the current, world-record brown bear is living, and why hunters haven't been able to bag him...how two-plane hunts offer 80 to 100 percent success ratios...the story behind the rip-off $400 fly-out hunt special, and more.

Hunt Area Specifics
In-depth reports on a specific game management units, what's available, type of terrain, weather, success figures for each species of big game animals, and more. This is information that would take you weeks to acquire on your own.

The Best of the Best
Alaska hunting guides and outfitters who are providing the very best guided trophy and do-it-yourself hunts. In-depth profiles on the guides whose clients are regulars in the Boone and Crockett, Pope and Young and Safari Club record books.

Secrets of Alaska's Hunting Guides
Tips gleaned from veteran guides with decades of field experience. Their observations and tips can spell the difference between success and failure.

Alaska Hunter News Updates
The most current news of the Alaska hunting industry, disciplinary actions, outfitter problems, USFWS sting operations on registered guides and renegade outfitters, new hunt openings, hunt closures, and Department of Fish and Game management decisions.

Marine Mammal Coverage
Ready for walrus, seal or polar bearhunting? The Alaska Hunter will keep you up-to-date on the status of

the Marine Mammal Protection Act, and who the top guides will be so you'll be ready when the seasons open.

Guide/Outfitter Issues
The inside stories behind the guides' push for dominance in the hunting market. How Alaska's big game populations are in trouble from unregulated hunting by renegade outfitters. The detrimental effect some air taxi operators are having on your hunting success.

Political Forum
Up-to-date reports on important political decisions and actions that affect you and your Alaska hunting plans. This is especially important as Alaska moves toward deregulation of guide areas, Native Sovereignty, 1991 amendments, and removal of prime hunting lands by the National Park Service.

Discounts
- Last minute hunt cancellations
- Special hunt openings
- The best registration hunts
- Waterfowl/big game hunts
- Fishing/hunting combos and more

The information you'll receive each month is an unbeatable combination of experience and knowledge.

It's created for hunters like you by year-long resident Alaska hunters and writers. And they are directed by Chris Batin, one of Alaska's most experienced hunting writers and editors.

Batin is author of the award-winning, "Hunting in Alaska: A Comprehensive Guide," and former editor of *Alaska Outdoors* magazine and *The Alaska Professional Hunter* newsletter. He has received over 30 awards for his reports in national and regional publications, including the Journalist of the Year from the Alaska Professional Hunters

Association and Sportswriter of the Year from The Alaska Outdoor Council. With over 15 years of experience covering the Alaska hunting scene, Chris is both as an active participant and veteran journalist. He is considered by many of the country's top outdoor writers as one of Alaska's most knowledgeable hunting editors.

Compare us with other publications on the market. A year's subscription is only **$49**, which includes first-class postage to your home or office.

If you want the very best of Alaska big game hunting, you can't afford to be without a subscription to The Alaska Hunter.

Don't miss a single issue. Send in the attached order form or call toll free today and be among those who benefit from **The Alaska Hunter**®

The Alaska Hunter.........**$49 per year.**

Hunting in Alaska
A Comprehensive Guide

By Christopher Batin

"(Hunting in Alaska) is the standard by which other Alaska hunting books will be judged."
Bob Robb,
Petersen's Hunting

Hunting in Alaska is a rich source of Alaska-tested hunting ideas & strategies that work!
- 416 information-packed pages, 138 photos, many award winning
- 51 maps & illustrations
- Expert advice on hunting sheep, bear, moose, caribou, waterfowl, and more!
- Detailed, where-to-go information and harvest statistics for each species in each Game Management Unit

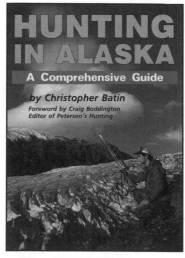

ISBN 0-916771-02-4

- Detailed maps and Game Management Unit descriptions that will familiarize you with Alaska's wilderness hunting hotspots and game concentrations.
- Planning a do-it-yourself hunt.
- Secret bear hunting techniques used by one guide who is nearly 100 percent for big brown bear, and who has put several in the record books, including a 30-incher.
- Criteria for choosing an Alaska big game guide.
- Learn secrets of taking wolves along salmon streams

For years, successful guides and hunters have known that it takes scientific knowledge and specific strategies to successfully harvest Alaska's most coveted big game trophies.

Now, for the first time, **Hunting in Alaska: A Comprehensive Guide** offers you over 1,000 of these hunting secrets and tips. Master guides and big game experts provide decades of first-hand experience, ensuring your Alaska hunt is a complete success.

Based on 15 years of Alaska hunting experience and research, "Hunting in Alaska: A Comprehensive Guide" **provides you with a wealth of never-before available information on:**
- High Bush and Low Bush Thrashing: Tactics scientifically proven to call in trophy moose.
- Specifics on hunting Kodiak and Alaska Peninsula Brown Bear
- Scientific data on the habits of full-curl Dall sheep, where they're found and how to hunt them, including interviews with guides who regularly take record-book sheep.
- 10-year trends on game populations, hunter statistics and harvest totals that give you pre-hunt knowledge of your chances for success in each of Alaska's 26 Game Management Units.

- Understanding seasonal migration habits of big mountain goats and goat hunting methods that have helped one guide bag over 40 trophy goats for his clients.
- Specialized equipment needs for guided, unguided, backpack and float hunts.
- Over 1,000 listings of where you can hunt Alaska's big and small game and waterfowl.
- Care of trophies and meat.
- How to hunt ridges, over bait, berry patches, and tidal flats for trophy black bear.
- Extensive chapters on duck, goose, sea duck and crane hunting, small game, grouse, ptarmigan.
- Four award-winning stories on Alaska Hunting Excitement, Ethics, Camaraderie, and Adventure.
- Big game behavioral and natural history information of special interest to you as a hunter. Historical synopses of Alaska big game species, including transplants and current distribution information.

Hunting in Alaska:
A Comprehensive Guide
Softcover **$24.95**
Hardcover **$29.95**

Bear Heads & Fish Tales

By Alan Liere

Patrick F. McManus, internationally recognized humorist, book author and columnist for Outdoor Life magazine, has this to say in the foreword of Alan Liere's recent book on Alaska outdoor humor entitled, **"Bear Heads & Fish Tales"**:

"What's funny? Nobody knows for sure, but I would venture to say that it's that tiny, gritty bit of truth that produces the pearl of laughter. I do not mean to imply that author Al Liere In any way resembles an oyster. The man is a funny writer, which is the best thing you can say about a humorist. I personally plan to buy a gross of Bear Heads & Fish Tales. If we have another Great Depression, people will need something to cheer them up, and I figure a copy of this book will be as good as gold in the marketplace."

Bear Heads & Fish Tales is a collection of zany outdoor stories written by Alan Liere, Alaska's ambassador of mirth and humor to the funny bone. Learn the techniques for smoking fish, Alaska-style, by burning your neighbors garage; what words to say to your oil pan while sleeping under your car; tips on preparing wilderness gourmet meals such as Chicken Noodle Salmon or Humpy Rainwater Soup, how to stuff a mature bull caribou into the cargo space of a Subaru hatchback and much more.

"This book is for anyone who has ever wielded a fishing rod, a shotgun, or a wiener stick," says Liere. "It's for those who experience deflated air mattresses, rubber rafts, and egos— sometimes all on the same outing. **Bear Heads & Fish Tales** is for anyone who believes in that fine line between tragedy and comedy and knows with all their heart that maturity is highly over-rated."

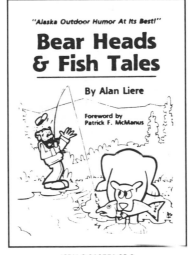

"Alaska Outdoor Humor At Its Best!"

Bear Heads & Fish Tales

By Alan Liere

Foreword by Patrick F. McManus

ISBN 0-916771-05-9

The 13 stories in this 139-page book are based on Liere's real-life personal misadventures and hilarious insights. In "King Tut's Revenge," Liere expounds on his childhood phobia regarding mummy-type sleeping bags. "Thanks, Aunt Judy" reveals tips on how Liere has learned to survive Alaska mosquitoes through such evasive tactics as "The Screamin' Exit" and the liberal use of garlic. And with a humorous eye, he examines that glossy, hope-inducing product of creative writing and adjective overuse known as "The Alaska Outdoor Brochure."

Each story is illustrated by outdoor cartoonist Jeff Schuler. The combined efforts of both author and cartoonist effectively capture the side-splitting antics and foibles of sportsmen in the Alaska outdoors, the Northcountry's grandest comic playhouse.

Bear Heads & Fish Tales **$9.95**

Alaska Angler® Information Service

Want to know the best rivers to catch all five species of Pacific salmon? Anxious to discover the Top 10 do-it-yourself trips for wild, 8 to 10-pound rainbow trout? Or a listing of Alaska's five-star lodges that serve you early-morning coffee in bed and at night, place European chocolates on your pillow?

The answers to these and other Alaska sportfishing questions can be answered by calling the **Alaska Angler Information Service**.

The Information Service provides "answers for anglers" who are planning a fishing trip to the 49th state.

"There's a common misconception that Alaska fishing is good year-round, no matter where or when you go," says Chris Batin, editor of **The Alaska Angler®** . "Alaska has over 3 million lakes and 3,000 rivers covering a land mass one-fifth the size of the continental United States. Planning is crucial for success. A miscalculation of several days can have anglers staring at fishless water rather than a stream filled with salmon."

He stressed the information service is not a booking agency.

"Objectivity is the key to the Alaska Angler Information Service," Batin said. "We do not receive any remuneration or benefit from recommending one stream or fishing service over another. This ensures that our customers receive objective information on fishing opportunities, guides and lodges that surpass industry standards for service, quality and professionalism. We can provide all the information anglers need, from the best flies for a particular watershed, water conditions to expect, type of hatches, and even the flora and fauna in the area."

Travel agents and booking agents are often unfamiliar with Alaska's myriad sportfishing options.

"Many travel agents sell a limited selection of trips that offer the best commissions for them," he said. "It's not cost effective for them to recommend quality, inexpensive trips, even though it may be perfect for the angler's needs. The Alaska Angler Information Service provides unbiased information so the angler can personally decide whether to spend $25 or $4,000 for a trip.

The crew of **The Alaska Angler** spends over 180 days a year fishing Alaska, searching out the best do-it-yourself and full-service adventures for the company's information service, periodicals and books.

The cost is **$25** for **15 minutes of consultation**. Before consultation begins, callers provide a Mastercard or Visa credit card number. To expedite matters, have ready your list of questions. To benefit from the Alaska Angler Information Service, call **1-907-455-8000** 10 a.m. to 6 p.m. Alaska Standard Time, Monday—Friday.

Ship to:_____

Address: _____

City _____

State _____ Zip _____

Daytime Phone( )_____

Quantity	Item	Price	Total
_____	Chris Batin's 20 Great Alaska Fishing Adventures.........................	$19.95	_____
_____	Fishing Alaska on Dollar$ a Day..	$19.95	_____
_____	How to catch Alaska's Trophy Sportfish, softcover.......................	$24.95	_____
_____	How to catch Alaska's Trophy Sportfish, Limited Edition, hardcover......	$45.	_____
_____	Hunting in Alaska, softcover..	$24.95	_____
_____	Hunting in Alaska, hardcover...	$29.95	_____
_____	Bear Heads and Fish Tales...	$9.95	_____
_____	The Alaska Angler® (one-year subscription)............................	$49. ppd	_____
_____	The Alaska Hunter® (one-year subscription)............................	$49. ppd	_____
_____	The Alaska Angler® custom binder..	$12. ppd	_____
_____	The Alaska Hunter® custom binder..	$12. ppd	_____
_____	Back issues of The Alaska Angler®	$8.50 each ppd	_____
	____ , ____ , ____ , ____ , ____ , ____ , ____ , ____ , ____	3 for $21. ppd	_____
_____	Back issues of The Alaska Hunter®	$8.50 each ppd	_____
	____ , ____ , ____ , ____ , ____ , ____ , ____ , ____ , ____	3 for $21. ppd	_____
_____	"Alaska Angler® " poplin leisure cap, one size fits all..................	$14. ppd	_____
	Circle color: Teal Green Red		
_____	"Alaska Angler® " leisure cap, one size fits all..........................	$16. ppd	_____
	Circle color and fabric: Teal Green Red Corduroy Ripstop Nylon		
_____	"Alaska Angler" Polo shirt, Circle size and color....................	$38.50 ppd	_____
	Teal Green Red Purple Men's sizes: S M L XL		

Gift Section

Book(s) personalized to: (please print)

Name _____

Title of book(s) _____

_____

Book(s) personalized to:

Name _____

Title of book(s) _____

_____

Book(s) personalized to:

Name _____

Title of book(s) _____

_____

Book Shipping Charges

Priority Mail delivery (1 to 2 weeks)......$6. _____
each additional book Priority Mail...............$3. _____
Bookrate delivery (4 to 5 weeks)............$4. _____
each additional book Bookrate...................$2. _____
Newsletters, binders, apparel postage paid....0.
Canada, add to above charges................$3. _____
Foreign countries, Airmail, per book....$15. _____
Airmail, per newsletter subscription..........$20. _____

ORDER AND SHIPPING TOTAL _____

Payment Method

Enclose your personal check, money order or credit card info.

☐ Check   ☐ Money Order   ☐ VISA   ☐ Mastercard

Card Acct. Number_____

Exp. Date — Signature _____